Guardians of the Avenue Part 2:
Biographies of African-American Legends of the Indianapolis Police Department

By Patrick R. Pearsey

2017

Dedicated to Richard Crenshaw

A pioneer at the Indianapolis Police Department in law enforcement and also in his research of its history.

Cover photo: Indianapolis Police Department recruits John R. Larkins (right) and Albert "Tom" Cotton, December 1968.
Inside cover: L-R: Clarence Lewis, Thomas Williams and Chester Coates.

Forward

This book is a continuation of my previous book under the same title. It is a collection of biographical profiles and career summaries of African-American officers of the Indianapolis Police Department who are now deceased. There are two living retired officers profiled however; Captain Clarence A. White and Sergeant Jacqueline J. Winters. They are the oldest living African-American IPD retirees of their sex. Their clear recollections of life on the department in the 1950's to the 1970's were too valuable to not include.

My primary source is the Indianapolis Recorder, a Black owned publication which kept the community informed about crime and punishment and the officers who enforced the law. They also logged all appointments, retirements, promotions and demotions – a virtual personnel file.

I am indebted to Mr. Richard Crenshaw, retired Major of IPD and winner of the Medal of Valor for pulling a fatally wounded comrade to cover. He published his own account of this subject in *"A History of the*

Indianapolis Police Department's Black Police Officers" in 2005. He graciously allowed me to use vintage photographs from his book for this volume.

I am grateful to the late Bill Lichtenberger, who retired from IPD and spent years researching its history. He preserved irreplaceable portraits of officers dating to the 1890's. Thanks also to Sergeant Jo A. Moore, former archivist of the Indianapolis Metropolitan Police Department's Lichtenberger History Room for her support. I hope this history fills a gap in our department's history.

Patrick R. Pearsey
IMPD Archivist

List of Biography Subjects

Contents

Turnkey Conrad Burley 13
Patrolman Benjamin Young 16
Patrolman William Whitaker 18
Patrolman Philip Franklin 18
Patrolman Thomas Hart 20
Detective Benjamin Tobias Thornton 22
Patrolman Carter Temple Jr. 41
Patrolman Nathan T. Ward 55
Patrolman Samuel P. Herron 58
Patrolman Richard W. Wells 61
Patrolman Samuel J. McClure 65
Patrolman Horace Heston 66
Patrolman Allen Dudley 68
Patrolman Ephraim Palmer 69
Patrolman George Washington Cheatham 70
Patrolman Edward Harris 73
Sergeant Joshua Spearis 77
Patrolman William Albert Hogan 80
Patrolman Frank Hurt 81
Patrolman Simpson T. "Sim" Hart 83

James William Winn..86

Patrolman Daniel Carter..88

Patrolman William H. Wheeler..91

Patrolman James W.H.Crabtree..94

Patrolman James Admire..97

Patrolman George W. Rankin..99

Patrolman Gabriel L. Jones 102

Patrolman Earl E. Titus 105

Patrolman Carter Fredrick Payton Temple...................................107

Patrolman Benjamin W. Lee..115

Patrolman Lewis Weaver Montgomery 118

Patrolman George H. Goins..120

Patrolman John W. Cousins..122

Detective Sergeant John M. Mosbey.......................................124

Detective Sergeant Edward Byron Trabue................................126

Patrolman Ralph LaRue..128

Patrolman Nelson Grandison 131

Patrolman William Whitfield...133

Detective Sergeant Thomas W. Hopson 140

Patrolman John Coleman..144

Policewoman Mary Ena (Roberts) Mays....................................147

Policewoman Emma (Christy) Baker..156

Lieutenant George William Sneed..166

Detective Sergeant Claude C. White.......................................182

....188
Patrolman James S. Vincent..188
Detective Sergeant Clarence "Plez" Jones 190
Detective Sergeant Roy Sonnie Kennedy......................195
Detective Sergeant Frederick "Fred" Harrison Starks 200
Lieutenant James "Preston" Heater...............................206
Sergeant Jesse "Jack" Hadley..210
Policewoman Mayme E.(Pettiford) Shelton....................216
Officer Hester H. "Hettie" (Johnson) Brewer Vaulx 219
Patrolman Admiral D. Harris..223
Patrolman George Thomas "Slim" Brown......................225
Patrolman George Blunt Paxton......................................228
Patrolman George W. Helm 230
Patrolman Harry B. Manuel..232
Patrolman Turner "Rail" Robinson..................................233
Patrolman George W. Spinks..236
Sergeant Norvel Bennett 237
Det. Sgt. Ferdinand Desoto Holt......................................241
Patrolman John Frank Buchanan 243
Sergeant John R. Glenn..245
      Patrolman Guy Luster 249
Patrolman Robert Edward "Eddie" Butler.....................252
Deputy Chief Spurgeon Dewitt Davenport....................257
Lieutenant Osa Garland Woodall 275

Patrolman Gilbert Jones 279

Detective Sergeant David N. Clark Jr. 283

Patrolman Clyde L. Ashby 287

Sergeant Alexander H. Posey 289

Patrolman Grant William Hawkins 293

Detective Sergeant Clarence W. Lewis 297

Policewoman Sara Alice Mize Jones 300

Policewoman Georgia M. (Broach) Rogers 302

Sergeant Thelma M.(Evans) Graves 306

Sergeant William W. DeJarnette 312

Detective Sergeant James W. Rogers 314

Detective Sergeant Albert R. Booth 317

Lieutenant Oscar B. Donahue 326

Lieutenant Garland Jones Sr. 329

Patrolman John T. Bailey 332

Captain Anthony Watkins 334

Detective Sergeant Alfred L. Finnell 339

Lieutenant Thomas H. Williams 342

Patrolman William T. "Bill" Lee 344

Sergeant Thelma Marie (Johnson) Sansbury 346

Lieutenant Chester Coates 358

Patrolman Luther Kurtz 365

Sergeant William Fairfield Rapier 368

Lieutenant Roger Nelson Harrison 373

Deputy Chief James Vernon Dabner 376

Patrolman Clarence Glover Snorden 379

Sergeant Bailey Coleman 382

Lieutenant Thomas Warry Bryant Jr. 385

Patrolman James Joseph McElroy 388

Sergeant Averitte Wallace Corley 389

Sergeant Richard Combs 399

Detective James M. Highbaugh 401

Patrolman James E. Mitchell 403

Patrolman Jack L. Yager 404

.... 406

Officer Clara (Clay) Dodson Williams 406

Officer Celestine G. (Vincent) Clark 408

Patrolman Johnny Clinton Nevilles 413

Policewoman Ella C. (King) Coleman 414

Officer Overa Catherine (Harris) Ward 417

Policewoman 419

Thelma Irene (Williams) Donahue 419

Officer Bessie Mae (Watkins) Matthews 421

Patrolman Albert Alan Sheridan Jr. 424

Patrolman James F. "Bruiser" Gaines 426

Sergeant Colion C. "Champ" Chaney 430

Lieutenant David Square Jeter Sr. 438

Officer Emelie Estherjane (Chowning) Weathers-Kerr 440

Policewoman Sarah Lee Jones..444

Detective Sergeant Albert S. Taylor..................................447

Patrolman Phillip Connaly Parker....................................449

Officer Barbara (Taliaferro) Sneed Chism......................451

Policewoman Maria (Legg) McElroy................................456

Patrolman Warren Edward Greene..................................461

Policewoman Joan M. Rayford 468

Detective Willie Norman Larkins 479

Major Cicero Claude Mukes 489

Detective William E. Durham...495

Detective Joe Cephas Berry 496

Sergeant Joe W. McCoy...497

Detective Sergeant Clarence R. Grant..............................500

Policewoman Rosemary Anthony Simpson....................503

Richard Cartwright Jeter 505

Patrolman Lyman T. Battle 506

Detective Ned H. Wyatt 508

Patrolman Ronald R. Coleman 509

Detective Ernest Lee Miller 511

Sergeant Willie J. Jackson 517

Asst Chief Robert G. "Bobby" Allen 519

Sergeant Jacqueline Jean Winters 521

Captain Clarence A. White 537
Detective James Melvin Compton...........................584

Detective Otha Stanley "Stan" Anderson...............586

Sergeant James Lewis Johnson........................... 589

Faces of IPD

Penny Davis and James D. Toler, first African-American Chief of Police of the Indianapolis Police Department (1992).

Captain Tim Martin with Detective George Long.

Patrolman Robert Jackson, Lockup.

Recruits from rookie class of February 16, 1963, from left, unidentified, William Myers, Howard Joe Allen and Patricia Nelis.

BIOGRAPHICAL SECTION

Conrad Burley is the first documented African-American to serve on the police department of Indianapolis. He was a turnkey or jailer and during his 5 months of employment, never saw duty on the streets of Indianapolis as a police officer. This is a distinction from the men who were hired 3 years later in 1876.

Turnkey Conrad Burley

Born: About 1842 Kentucky
Died: December 27, 1895 Indianapolis, Indiana
Date Appointed: May 21, 1873
Date Separated: August 18, 1873

Conrad Burley arrived in Indianapolis, Indiana by 1865.[1] He was born in Kentucky about 1842-45 according to the 1880 Indianapolis Census.[2]

---

[1] 1865 Indianapolis City Directory
[2] Year: 1880; Census Place: Indianapolis, Marion, Indiana; Roll: 295; Family History Film: 1254295; Page: 159A; Enumeration District: 111; Image: 0019.

In July of 1873, Conrad Burley was working for the Indianapolis Police Department according to the below news item from July 1st.

"The prisoners in the station house last night attempted to overpower Conrad Burley, the colored policeman, while he was in the act of putting an arrest in the "big room." Burley punished several of them severely, while their comrades slunk away from the contest." [3]

In 1873, Conrad Burley was superintendent of the Zion's Baptist church in Indianapolis. Later in the summer of 1873, Burley's employment as turnkey with the Metropolitan Police Department was terminated.

August 9, 1873:
"Turnkey Burley, of the city jail, has been suspended for sleeping while on duty." [4]

---

[3] "Minor Mention", The Indianapolis News – July 1, 1873, 3, http://indiamond6.ulib.iupui.edu/cdm/compoundobject/collection/IN/id/5100/rec/1

[4] "Personal", The Indianapolis News, August 9, 1873, 4, http://indiamond6.ulib.iupui.edu/cdm/compoundobject/collection/IN/id/5275/rec/1

August 18, 1873:
"*At a meeting of the Board held Saturday afternoon the resignation of office Ed. Mc Clintock was accepted, but as yet no one has been appointed to fill the vacancy. William Porter was appointed Turnkey at the city jail vice Conrad Burley dismissed.*" [5]

From 1878 until 1894, Conrad Burley held the elected position of Constable in Indianapolis. The 1880 census of Indianapolis lists Conrad Burley, Black male, age 39, born Kentucky and his daughter Bessie, age 8. His occupation then was "Constable". [6] His first wife, Mary Harvey, had died in childbirth, March of 1876. [7]

She and the child were buried in Crown Hill Cemetery. Conrad married a Sarah Hart on September 5th of that year in Indianapolis. She died in November 1900.

---

[5] "The Police Board", The Indianapolis News – August 18, 1873, 3,
http://indiamond6.ulib.iupui.edu/cdm/compoundobject/collection/IN/id/5425/rec/11

[6] 1880 U.S. Census, Indianapolis, Marion, Indiana; Roll: 295; Family History Film: 1254295; Page: 159A; Enumeration District: 111; Image: 0019, Ancestry.com

[7] Findagrave.com

Burley was Republican candidate for Constable of Indianapolis, 1884. Conrad Burley, "colored", died December 27, 1895, aged 49 in Indianapolis.[8]

Patrolman Benjamin Young

Born: October 1839 Kentucky[9]
Died: June 1914 Indianapolis, Indiana
Date Appointed: May 13, 1876
Date Separated: By 1880
Benjamin Young was working as a farm laborer in Indianapolis, September of 1870. He was one of four men hired by the Metropolitan Police Department on May 13, 1876.[10] He was reappointed May 31, 1878. He appears to have left the force between 1877 and 1880, when he was again farming, now in Perry Township of Marion County, Indiana.[11] Benjamin Young died in Indianapolis, June 1914.

---

[8] Indiana Deaths 1882-1920, H-6 on page 12, Ancestry.com
[9] Source Citation: Year: 1900; Census Place: Indianapolis, Marion, Indiana; Roll: 390; Page: 3A; Enumeration District: 0175; FHL microfilm: 1240390.
[10] "Police Appointments", The Indianapolis News – May 13, 1876, 4, http://indiamond6.ulib.iupui.edu/cdm/compoundobject/collection/IN/id/9844/rec/1

Obituary – June 6, 1914 *Indianapolis Recorder*

An Active Life Ended

"Benjamin Young was a resident of this city since the war of '61. He served three and half years in the 109th Regiment Ky. Inf, and was a member of Martin R. Delaney Post, No.70 He was a charter member of the Olivet Baptist Church and made the motion which brought about the permanent organization. He was a Christian for 55 years and was one of the first colored policemen appointed in this city. He leaves three children, Rev. Frank F. Young, Bert Young and Mrs. Effie Young Ray. He was a property owner and was well respected. The Rev. C. W. Lewis conducted the services." [12]

Patrolman William Whitaker

---

[11]   1880 U.S. Census, Marion County, Indiana. Census Place: Perry, Marion, Indiana; Roll: 294; Family History Film: 1254294; Page: 560B; Enumeration District: 103; Image: 0302, Ancestry.com

[12]   "An Active Life Ended", *Indianapolis Recorder*, June 6, 1914, 4, http://indiamond6.ulib.iupui.edu/cdm/compoundobject/collection/IRecorder/id/27199/rec/1

Date Appointed: May 13, 1876[13]
Reappointed May 31, 1878.
Date of Separation/Retirement: 1881

<u>August 30, 1877</u>:   William Whitaker, "colored policeman", brought suit against George Schrote for $5,000 in damages, for being shot in the arm.

Patrolman Philip Franklin

Born: About 1852 Tennessee[14]
Died:
Date Appointed: May 13, 1876[15]
Date of Separation/Retirement: By 1879

Working as a plumber in Indianapolis, 1879.[16] Philip Franklin owned a place

---

[13]   "Police Appointments", The Indianapolis News – May 13, 1876, 4,
http://indiamond6.ulib.iupui.edu/cdm/compoundobject/collection/IN/id/9844/rec/1

[14] Year: 1880; Census Place: Center, Marion, Indiana; Roll: 294; Family History Film: 1254294; Page: 601C; Enumeration District: 105; Image: 0383.

[15]   "Police Appointments", The Indianapolis News – May 13, 1876, 4,
http://indiamond6.ulib.iupui.edu/cdm/compoundobject/collection/IN/id/9844/rec/1

[16]   1879 Indianapolis City Directory

known as Coney Island on the Canal and on March 10, 1893, he left it in charge of a "White woman".

When he returned at 5 p.m., she told him that his house had been invaded by a group of seven "toughs", who drank beer and destroyed his furniture. Franklin became engaged in an argument with Carl Vorhis and before it was over, Franklin shot at him three times, the last bullet lodging in Vorhis' thigh. Franklin was arrested for assault and battery.[17]

In October of 1895 Philip Franklin was an attorney and plumber living in Haughville. He reported his bicycle missing that month, which Detective Ben Thornton found in a bicycle shop. The owner of the shop wanted money for a repair bill and a fight ensued with Franklin, who was found guilty of assault. Franklin filed an appeal.[18] On

---

[17] "A Disturbance at Coney Island", The Indianapolis News - March 11, 1893, 1,
http://indiamond6.ulib.iupui.edu/cdm/compoundobject/collection/IN/id/44548/rec/1
[18] "In the Suburbs", The Indianapolis News – October 30, 1895, 7,
http://indiamond6.ulib.iupui.edu/cdm/compoundobject/collection/IN/id/49622/rec/1

May 2, 1925 in Indianapolis, a man named Philip Franklin, "colored" was arrested for operating a "blind tiger" (a speak-easy).[19]

Patrolman Thomas Hart

Born: 1834 North Carolina[20]
Died: July 15, 1881 Indianapolis, Indiana[21]
Date Appointed: May 13, 1876
Date of Separation/Retirement: July 15, 1881 (death)

Thomas Hart, born about 1834 in North Carolina, came from Salem, Indiana to Indianapolis in 1862. He was appointed to the Indianapolis Police Department on May 13, 1876[22], being the first African-American

---

[19] "Four Held in Tiger Raids", The Indianapolis News – May 4, 1925, http://www.newspapers.com/image/39566585/?terms=%22phili p%2Bfranklin%22

[20] Source Citation: Year: 1880; Census Place: Indianapolis, Marion, Indiana; Roll: 295; Family History Film: 1254295; Page: 452B; Enumeration District: 120; Image: 0606, Ancestry.com

[21] "A Faithful Officer and Good Citizen Gone", The Indianapolis Leader – July 23, 1881, https://newspapers.library.in.gov/cgi-bin/indiana?a=d&d=IL18810723.1.4#

[22] "Police Appointments", The Indianapolis News – May 13, 1876, 4, http://indiamond6.ulib.iupui.edu/cdm/compoundobject/collection/IN/id/9844/rec/1

to join (along with three others). On June 1, 1881, Officer Thomas Hart was assigned to patrol the Fourth District.[23] Thomas Hart, policeman, was buried July 17, 1881. He was a Mason. His son Simpson "Sim" Hart also served with IPD from 1890 until his death in December 1909.

[24]

Detective Benjamin Tobias Thornton

---

[23] "The Police Assignments", The Indianapolis News – June 2, 1881, 3, http://indiamond6.ulib.iupui.edu/cdm/compoundobject/collection/IN/id/16521/rec/2

[24] IMPD Historical Photograph Archives

Born: December 18, 1849 near Winchester, Virginia[25]
Died: June 18, 1900, Indianapolis, Indiana[26]
Date Appointed: May 24, 1876[27]
Date of Separation: June 18, 1900 (death)

(Unless otherwise noted, the details of Benjamin T. Thornton's life comes from his lengthy obituary in the Indianapolis News, June 19, 1900).

Benjamin T. Thornton was born December 18, 1849 near Winchester, Virginia, a slave. At age 12, he was working for an abusive master named John H. Crebs, who kicked him in the chin that day because another slave had ran away. After one aborted escape attempt, he was sent to stay in a room. Instead, he ran out into the dark, running blindly through fields and creeks.

---

[25] "Detective Thornton Dead", The Indianapolis News – June 19, 1900, 5,
http://indiamond6.ulib.iupui.edu/cdm/compoundobject/collection/IN/id/68028/rec/5
[26] Ibid
[27] "Police Appointments", The Indianapolis News – May 24, 1876, 4,
http://indiamond6.ulib.iupui.edu/cdm/compoundobject/collection/IN/id/9664/rec/1

Young Ben stumbled in the midnight gloom over the body, having walked into a battlefield. He swore on the spot to serve the Union in order to honor the men fighting for his freedom.

Making his way to the Union army lines, he found the 16th Indiana Regiment, which took care of him. He heard about Richmond, Indiana from the soldiers who lived there and when the war ended, made his way to that small city. He spent time in Indianapolis & Kansas City, Missouri, before returning to Indianapolis in the early 1870's.

Thornton was a member of the Republican Party and on May 18, 1874 he was nominated by acclamation at the Center Township convention for the office of Center Township Constable.[28] He did not get elected and applied for a position with the Metropolitan Force of Indianapolis. He was sworn in as a member of the department, May 24, 1876.[29]

---

[28] "Township Constable", The Indianapolis News – May 18, 1874, 3, http://indiamond6.ulib.iupui.edu/cdm/compoundobject/collection/IN/id/7251/rec/1

[29] "Police Appointments", The Indianapolis News – May 24,

Officer Thornton spent 1876-1877 as the night shift jailer or "turnkey" at Police Headquarters at the corner of Pearl and Alabama Streets.

Just after midnight, Christmas Day, 1877, a mob of people, African-Americans, approached the door to his office, which opened into an alley north of the building. They were seeking to lynch a prisoner, William Greenley, arrested the previous day for allegedly murdering Mrs. Ida Kersey.

The leader of the mob knocked on the door. Ben managed to recover his composure before he opened the door. He had his other hand on his mace (billy club). The leader of the mob asked if Greenley was at the station house. "He is", replied Ben. "What do you want with him?"

"We want to hang him for the murder of Ida Kersey", the leader replied, trying to force his way past Ben. Without saying a word,

1876, 4,
http://indiamond6.ulib.iupui.edu/cdm/compoundobject/collection/IN/id/9664/rec/1

Ben knocked him down with his mace. Two other men, who were moving toward the door, also went down under Ben's mace.

The remaining members of the mob, taken aback by the resistance shown, fled down the alley. The lynch mob was masked but Ben recognized a couple of their voices.[30]

On December 26, 1877, Thornton was given street duty, walking the same beat as Officer Carter Temple. This was probably a result of him using his head to prevent a lynching. On July 2, 1879, while engaged in crowd control at a fire scene, a man who Thornton had connected to a theft stabbed him in the left temple with a pen knife, causing him to bleed profusely.

He received medical attention and the suspect was arrested. On August 26, 1886, Thornton was appointed to the IPD Detective Squad. He was the first and only African-American member of this squad until 1919.

One of his greatest assets as a detective was his thorough knowledge of the criminals in

---

[30] *The Indianapolis Journal* – May 24, 1896

Indianapolis and their activities. Det. Thornton solved several murders, including the slayer of Willie Roberts in a saloon.

Through his investigation, John Coleman was arrested in St. Louis, Missouri for the murder and Thornton left to pick him up on October 15, 1890. "In our business, the least little thing sometimes leads to the greatest results", Thornton frequently said.[31]

"I remember how we worked 2 or 3 years ago to capture a gang of thieves who were terrorizing the town. Robbery after robbery occurred and we could get no clew, and it was anything but encouraging. Men were held up, houses were robbed at the rate of 5 to 8 a day. One day I got a 'tip'. I drove 15 miles to secure possession of a pair of 15 cent gloves that had been stolen. The gloves turned out to be a valuable clew which, when followed, resulted in the capture of the Fred Piper gang. (September 8, 1892 interview at roll call).[32]

---

[31] "Old Bloch, Ought-to", The Indianapolis News – September 8, 1892, 5,
http://indiamond6.ulib.iupui.edu/cdm/compoundobject/collection/IN/id/40296/rec/1

[32] "Old Bloch, Ought-to", The Indianapolis News – September 8, 1892, 5,

Engraving from Cleveland Gazette, January 28, 1888[33]

On October 5, 1891 at a Republican political rally on the "Yellow Bridge", the crowd, estimated at over 1,000, became unruly; refusing to let several men speak. Thornton at one point mounted the podium and said

---

http://indiamond6.ulib.iupui.edu/cdm/compoundobject/collection/IN/id/40296/rec/1

[33] From "The Ohio Historical Society" – The African American Experience in Ohio 1850-1920 Internet site, accessed May 13, 2014.
http://dbs.ohiohistory.org/africanam/page1.cfm?ItemID=15712

"This is a free country and these men have a right to speak here." Stones were thrown at him as he stepped down, which missed. As two patrolmen charged into the crowd and had their uniforms cut into ribbons, the mob closed in on Det. Thornton. Thornton drew his pistol and fired it into the air twice, which sent the mob running. The Indianapolis News credited Thornton's bravery with saving lives.[34]

The Charles Eyster Murder Case

In 1893, a druggist named Charles E. Eyster was shot to death in his store. Det. Thornton arrested two African-Americans named John Parker and Edward McAfee but by June 1893, became convinced they were innocent of the crime. He informed the Superintendent of Police of this.

IPD Officer Nathan Ward filed charges against Det. Thornton of working on behalf of the defendants instead of the State.[35] He

---

[34] "A Bad Political Riot", The Indianapolis News - October 6, 1891, 8, http://indiamond6.ulib.iupui.edu/cdm/compoundobject/collection/IN/id/35218/rec/1

[35] "Charges Against Thornton", The Indianapolis News – June

was suspended for 10 days and reprimanded (the only time in his career), "for telling the truth", as he described it later. Thornton then testified before a grand jury as to the innocence of Parker and McAfee. They were sentenced to death in 1893[36] but received a new trial in Franklin, Indiana in 1894.

In the retrial, May 3, 1894, Thornton testified on behalf of the defense and after being cross examined by the Marion County Prosecutor, Thornton's response generated applause from the court room audience, who felt he had gotten the best of the exchange. They received life sentences, but McAfee was paroled by Governor Mount in 1897 after a petition of friends and prison authorities.[37] [38]

19, 1893, http://indiamond6.ulib.iupui.edu/cdm/compoundobject/collection/IN/id/41415/rec/8

[36] "The Execution of Parker and M'Afee Postponed", The Indianapolis News – October 13, 1893, 2, http://indiamond6.ulib.iupui.edu/cdm/compoundobject/collection/IN/id/44419/rec/15

[37] "Edward M'Afee's Death", The Indianapolis News – October 11, 1899, http://indiamond6.ulib.iupui.edu/cdm/compoundobject/collection/IN/id/67397/rec/1

[38] Indiana State Prison South records.,

Benjamin Thornton was assigned to investigate the arson fire. At 3 a.m. on April 29, 1897, the stable of J.C. Adams, rear of 750 North Delaware Street, was almost destroyed by fire. Ben Thornton examined the burned barn and noticed two fragments of partially burned matches on the window sill where the arsonist had been seen.

The previous fall, he had investigated the arson of a Mr. McKee's barn and found matches at the scene. He did a study and found that these types of matches were made in Sweden. They were of a yellowish color and contained more than an ordinary parlor match. The McKee barn was located just across from Fraser's barn. Now, he found the same kind of matches in the burned out remains of J.C. Adams' barn. He also found the same types of matches in the pockets of William Edwards.[39]

Ben arrested Edwards the night of the fire and charged him with arson. Edwards had

---

http://www.indianadigitalarchives.org/ViewRecord.aspx?RID=0993D7EC52F0B2BB739265E6F41A0C92

[39] *The Indianapolis News* – May 29, 1897 & The Cincinnati Enquirer, May 30, 1897

been employed by Fraser for two years. The police said that he had been an arson suspect for some time and that there had been fires in the neighborhoods he had previously been employed at. They also believed the fires of the barns of Winfield Miller, Fred Mayer, Cortland Van Camp, Henry Drew and L.S. Ayres were arson cases.[40]

Edwards said "The charge against me is false. I never burned a barn in my life." He was scheduled to appear in Police Court on May 7, 1897.[41] Mr. Fraser testified during the five day trial that he had made a special order for the matches from his grocer.

On May 28th, Ben Thornton testified at length about his study of certain matches which figure in this case. He said that since last fall, he has been making a special study of matches, under the microscope and otherwise, trying to find clues in arson cases.[42] At the end of the trial, William

---

[40] *The Indianapolis News* – April 30, 1897, p.7
[41] *The Indianapolis News* - May 7, 1897, p.2

Edwards was exonerated in Criminal Court. The evidence was judged to be largely circumstantial. [43] This case is noteworthy for Detective Ben Thornton's use of forensic science in a criminal trial.

In 1898, the Indianapolis Police Department set up its first Criminal Identification Bureau. It used a criminal identification system known as the Bertillon system. This system, named for the French police photographer who developed it, would be widely used across the United States to identify criminals.

It consisted of taking a number of measurements of the head and various other body parts, the width and length of hands, feet, etc. which were supposed to be a method of making positive identification. Jerry Kinney and Benjamin Thornton set this system up for IPD and it was used until 1931 when it was finally replaced by the forensic science of fingerprints.[44]

---

[42] *The Indianapolis News* – May 29, 1897, p.3
[43] *The Indianapolis News* – June 3, 1897, p.2
[44] "Indianapolis Police Department – A Proud Tradition

A box of instruments for use with the Bertillon system arrived at police headquarters in March 1898. IPD set aside two rooms in their headquarters to house the Criminal Identification Bureau.[45]

Detective Benjamin Thornton - 1896

Ben Thornton's last case was that of Edward Ruthven, sought by Cleveland police for murder. Thornton staked out the

---

of Service", (2000), p.19
[45] The Indianapolis News – March 24, 1898, p.9

house Ruthven was suspected to be holed up in, in Indianapolis for two days, in a pouring rain. He already had a bad cold.

Thornton wanted to be present when IPD arrested Ruthven but he was ordered home by Captain Kinney due to his illness. He always had a problem with asthma and soon developed pneumonia. He died on June 18, 1900, aged 50.[46]

The Indianapolis News - SATURDAY, JUNE 19, 1900[47]

BENJ. THORNTON DEAD

"Noted Detective. His Death was A Surprise to the Public.
"Detective Benjamin Thornton, one of the most celebrated colored police officers in the United States, died at his home, 525 Bright street, at 11:30 o'clock Monday night of

---

[46] "Detective Thornton Dead", The Indianapolis News – June 19, 1900, 5,
http://indiamond6.ulib.iupui.edu/cdm/compoundobject/collection/IN/id/68028/rec/5

[47] "Detective Thornton Dead", *The Indianapolis News* – June 19, 1900, 5,
http://indiamond6.ulib.iupui.edu/cdm/compoundobject/collection/IN/id/68028/rec/1

asthma. He had been confined to his home for less than a week.

The illness that preceded his death was in a great measure due to the zealous performance of his duties. Three weeks ago he received information that enabled him, in company with Detective Splan, to locate a lot of stolen bicycles, and for two or three days the two officers were driving about the country searching for the thieves.

During these trips he contracted a cold. He received the tip that Edward Ruthven, the colored man wanted by the Cleveland authorities to answer the charge of murder, and for two nights he was on watch near the house in which he was caught. On the day of the capture he reported and wanted to accompany the squad of detectives that made the arrest, but Capt. Kinney ordered him to go home.

Benjamin Tobias Thornton was born in slavery at Winchester, Va., December 18, 1849, his parents having belonged to a family named Krebbs. When he was twelve years of age he ran away to keep from being whipped and passed through the lines of Col

Grin Perry's regiment which was encamped at Winchester. One of the soldiers caught him up in his arms and he was taken to headquarters where the colonel formally adopted him as a mascot of the regiment, telling him he could remain with his men. At the close of the war he was taken to Washington, and after the regiment with which he cast his lot was mustered out of the service, he located at Richmond in this state, where he was employed in the family of a man named Jewell. He remained there about a year and came to Indianapolis and went to work for Jason Cary in a cooper shop.

When he was sixteen years of age he went to Kansas City, where he was also employed in a cooper shop. He also attended school there at odd times and it was while in that city he first met his wife, who was Essie M. Moore He returned to Indianapolis and after a short time, in which he kept a set of books and drove a sprinkling cart, he was appointed to the police force.

There are few men who have been as universally respected and who have maintained as high a degree of integrity as

Ben Thornton. His brother officers without exception say that he has always been faithful to his duty and his record in the department bears this out. Only once in his career was he reprimanded, and he contended always that on that occasion he was censured for telling the truth. The incident grew out of the killing of Charles Eyster by Parker and McAfee a great many years ago.

He was universally respected by his friends and acquaintances and enjoyed an enviable reputation as a citizen and an officer. During his career as a detective he made many celebrated arrests, and a most peculiar circumstance of his life is that he was stabbed by a colored desperado the same day that President Garfield was shot.

Among those he captured were Philip Cooper and his wife who robbed J. W. Murphy of $2,000 worth of diamonds. He also I recovered valuable diamonds stolen from George F. Adams and arrested the thief, He was instrumental in the capture of the Southgate bank robbers and handled many other celebrated criminals during his life.

He was a charter member of Lincoln Union Lodge, I.O. of O. F., and was secretary for several years. At the time of his death he was a grand director in the Biennial movable committee, He was also prominently connected with Pride of the West Lodge No. 2, Knights of Pythias. The funeral was held from Bethel A M. E. church, Thursday afternoon. All day Wednesday and Thursday morning, the body lay in state, and it was viewed' by thousands of people.

There were numerous floral offerings, among them a beautiful design in the shape of a patrolman's star, four feet high and thirty-four inches wide, contributed by the police department. Mr. Thornton always admired a star and crescent design and was the possessor of a jewel of this shape set with diamonds. This was tile design sent by the detective force.

The pall bearers were, Captain Kinney and detective Span of the detective force, patrolmen Harris and Richards; Edward Harris and Dr. B. J. Morgan of the Ugly Men's club; N. Hill and C. A. Webb of

Lincoln Union lodge and Benj. Wade and Edmund White of the Patriarchie.

Grand directors Lee of Atlanta, Ga., and Temple of St. Louis. Mo., attended as representatives of the biennial committee the funeral procession was headed by a detail of twenty-four patrolmen under the command of Captain Kruger, followed by the Indianapolis Military band, the Uniformed Patriarche, then the lodges and Household of Ruth.

The procession was the largest seen in this city for many years. At the church, the services were con ducted by the pastor Rev. C. W, Newton, assisted by visiting ministers. The services were brief but solemn, and the speaker dwelt in laudable terms of the life's work of this good citizen, and affectionate husband and father. The burial was in Crown Hill."

Carter Temple Jr. [48]

Patrolman Carter Temple Jr.

Born: February 14, 1843 Logan County, Kentucky[49] [50]

---

[48] Photograph courtesy of Reginald Temple, great-grandson of Carter Temple Jr., received February 1, 2015.

[49] Year: 1900; Census Place: Indianapolis, Marion, Indiana; Roll: 388; Page: 1A; Enumeration District: 0074; FHL microfilm: 1240388.

[50] Temple Family Bible gives birth date.

Died: February 13, 1929 Indianapolis, Indiana
Date Appointed: May 13, 1876
Date of Separation/Retirement: 1900

In 1920, Carter Temple Jr. had to submit an affidavit to receive a pension for his Civil War service. It contains interesting details about his life. This is provided through the courtesy of his great-granddaughter, Cecelia Boler.

In 1920, Carter Temple Jr. (Alias Carr Hopkins) says:
"I was born in Logan Co., KY, November 13, 1843. My father was named Carter Temple. My mother was Sarah Hayden. I fell to the possession of Sam Hopkins, and that is how I came to go into the service under the name of Hopkins.

After the war, I took my father's name. I have a half-brother living. He is George Temple and he is here in Indianapolis. I have no sister at all. I have never married, but once. I married her, Martha A. Blackwell, a single girl, here in Marion Co. April 13, 1871. We have lived here together without separation or divorce. We have had five children, but all are dead, but one. He is Carter F.P. Temple and he is our youngest child. He was born Feb.17, 1879.

I came to Indianapolis on March 27, 1866, immediately after my muster out and I have lived here ever since. I lived in Logan County, 10 miles from Russellville, until I enlisted. I lived on the farm of my owner, Sam Hopkins, and I left that farm to enlist.

I had no wife in slavery and lived with no woman at all until I married my present wife. I was not quite 21 years old when I enlisted. I ran away from Logan Co. and went to Tennessee. I got with the 106th Ohio infantry and I drove a team for them until November when I enlisted in the 14th. No, I was not an enlisted man in the 106th, but they promised me pay, but I never got any pay for it at all. It was company A, 106th Ohio that I was with. I was there as Carr Hopkins too."

December 16, 1876: Carter Temple Jr. shot and wounded a fleeing felon named Crum Brown on Lafayette Road.

<u>December 11, 1877:</u> Arrested Edward Harvey, who had just shot his wife Nan three times, wounding her. [51]

<u>June 1, 1881:</u> Assigned to Fourth District, along with Benjamin Thornton.[52]

<u>June 20, 1882:</u> Appointed as "muscle for control of prisoners" and assigned to patrol wagon duty.[53]

<u>November 1882:</u> Paid $2.00 a day for 15 days work.[54]

---

[51] "An Attempt to Kill", The Indianapolis News – December 12, 1877, 1,
http://www.newspapers.com/image/37769682/?terms=%22officer%2Btemple%22

[52] "The Police Assignments", The Indianapolis News – June 2, 1881, 3, http://indiamond6.ulib.iupui.edu/cdm/compoundobject/collection/IN/id/16521/rec/2

[53] The Indianapolis News – June 20, 1882, p.3, accessed March 27, 2014,
www.newspapers.com/image/34619604/?terms="carter%2Btemple"

[54] Index to the Miscellaneous Documents of the House of Representatives for the 48th Congress, 1883-1884,Payroll of officers and men of the police force, p.495, accessed May 24, 2014,
http://books.google.com/books?id=DVRHAQAAIAAJ&pg=RA1-PA495&lpg=RA1-PA495&dq=%22horace+heston%22++%22indianapolis%22&source=bl&ots=RREcmOx0Wr&sig=KIj-rbovMrhXIJdDCUhqfZEWy-A&hl=en&sa=X&ei=Dyd_U5i3OcqrsATDlYDQCA&ved=0CDQQ6AEwBA#v=onepage&q=%22horace%20heston%22%20&f=false

Carter Temple Jr. - 1890[55]

April 5, 1883: When the Metropolitan Force was reorganized, Carter Temple was reappointed to it.

Carter Temple Jr. – 1889

---

[55] IMPD Historic Photographic Collection

October 10, 1893:   Carter Temple, after getting off an electric street car, was struck by another car at Alabama and Massachusetts Avenue, breaking two ribs on the right side. He received injuries to his head and face.[56]

May 7, 1896:   While patrolling early this morning, Patrolman Carter Temple saw a man lurking in the front yard of Mayor Thomas Taggart's home, on Capitol Avenue. Carter got up close behind the man and demanded to know what he was doing. "None of your damn business" replied the man. Looking closely at the man's face, Temple saw it was Mayor Taggart's and there was a smile on it.[57]

October 8, 1896: The "Colored Odd Fellows" held a parade in Indianapolis and asked the police department if they could assign some police officers to it. Superintendent Colbert assigned 9 African-American officers to lead the parade and put Officer Carter Temple in

---

[56] "Carter Temple Injured", The Indianapolis News – October 10, 1893, 2, http://indiamond6.ulib.iupui.edu/cdm/compoundobject/collection/IN/id/44745/rec/2

[57] "Temple With His Revolver", The Indianapolis News – May 7, 1896, 6, http://indiamond6.ulib.iupui.edu/cdm/compoundobject/collection/IN/id/52593/rec/2

charge of it. There were nearly 500 persons in the parade. Carter Temple was an Odd Fellow as were a number of other African-American officers with IPD.[58]

Carter Temple was born in 1843 in Logan County, Kentucky as a slave. He ran away prior to joining the U.S. Army in 1863 at Gallatin, Tennessee. Under the alias Carr Hopkins, he enlisted in Company C of the 14th United States Colored Troops. He saw action at the Battle of Nashville, 1864 before being mustered out in 1866.[59] He came to Indianapolis in 1871.

He had a half-brother named Fred Hopkins (1832-1899) who moved to Vicksburg, Mississippi, probably as a slave and ended up working for the Confederate Army in some capacity, possibly during the Siege of Vicksburg, May-July 1863. After the war,

---

[58] "Odd Fellows in Session", The Indianapolis News – October 8, 1896, 6,
http://indiamond6.ulib.iupui.edu/cdm/compoundobject/collection/IN/id/50406/rec/1

[59] National Archives and Records Administration (NARA); Washington, D.C.; Compiled military service records of volunteer Union soldiers who served with the United States Colored Troops, infantry organizations.; Microfilm Serial: M1822; Microfilm Roll: 8. (Gives birthplace).

he served as police officer and detective for the Vicksburg Police Department, from before 1870 until all African-American police officers were forced to resign in 1884. He is probably the first African-American police officer in the state of Mississippi.

Carter Temple Jr. wed Martha A. Blackwell, April 13, 1871 in Indianapolis, Indiana. In September 1872, Carter purchased lot #59 in Elliott's subdivision of Indianapolis from Emma R. Colwell for $425. He built a fine home at 550 Minerva Street, which stood until 1979 in Indianapolis. It was razed to make way for part of IUPUI.

He apparently owned cattle as on November 17, 1875; the Indianapolis News noted that he was the first person to suffer the penalty of letting his stock run at large within the city limits. He was one of the founders of the Martin R. Delaney Post of the Grand Army of the Republic (G.A.R.) and in December of 1887, was elected its commander. This was a patriotic organization of former Civil War Union Army soldiers.

Carter Temple Jr. aspired to be an "actor man" as he called it, but after one performance in a minstrel show, he quit to become a police officer. [60] Temple joined the Indianapolis Police Department in 1876.

He was issued badge #13 and upon his retirement in 1900, the badge was not used until 1903 when the Board of Safety appointed several officers. All refused to wear #13 due to a fear of bad luck. The 1903 property tax records of Indianapolis showed the value of Carter Temple Jr.'s real estate at $4,600, ranked #14 in Indianapolis among African-Americans. He was considered one of the most prosperous men of his race in town.

---

[60] "Brief Biographies of Great Men", The Indianapolis News – April 7, 1890, 8,
http://indiamond6.ulib.iupui.edu/cdm/compoundobject/collection/IN/id/29611/rec/1

Carter Temple Jr. Family about 1920[61]
L-R Front Row: Maggie Varnum, Bertha and Juanita.
Back Row: Carter Temple Jr., Bob Ferguson

He passed away at age 86, February 13, 1929.

---

[61] Photo courtesy of Cecelia A. Boler.

Top photo: Reginald Temple, great-grandson of Carter Temple with a composite photo of all IPD officers from 1895.

L-R: Chief Hite, IMPD Chaplain David Coatie, IMPD Civilian Patrick Pearsey and Cecelia Boler, great-granddaughter of Carter Temple Jr.

L-R: Public Safety Director Troy Riggs, Author Pearsey, Cecelia Boler.

On February 2, 2015, the Indianapolis Metropolitan Police Department dedicated the first historical exhibit dedicated to the contributions of African-American police officers in its history.

At the dedication ceremony, Chief of Police Rick Hite, Public Safety Director Troy Riggs, Cecelia A. Boler, great-granddaughter of Officer Carter Temple Jr., and the author, Patrick Pearsey, made remarks for the occasion.

They commemorated Officer Temple, one of the five men who on May 13, 1876 became the first Black police officers in the city's history.

Patrolman George W. Hilliard

Born: January 1846 Halifax County, N.C.
Date Appointed: May 31, 1878
Date of Separation/Retirement: May 26, 1879 (dropped from force)

George W. Hilliard claimed Cherokee blood on both sides of his family, which were Free Blacks, ordered to leave North Carolina within 90 days or become slaves. He made an attempt to be a member of the Cherokee Nation on August 18, 1908 when he submitted an affidavit. He then lived at 441 N. Indiana Avenue. [62] George was employed as an engineer of a stationary plant, 1887-1910 in Indianapolis.

---

[62] Records Related to Enrollment of Eastern Cherokee by Guion Miller, George W. Hilliard, #34532.

Nathan Ward ca.1890[63]   Nathan Ward 1896

Patrolman Nathan T. Ward

Born: March 1853 Union County, Indiana[64]
Died: March 20, 1908 Indianapolis, Indiana
Date Appointed: May 31, 1878
Date of Separation/Retirement: November 10, 1901

Buried in Crown Hill Cemetery, plot 37, lot 594.[65]
Nathan T. Ward was 5'11" in height.

---

[63] IMPD Historical Photograph Archives
[64] Year: 1900; Census Place: Indianapolis, Marion, Indiana; Roll: 387; Page: 7A; Enumeration District: 0037; FHL microfilm: 1240387.
[65] Findagrave.com.

May 26, 1879: "The discharge of Nathan Ward, a colored man and one of the most efficient officers on the police force, by the new police board, did not meet with the approval of the citizens of the third ward, where his beat lay. Prominent citizens are going to bring pressure to have him reinstated."[66]

May 30, 1879: "The police board, it is understood, has concluded to yield under the pressure brought to bear in favor of Nathan Ward, and will drop Edward P. Doody, turnkey at the Sixth Street station house, reinstate John Minor, and thus make a place for Ward. A portion of the burden of blame laid on their shoulders will then be lifted."[67]

April 5, 1883: Considered for appointment to newly reorganized Metropolitan Force.

March 12, 1889: Reappointed to Metropolitan Force.

March 22, 1893: The Indianapolis News reported on a rumored political feud

---

[66] "City News", The Indianapolis News - May 29, 1879, http://indiamond6.ulib.iupui.edu/cdm/compoundobject/collection/IN/id/13061/rec/13

[67] "Additional City News", The Indianapolis News – May 30, 1879, http://indiamond6.ulib.iupui.edu/cdm/compoundobject/collection/IN/id/13776/rec/14

between Officer Nathan Ward (Democrat) and Detective Benjamin Thornton (Republican). The two had worked on the Eyster murder case that year and came up with different conclusions. Thornton said that reports that he has instigated efforts to have Ward removed from the department are untrue.[68]

He filed charges in June 1893 against Detective Benjamin Thornton for conduct unbecoming related to the Charles Eyster murder case.[69]

November 10, 1901: "Nathan Ward, colored policeman, dismissed from force for intoxication."[70]

September 23, 1907: Employed as a professional bail bondsman.

March 28, 1908: "Nathan T. Ward, was born at Union County, Ind., 1853 and

---

[69] "Charges Against Thornton", The Indianapolis News – June 19, 1893, http://indiamond6.ulib.iupui.edu/cdm/compoundobject/collection/IN/id/41415/rec/8

[70] "Trial of Patrolman Ward", The Indianapolis Journal – November 10, 1901, 8, https://newspapers.library.in.gov/cgi-bin/indiana?a=d&d=IJ19011109.1.3&srpos=8&e=-------en-20--1--txt-txIN-%22nathan+ward%22-----#

departed this life Friday morning at the age of 54 years. He served on the Indianapolis Police force for 19 years and for a number of years held the position of Police Court Bondsman. The funeral services were held Monday afternoon from Bethel Church Rev. Geo. Sampson officiating. He was a member of Pride of the West Ledge No. 2. K. of P." [71]

Patrolman Samuel P. Herron

Born: April 9, 1850 Kentucky[73]
Died: January 4, 1905 Indianapolis, IN.
Date Appointed: May 26, 1879
Date of Separation: September 22, 1879

---

[71] *Indianapolis Recorder* – March 28, 1908, 2, http://indiamond6.ulib.iupui.edu/cdm/compoundobject/collection/IRecorder/id/14672/rec/2
[72] Findagrave.com – photo of tombstone
[73] Year: 1900; Census Place: Indianapolis, Marion, Indiana; Roll: 388; Page: 1B; Enumeration District: 0076; FHL microfilm: 1240388.

September 22, 1879: Discharged by the Police Board after shooting Hill Ferguson in the line of duty on September 20th.

He was employed as a saloon keeper, 1880. Buried Crown Hill Cemetery, section 43, lot 5071. Dates of birth and death come from his tombstone. [74]

Patrolman Henry Holt

Born: 1852 Kentucky
Died: July 1904 Indianapolis, Indiana
Date Appointed: May 31, 1880
Date of Separation/Retirement: 1886

Buried Crown Hill Cemetery, section E, lot 3029. Buried July 30, 1904. [75]

October 2, 1881: On Sunday morning this date, Patrolmen Benjamin Thornton and Henry Holt arrested a man named James Fry for disturbing the peace. Holt took Fry back to the station house and at the corner of Indiana Avenue and Mississippi Street, Fry made an escape attempt. He struck

---

[74] Findagrave.com – photo of tombstone
[75] Ibid.

Holt, cutting him in the face three times with a knife and took off running. He managed to escape despite several shots being fired at him by Officer Holt. Holt was not seriously injured.[76]

<u>July 20, 1882</u>: Accused of striking a man named Albert Swope, who later died (along with a White officer), Patrolman Holt was questioned by the coroner. Holt denied any violence. Additional witnesses testified that Swope was very ill and weak before police arrived and Holt put his shoes on and dragged him out to the front of 495 California Street to the await the arrival of "Tally Ho" (police wagon). Holt was cleared.[77]

<u>September 12, 1882</u>: After being suspended for an apparent political reason, Officer Henry Holt was described by the Indianapolis News as "one of the most vigilant and efficient colored men attached to the police force."

---

[76] "Officer Holt Stabbed", The Indianapolis Leader – October 8, 1881, 4, https://newspapers.library.in.gov/cgi-bin/indiana?a=d&d=IL18811008.1.4&srpos=12&e=-------en-20--1--txt-txIN-%22henry+holt%22-----

[77] "The Swope Homicide", The Indianapolis News – July 20, 1882 , 4, http://indiamond6.ulib.iupui.edu/cdm/compoundobject/collection/IN/id/18110/rec/1

<u>November 1882:</u> Paid $30 for 15 days work.[78]
<u>August 4, 1885:</u> Appointed driver of the police patrol wagon by the Police Board. [79]

Buried in Crown Hill Cemetery, section E, lot 3029.[80]

Patrolman Richard W. Wells

Born: 1855 Kentucky
Died: February 4, 1901 Indianapolis, Indiana
Date Appointed: By 1880
Date of Separation/Retirement: 1884

<u>April 1871:</u> Richard Yaw age 55, slightly drunk, is assaulted by four youths from a

---

[78] Index to the Miscellaneous Documents of the House of Representatives for the 48th Congress, 1883-1884, Payroll of officers and men of the police force, p.495, accessed May 24, 2014,
http://books.google.com/books?id=DVRHAQAAIAAJ&pg=RA1-PA495&lpg=RA1-PA495&dq=%22horace+heston%22++%22indianapolis%22&source=bl&ots=RREcmOx0Wr&sig=KIj-rbovMrhXIJdDCUhqfZEWy-A&hl=en&sa=X&ei=Dyd_U5i3OcqrsATDlYDQCA&ved=0CDQQ6AEwBA#v=onepage&q=%22horace%20heston%22%20&f=false

[79] The Indianapolis News – August 5, 1885, 4,
http://www.newspapers.com/image/34593156/?terms=%22henry%2Bholt%22

[80] Birth and death dates from Findagrave.com

school for African-Americans on the way home. He drives them off, but as he reaches his home he is hit by a rock thrown by a youth – Richard Wells, aged 18-20. Yaw died at 9:30 p.m. and Wells was arrested for 2nd degree murder.[81] The trial of Richard Wells started May 17th.[82] [83] He was found guilty on June 5th, sentenced to 2 ½ years at Michigan City Prison. He ended up serving his time at the Boys School in Plainfield, Indiana.[84]

<u>September 22, 1875:</u> Richard Wells serves as secretary to The State Convention of Colored Men held at Indianapolis. [85]

---

[81] "Man Killed by a Colored Boy", The Indianapolis News – April 24, 1871, 4, http://indiamond6.ulib.iupui.edu/cdm/compoundobject/collection/IN/id/939/rec/1

[82] "The Courts", The Indianapolis News – May 17, 1871, 4, http://indiamond6.ulib.iupui.edu/cdm/compoundobject/collection/IN/id/1239/rec/21

[83] "The City", The Indianapolis News – May 18, 1871, 4, http://indiamond6.ulib.iupui.edu/cdm/ref/collection/IN/id/1456/rec/22

[84] Department of Correction-Boys' School 1867-1937, http://www.indianadigitalarchives.org/ViewRecord.aspx?RID=A97AA147BCF10B2EDC9084E65DC7BA14

[85] "The Black Laws", The Indianapolis News – September 22, 1875, 2, http://indiamond6.ulib.iupui.edu/cdm/compoundobject/collection/IN/id/8779/rec/1

Employed as a janitor in 1877[86], Wells was a member of IPD in June of 1880 according to the census of that year.

June 1, 1881: Assigned to the Third District along with Henry Holt, African-American.[87]

November 1882: Paid $28 for 14 days of work.[88]

1884: Richard Wells left the Metropolitan Force.

June 25, 1890: Richard W. Wells received at Michigan City State Prison. He is released October 23, 1891.[89]

---

[86] 1877 Indianapolis City Directory

[87] "The Police Assignments", The Indianapolis News – June 2, 1881, 3. http://indiamond6.ulib.iupui.edu/cdm/compoundobject/collection/IN/id/16521/rec/2

[88] Index to the Miscellaneous Documents of the House of Representatives for the 48th Congress, 1883-1884,Payroll of officers and men of the police force, p.495, accessed May 24, 2014, http://books.google.com/books?id=DVRHAQAAIAAJ&pg=RA1-PA495&lpg=RA1-PA495&dq=%22horace+heston%22++%22indianapolis%22&source=bl&ots=RREcmOx0Wr&sig=KIj-rbovMrhXIJdDCUhqfZEWy-A&hl=en&sa=X&ei=Dyd_U5i3OcgrsATDIYDQCA&ved=0CDQQ6AEwBA#v=onepage&q=%22horace%20heston%22%20&f=false

[89] Department of Correction-Prison North 1858-1897, http://www.indianadigitalarchives.org/ViewRecord.aspx?RID=FC14544C64306FB7FDD08DF700371853

He worked for the National Malleable Iron Works in Haughville and died of a heart attack there.

WELLS HAD A HISTORY.
Man Who Fell Dead Went from Political Success to Prison.

"Richard Wells, who dropped dead while at work at the Malleable Casting's Company's' plant, at Haughville, had lived in this city from early boyhood, and at one time was regarded as one of the city's most promising men. He finished a course in the common and high schools, and was an expert mathematician. Early in the 80's he engaged in politics, and was Influential in wielding the colored vote.

He served several years as a turnkey at the Jail, was elected city market master at the west market.

Defalcations were traced to Wells, who was arrested, and after two trials, convicted and sentenced to a term in the prison north. Wells returned to the city at the expiration of his prison term. He at one time owned several valuable pieces of property, which were lost in the effort to save him from prison. His only relatives are a brother and a sister. The whereabouts of the former is unknown. He was forty-eight years old." [90]

Patrolman Samuel J. McClure

Born: 1846 South Carolina
Died: June 1, 1920 Chicago, Illinois [91]
Date Appointed: June 1, 1881
Date of Separation/Retirement: 1883

Samuel McClure was appointed to the Metropolitan Police Department June 1, 1881 as an "extra" policeman.[92] By 1883 he had been hired by the Merchant Police, a separate entity from the Metropolitan Force. He remained on the Merchant Police

---

[90] "Wells had a History", The Indianapolis News – February 5, 1901, 9,
http://indiamond6.ulib.iupui.edu/cdm/compoundobject/collection/IN/id/68817/rec/1
[91] "Illinois, Cook County Deaths, 1878-1922," index, FamilySearch (https://familysearch.org/pal:/MM9.1.1/N779-5YZ : accessed 24 May 2014), Samuel Mcclure, 01 Jun 1920; citing Chicago, Cook, Illinois, Cemetery, cn 18729, Cook County Courthouse, Chicago; FHL microfilm 1309238.
[92] "The Police Assignments", The Indianapolis News – June 2, 1881, 3,
http://indiamond6.ulib.iupui.edu/cdm/ref/collection/IN/id/16521/rec/6

as late as 1909. He is buried in Crown Hill Cemetery.[93]

Patrolman Horace Heston

Born: September 1853 Kentucky
Died: August 20, 1906 Indianapolis, Indiana[94]
Date Appointed: June 1, 1881
Date of Separation: About 1883

Buried in Crown Hill Cemetery, section 37, lot 190.[95]

In 1880, Horace Heston was working as a shoemaker.[96] In June 1881 he was appointed as the Night Turnkey at police headquarters. [97] He received his commission as a Notary Public on June 2, 1881.[98]

---

[93] Findagrave.com
[94] Ancestry.com. Indiana Deaths, 1882-1920 [database online]. Provo, UT, USA: Ancestry.com Operations Inc, 2004. The source of this record is the book H-13 on page 14 within the series produced by the Indiana Works Progress Administration.
[95] Findagrave.com
[96] Year: 1880; Census Place: Indianapolis, Marion, Indiana; Roll: 294; Family History Film: 1254294; Page: 127A; Enumeration District: 110; Image: 0727.
[97] The Indianapolis Journal – June 4, 1881, https://newspapers.library.in.gov/cgi-bin/indiana?a=d&d=IL18810604.1.4&srpos=5&e=-------en-20--1--txt-txIN-%22henry+holt%22-----#

November 1882: Paid $E30 for 15 days work as Turnkey.[99]

April 1884: Defeated for office of Constable on Republican ticket.

1902-1904: Arrested several times for policy making (gambling).

July 1903: Serving as a Republican precinct committeeman of the First Precinct, Fifth Ward.

After his death, the home of Horace Heston, 635 Blake Street, reputed to be a "policy

---

[98] Annual Reports of the Officers of State of the State of Indiana, Part 1
By Indiana, 108, accessed May 23, 2014,
http://books.google.com/books?id=R3ax4VWshxIC&pg=PA108&lpg=PA108&dq=%22Horace+heston%22++%22indianapolis%22&source=bl&ots=1jHog-Ln_w&sig=C7gW3wd6MEJC7xeHrNRj-oMZF6w&hl=en&sa=X&ei=0SV_U924KKPLsQSi3YHAAQ&ved=0CCYQ6AEwAA#v=onepage&q=%22Horace%20heston%22%20%20%22indianapolis%22&f=false

[99] Index to the Miscellaneous Documents of the House of Representatives for the 48th Congress, 1883-1884,Payroll of officers and men of the police force, p.495, accessed May 24, 2014,
http://books.google.com/books?id=DVRHAQAAIAAJ&pg=RA1-PA495&lpg=RA1-PA495&dq=%22horace+heston%22++%22indianapolis%22&source=bl&ots=RREcmOx0Wr&sig=KIj-rbovMrhXIJdDCUhqfZEWy-A&hl=en&sa=X&ei=Dyd_U5i3OcqrsATDlYDQCA&ved=0CDQQ6AEwBA#v=onepage&q=%22horace%20heston%22%20&f=false

king" of Indianapolis, was purchased and used as a home for young Black women.

Patrolman Allen Dudley

Born: 1858
Died: May 14, 1893 Indianapolis, Indiana[100]
Date Appointed: June 1, 1881 [101]
Date Separated: 1882

Hired June 1, 1881 as a Second District Nightman along with Ed Harris. The Indianapolis News described him as making a fine appearance in uniform and from his manner will doubtless make an "efficient officer."
February 1886: Republican candidate for Constable.

Patrolman Ephraim Palmer

---

[100] Ancestry.com. Indiana Deaths, 1882-1920 [database on-line]. Provo, UT, USA: Ancestry.com Operations Inc, 2004. The source of this record is the book H-4 on page 347 within the series produced by the Indiana Works Progress Administration.
[101]   The Indianapolis Journal – June 4, 1881, https://newspapers.library.in.gov/cgi-bin/indiana?a=d&d=IL18810604.1.4&srpos=5&e=-------en-20--1--txt-txIN-%22henry+holt%22-----#

Born: 1842 Boone County, Missouri
Died: December 18, 1918 Danville, Vermillion County, IL.
Date Appointed: May 31, 1880
Date of Separation: September 16, 1889

Six feet, two inches tall, Ephraim was a veteran of the Civil War, enlisting March 21, 1864 in Company K of the 68th United States Colored Troops.[102] He was discharged February 5, 1866. After leaving the Metropolitan Police Force of Indianapolis, Ephraim lived in Indianapolis. On December 29, 1904, he was admitted to a home for disabled soldiers in Marion, Indiana. He was discharged April 21, 1906.[103] His widow Mary E. Palmer filed for a widows pension March 10, 1919. He is buried in the Danville, Illinois National Cemetery, plot 10, 2681 R1.[104]

---

[102] National Park Service. U.S. Civil War Soldiers, 1861-1865 [database on-line]. Provo, UT, USA: Ancestry.com Operations Inc., 2007.
[103] Original data: Historical Register of National Homes for Disabled Volunteer Soldiers, 1866-1938; (National Archives Microfilm Publication M1749, 282 rolls); Records of the Department of Veterans Affairs, Record Group 15; National Archives, Washington, D.C.
[104] Findagrave.com

The Police Board suspended his police powers on September 16, 1889 after his arrest for assault and battery. He was the market horse officer.[105]

Patrolman George Washington Cheatham

Born: 1849 Kentucky[106]
Died: January 1917 Indianapolis, IN.
Date Appointed: May 21, 1880[107]
Date Separated: 1883

---

[105] "Powers Granted and Revoked", The Indianapolis News – September 16, 1889, 1, http://indiamond6.ulib.iupui.edu/cdm/compoundobject/collection/IN/id/30837/rec/1

[106] "United States Census, 1910," index and images, FamilySearch (https://familysearch.org/pal:/MM9.1.1/MKP5-RV9 : accessed 24 May 2014), George W Cheatum, Indianapolis Ward 4, Marion, Indiana, United States; citing enumeration district (ED) 92, sheet 5B, family 153, NARA microfilm publication T624, FHL microfilm 1374380

[107] Proceedings of the Common Council, 58, accessed May 24, 2014, http://books.google.com/books?id=dX04AAAAMAAJ&pg=PA100&lpg=PA100&dq=%22george+w.+cheatham%22++%22indianapolis%22&source=bl&ots=SkZzWDCnte&sig=aMWzrVWoojFQgth5jfbbLUj_E4&hl=en&sa=X&ei=sTCAU5WNOdCMyASNIYKICw&ved=0CDQQ6AEwAw#v=onepage&q=cheatham&f=false

Buried in Crown Hill Cemetery, section 47, lot 162.[108]

June 18, 1881: Praised in The Indianapolis Leader for his work as Turnkey of the Sixth Street Station in the previous year. Not only was there no complaints about him but he had saved the city money in fuel costs.[109]

July 14, 1890: Declares his candidacy for the State Legislature in the Indianapolis News.[110]

February 28, 1892: During a transit strike where riots occurred and many city policemen resigned, G.W. Cheatham of the Merchant Police was sworn in as a member of the regular Metropolitan Force.[111]

June 6, 1900: After a dispute over purchasing uniforms, G.W. Cheatham and 22 other members of the Merchant Police

---

[108] Findagrave.com
[109] The Indianapolis Leader – June 18, 1881, 4, https://newspapers.library.in.gov/cgi-bin/indiana?a=d&d=IL18810618.1.4&srpos=2&e=-------en-20--1--txt-txIN-%22george+w.+cheatham%22-----#
[110] The Indianapolis News – July 14, 1890, 3, http://indiamond6.ulib.iupui.edu/cdm/ref/collection/IN/id/30612/rec/4
[111] "The Mob Spirit Again", The Indianapolis News – February 29, 1892, http://indiamond6.ulib.iupui.edu/cdm/ref/collection/IN/id/39447/rec/2

resigned and formed the Indianapolis Merchants Detectives' Association.[112]
1910: Still a member of the Indianapolis Merchants Police Force.[113]

1904

Patrolman Edward Harris

---

[112] "Won't Wear Uniforms", The Indianapolis Journal – June 6, 1900, 12, https://newspapers.library.in.gov/cgi-bin/indiana?a=d&d=IJ19000607.1.12&srpos=1&e=-------en-20--1--txt-txIN-%22george+w.+cheatam%22-----#

[113] 1910 Indianapolis City Directory, http://www.mocavo.com/Indianapolis-City-Directory-1910/416594/64

Born: May 1850 Mt. Sterling, KY. [114]
Died: April 1, 1908 Indianapolis, IN.
Date Appointed: May 31, 1880
Date of Retirement: August 1905 (retired)

Buried Crown Hill Cemetery, section 47, lot 302.

Ed Harris was born a slave. At age 14, he ran away from his master and joined the Union Army. He served until the end of the war, being mustered out at Nashville, Tennessee. He stayed in Nashville until 1872, when he came to Indianapolis.

Officer Harris was 5'11" in height.

Early in his career, Officer Harris was assigned to a district that was known for the number of "toughs" that hung out at the saloons. He was ordered to do everything in his power to break up the gang. His first arrest was the chief bully of the gang. He took the prisoner to No. 5 Engine House and called for the wagon.

---

[114] Year: 1900; Census Place: Indianapolis, Marion, Indiana; Roll: 388; Page: 7B; Enumeration District: 0073; FHL microfilm: 1240388

While there, a number of the confederates of the arrested man gathered around and the bully insisted that the officer lay down his mace and revolver and fight. Harris did so and the prisoner regained consciousness after arriving at police headquarters in the wagon. This event sent a message and from then on, all of Ed Harris' prisoners went to jail without resisting. He never used his mace.[115]

He was reappointed March 12, 1889 and assigned to District 15.

<u>November 1882:</u> Paid $30 for 15 days work.[116]
<u>February 2, 1894</u>: Monthly salary, 69.75

---

[115] 1904 Indianapolis Sentinel
[116] Index to the Miscellaneous Documents of the House of Representatives for the 48th Congress, 1883-1884, Payroll of officers and men of the police force, p.495, accessed May 24, 2014,
http://books.google.com/books?id=DVRHAQAAIAAJ&pg=RA1-PA495&lpg=RA1-PA495&dq=%22horace+heston%22++%22indianapolis%22&source=bl&ots=RREcmOx0Wr&sig=KIj-rbovMrhXIJdDCUhqfZEWy-A&hl=en&sa=X&ei=Dyd_U5i3OcqrsATDlYDQCA&ved=0CDQQ6AEwBA#v=onepage&q=%22horace%20heston%22%20&f=false

Edward Harris - 1896

<u>May 11, 1901:</u> Receiving treatment at Martinsville, Indiana.
<u>1903:</u> Indianapolis Tax Duplicate shows Edward Harris owned real estate valued at $5,230, ranked 5th most valuable among African-American residents at that time.

Indianapolis Recorder April 4, 1908
EDWARD HARRIS DEAD
"Edward Harris a well-known transfer and storage man died Wednesday at his home 531 Hiawatha Street, after two day's illness. Mr. Harris was born a slave at Mt. Sterling, Ky. He came to this city thirty seven years ago, after having lost all his savings by a bank failure at Louisville; He went into the

express business. He accumulated rapidly and owned considerable real estate.

He had been a trustee of Bethel A. M E. Church for eighteen years. He leaves a widow, son and daughter The funeral observances will be held this afternoon at Bethel church at2 p. m. Rev. G. H. Shaffer, officiating He was not a member of any organization. Mrs. Anna Lewis is in the city from Louisville, to attend the funeral."[117]

Sergeant Joshua Spearis

Born: 1858[118]

---

[117] "Edward Harris Dead", The Recorder – April 4, 1908, 4, http://indiamond6.ulib.iupui.edu/cdm/compoundobject/collection/IRecorder/id/14677/rec/1

[118] Year: 1930; Census Place: Indianapolis, Marion, Indiana;

Died: November, 1945 Indianapolis, IN.
Date Appointed: April 14, 1883
Date of Retirement: July 1, 1934
6'2", 240 lbs.

<u>March 5, 1888:</u> Patrolman Joshua Spears was involved in the pursuit of a homicide suspect named Gus Williams. Williams shot and killed a Hardin Venable in a tavern and fled. Joined by Captain Colbert and Sergeant Lowe, the officers chased Williams with orders to shoot him if he tried to escape. They surmised he ran to his brother Ben Williams apartment. Through a tragic mix-up, when Ben Williams was spotted in the apartment, the officers thought he was Gus Williams.

Told to halt, Ben Williams instead fled through a window. When he got on the ground, Officer Spearis saw him in the dark and fired twice, hitting him with the second shot. Williams died and Officer Spearis was "nominally" arrested by Captain Colbert, taken to the police station and relieved from duty.

Roll: 609; Page: 9A; Enumeration District: 0336; Image: 573.0; FHL microfilm: 2340344.

<u>1888:</u> Discharged.

<u>March 19, 1894:</u> Reappointed to IPD.

<u>February 8, 1903</u>: A gang of five men, who stole over 500 chickens on the northwest side of town, were rounded up by African-American patrolmen James Crabtree, Lewis W. Montgomery and Joshua Spearis. [119]

<u>May 28, 1919:</u> Patrolman Joshua Spearis, colored, was advanced to the-same department. Both will rank as sergeants. Spearis has been probation officer in the Juvenile Court. Also, Edward Trabue (African-American) was promoted to Detective Sergeant.   They were the first African-Americans to reach the rank of Sergeant with IPD.[120]

July 7, 1934 *Indianapolis Recorder* "ENVIABLE SERVICE RECORD The retirement from the Indianapolis police force of Joshua Spearis', for thirty-three years member of the department, removes from active service an officer with a long and brilliant record. Mr. Spearis was

---

[119] "Greed for Chickens", The Indianapolis Journal – February 8, 1903, 3, https://newspapers.library.in.gov/cgi-bin/indiana?a=d&d=IJ19030208.1.3&srpos=1&e=08-02-1903-08-02-1903--en-20-IJ-1--txt-txIN-crabtree-----#

[120]   The Indianapolis News – May 28, 1919, http://www.newspapers.com/newspage/6887854/

scheduled to be relieved July 1 of his duties as a guardian of the law. He severs his connection with the force as a pensioner at the ripe age of 75, and at the end of an enviable career. As a public servant, Mr. Spearis was recognized throughout the entire period of his long incumbency by comrades and superiors for his great ability and natural efficiency.

These qualities of the retiring officer were commended in high terms by Michael F. Morrissey, chief of police. Mr. Spearis' record should serve as an excellent example for the two newly appointed race officers. It should also make for greater opportunities for service in the higher brackets of the Indianapolis Police department by competent members of our group. The system is in vogue in other progressive cities, why not in our own Indianapolis."[121]

---

[121] "Enviable Service Record", *Indianapolis Recorder* – July 7, 1934, 4, http://indiamond6.ulib.iupui.edu/cdm/compoundobject/collection/IRecorder/id/16857/rec/1

Patrolman William Albert Hogan

Born: August 15, 1854 Tennessee[122]
Died: May 5, 1939 Indianapolis, IN.[123]
Date Appointed: March 12, 1889
Date of Separation: Before 1894

<u>1889</u>: Driver of patrol wagon.[124] Patrolled District #4 that year.
<u>1900</u>: Working as express man.[125]

---

[122] Year: 1900; Census Place: Indianapolis, Marion, Indiana; Roll: 387; Page: 3A; Enumeration District: 0032; FHL microfilm: 1240387.
[123] Death Certificate provides birth & death dates. Ancestry.com.
[124] 1889 Indianapolis City Directory
[125] "Called in the Police", The Indianapolis Journal, August 7, 1900, 3, https://newspapers.library.in.gov/cgi-bin/indiana?a=d&d=IJ19000807.1.3&srpos=2&e=-------en-20--1--txt-txIN-%22william+a.+hogan%22-----

Patrolman Frank Hurt

Born: May 1859 Kentucky [126]
Died: January 15, 1905 Indianapolis, IN.
Date Appointed: On force by 1885
Date of Separation/Retirement: By 1900

<u>September 9, 1887:</u> Arrested a rape suspect.
<u>1889</u>: Assigned to District 17.

Frank Hurt was a gambler after he left the force, as evidenced by several arrests after 1900. Buried in Crown Hill Cemetery, section E, lot 3115. [127]

---

[126] Year: 1900; Census Place: Indianapolis, Marion, Indiana; Roll: 388; Page: 4A; Enumeration District: 0084; FHL microfilm: 1240388.
[127] Findagrave.com

Patrolman Simpson T. "Sim" Hart

Born: 1862 Salem, Indiana
Died: December 17, 1909 Indianapolis, Indiana
Date Appointed: February 1, 1890

---

[128] IMPD Lichtenberger History Room.

Date of Separation: December 17, 1909 (death)

Badge #33. 6'1", 210 lbs., Republican.[129]

February 2, 1894: monthly salary, $67.50.

One of the most exciting episodes in the career of Sim Hart was when he into an area known as "Little Canada" to get a suspect. He was at home with a dozen friends, who attempted to take the prisoner away from Hart. Hart fought them off and kept his prisoner.

November 27, 1907: Commended and thanked by the board for saving the life of Guilford Madden on November 7th, "Act of Bravery." [130]

Funeral of Sim Hart
"The funeral services of Mr. Simpson T. Hart, whose death occurred last Friday, Dec. 17, at his home, 425 W. 12th street, were held at Mt. Zion Baptist church, Tuesday morning at 10o'clock, Rev. G. W. Ward, officiating. Mr. Hart was a well-

---

[129] Public Safety Record, Indiana State Archives.
[130] Public Safety Record, Indiana State Archives.

known patrolman and at the time of his death was the oldest colored patrolman in active service in the city. Had he lived until Feb. 1, he would have rounded out twenty years of continuous services. He was regarded by his fellow officers as a model of bravery and faithfulness to duty, having served so long a period without a single reprimand. For a great part of this time he was route mate with Dan Carter, known as a terror to lawbreakers, especially along Indiana ave, and shared with him in many thrilling episodes.

Mr. Hart was born in Salem, Ind., in 1862 and was the son of Thomas Hart, who with William Whittaker, Benjamin Young and Carter Temple, was among the first colored patrolmen in the city. The Harts have been residents of this city for nearly fifty years. Mr. Hart suffered a paralytic stroke about a month ago, from which he never recovered. He is survived by a wife, a son and a daughter, two sisters and two brothers."[131]

---

[131] *The Indianapolis Star* – December 18, 1909, 3, http://www.newspapers.com/newspage/7307157/

James William Winn

Born: December 1860 Nicholasville, KY.
Died:
Appointed: 1891
Separated: April 18, 1906

James Winn's family moved to Xenia, Ohio when he was very young. He worked on a farm there until moving to Indianapolis in 1879. There, he got a job painting and hanging wall paper. One story related about James Winn's career was that about 1900, he was called to 10th and Middle Streets on a barber named Thomas Coley, who had run amuck, slashing several people with a razor.

Upon arrival, Coley approached Winn in a menacing manner, refusing to comply when Winn ordered him to halt. Coley continued to advance when Winn pulled his gun and fired into the ground at Coley's feet.

Coley stopped, threw the knife away and surrendered. However, as soon as Winn holstered his weapon Coley again started fighting and a hard fight ensued, won by Winn. He got a 2 year sentence for his actions that day.[132] Winn failed a physical and was released from the force in 1906.

---

[132] 1904 Indianapolis Sentinel

Patrolman Daniel Carter

Born: May 1853 Louisiana[133]
Died July 15, 1910 Indianapolis, Indiana[134]
Date Appointed: March 31, 1891
Date of Separation/Retirement: July 15, 1910 (his death)

Badge #29, 6'2", 180 lbs., Republican.[135]

---

[133] Year: 1900; Census Place: Center, Marion, Indiana; Roll: 389; Page: 3A; Enumeration District: 0110; FHL microfilm: 1240389.
[134] "Patrolman Dan Carter Dies", Indianapolis Recorder – July 16, 1910, 2, http://indiamond6.ulib.iupui.edu/cdm/compoundobject/collection/IRecorder/id/18704/rec/69

The Police Board placed him on retirement due to ill health, December 21, 1900[136]. Retired a 2nd time, April 11, 1902.[137] However, he was reappointed June 3, 1903.[138]

A write-up about the African-American officers on the department in February 1897 described how Dan "The Dark Secret" Carter cleaned up Columbia Avenue. Other officers had failed to get rid of some bad characters congregating here.

Superintendent Thomas Colbert instructed Dan Carter to camp there in July 1896 and take care of the problem. Within 7 months the troublemakers had moved onto other parts. Carter was described as one of the best natured men on the department.[139]

---

[135] Public Safety Record, Indiana State Archives.
[136] "Long Deliberations", The Indianapolis Journal – August 18, 1900, 3, https://newspapers.library.in.gov/cgi-bin/indiana?a=d&d=IJ19001222.1.3&srpos=13&e=-------en-20--1--txt-txIN-%22dan+carter%22-----#
[137] Public Safety Record, Indiana State Archives.
[138] "Safety Board Session", The Indianapolis Journal – June 4, 1903, 3, https://newspapers.library.in.gov/cgi-bin/indiana?a=d&d=IJ19030604.1.3&srpos=10&e=-------en-20--1--txt-txIN-%22dan+carter%22-----
[139] Unknown newspaper, February 21, 1897.

August 27, 1903: James Coulson, drunk, slapped Officer Dan Carter when he tried to arrest him. A "fierce" fight erupted and when it was over, Coulson looked like he'd been in an encounter with heavyweight champ Jim Jeffries, according to the Indianapolis News.[140]

In August of 1903 it was reported that Daniel Carter, one of the oldest policemen in Indianapolis, was going to assist Rev. J.L. Jackson with the newly established Christian Home for Rescue, for "colored boys". [141]

He was one of the best known IPD officers, regardless of color and had a reputation as a police officer that was "second to none".[142] He was known as the "Dark Secret" according to his obituary.

---

[140] The Indianapolis News – August 27, 1903, 3, http://www.newspapers.com/image/40139226/?terms=%22dan%2Bcarter%22

[141] "To Reform Colored Boys", The Indianapolis Journal – August 11, 1903, 7, https://newspapers.library.in.gov/cgi-bin/indiana?a=d&d=IJ19030811.1.7&srpos=3&e=-------en-20--1--txt-txIN-%22daniel+carter%22-----#

[142] "Patrolman Dan Carter Dies", Indianapolis Recorder – July 16, 1910, 2, http://indiamond6.ulib.iupui.edu/cdm/compoundobject/collection/IRecorder/id/18704/rec/69

Patrolman William H. Wheeler

Born: 1855: Jeffersonville, Kentucky
Died: December 30, 1932 Indianapolis, Indiana
Date Appointed: March 31, 1891
Date of Retirement: September 20, 1927

Badge #58 (lost), then #209, 5'8", 158 lbs., Republican.[144]

---

[143] IMPD Lichtenberger History Room.
[144] Public Safety Record, Indiana State Archives.

William Wheeler came to Indianapolis with his parents in 1863. He learned the trade of a cooper (barrel maker) and worked at that occupation for a number of years. He then worked as trainer at Henry Philip's stable until he joined the police department.

<u>October 29, 1895:</u> Received a letter notifying he was being dismissed along with other Republican policemen. He had been the wagon driver. His personnel record states he was dismissed for assault.[145]
<u>March 28, 1902:</u> Reinstated with IPD. Assigned as a wagon man.[146]

---

[145] Ibid.
[146] Ibid.

1905 photograph of an IPD officer, African-American, driving the chief's carriage. Identity uncertain but this may be William Wheeler, police chauffeur.

November 16, 1915: Police chauffeur Patrolman William Wheeler fractured his right arm while trying to crank the emergency auto in the police headquarters barn and was taken to City Hospital.[147]

He spent his early years with IPD attached to the police barns. He spent 25 years as a chauffeur of police patrols, which meant he drove police vehicles once the department became mechanized. He retired in 1927 after 36 years on the department. He became ill in October 1932. He died December 30, 1932 and was buried in Crown Hill Cemetery.[148]

---

[147] *The Indianapolis News* – November 17, 1915, 7, http://www.newspapers.com/image/7967165/?terms=%22william%2Bwheeler%22

[148] "William Wheeler Former Police Dies", *Indianapolis Recorder* – January 7, 1933, 1, http://indiamond6.ulib.iupui.edu/cdm/compoundobject/collection/IRecorder/id/15564/rec/1

Patrolman James W.H. Crabtree

Born: September 1860 Buxton, Canada
Died: June 27, 1913 Indianapolis, Indiana
Date Appointed: October 30, 1895
Date of Separation: December 27, 1911
Badge #174, 5'11", 180 lbs., Republican.[149]
Buried in Crown Hill Cemetery, section 18, lot 216.
<u>November 14, 1904:</u> Dismissed from IPD due to an assault charge November 2, 1904 for which he received a 10 day suspension.[150]
<u>April 4, 1906:</u> Reinstated with IPD.[151]

---

[149] Public Safety Record, Indiana State Archives.
[150] Public Safety Record, Indiana State Archives.
[151] Public Safety Record, Indiana State Archives.

When James W. Crabtree was 6 years of age, he left Canada and came to Indianapolis. He spent a number of years as a teamster and later as head sawyer in a saw mill. He was assigned to patrol the northeastern part of Indianapolis in 1897. There were a gang of juveniles congregating at 9th and Yandes on his beat. Responding to complaints, he got them under control.[152]

In 1902 Crabtree was assigned to a dog and pony show given by the Gentry Bros. at Capitol Avenue and 16th Street. A fight between a crowd of the circus people and an African-American became a race riot. Several members of Rufus Cantrell's grave robbing gang cut the tent ropes down so it fell on the crowd. Crabtree drove the trouble makers out and ordered others to leave. Nicknamed "The Black Limb of the Law", Crabtree sent numerous men to the prison.[153] Officer Crabtree was forced to retire along with other older men, on December 28, 1911.[154]

---

[152] Unknown newspaper, dated February 21, 1897.
[153] 1904 Indianapolis Sentinel.
[154] *The Indianapolis Star* – December 28, 1911, 3, http://www.newspapers.com/image/#6852080&terms=crabtree

Patrolman James Admire

Born: April 1859 Henry County, KY.[156]
Died: September 18, 1918 Indianapolis, IN.[157]
Date Appointed: December 15, 1897
Date of Separation: March 24, 1915

---

[155] IMPD Lichtenberger History Room.
[156] 1900; Census Place: Indianapolis, Marion, Indiana; Roll: 387; Page: 6B; Enumeration District: 0023; FHL microfilm: 1240387.
[157] Findagrave.com

Badge #118, 6'1", 215 lbs., Republican.[158]

James Admire went to Campbellsburg, Kentucky in 1871, where he worked for Captain James Howard, a steam boat builder, for two years. In 1885, he came to Indianapolis.

One story told about Admire was when he raided a crap game at 15th Street and the Canal and caught seven well known gamblers. Three of them resisted and were overcome after a tough fight, where Admire was forced to draw his revolver. James Admire and his partner broke up the notorious "Third Street" club at 12th and the canal. While Admire knocked on the front door, his partner went to the rear.

Admire entered and found that one of the 27 gamblers had his partner covered with a revolver. Admire shot at the man and he gave up. The rest of the men were arrested and paid heavy fines. B 1904, James Admire was working the 23fd District, known also as the Petersburg District. He had made 276 arrests by now.[159]

---

[158] Public Safety Record, Indiana State Archives.
[159] 1904 Indianapolis Sentinel

Buried Crown Hill Cemetery, section F, lot 6162.[160]

Patrolman George W. Rankin

Born: June 1863 Clark County, KY.[161]
Died: June 29, 1940 Indianapolis, IN.[162]
Date Appointed: August 6, 1898
Date of Separation: 1906

---

[160] Findagrave.com
[161] 1900; Census Place: Indianapolis, Marion, Indiana; Roll: 388; Page: 2A; Enumeration District: 0069; FHL microfilm: 1240388.
[162] "RANKINS, In loving remembrance", *Indianapolis Recorder* – June 28, 1941, 15, http://indiamond6.ulib.iupui.edu/cdm/compoundobject/collection/IRecorder/id/92091/rec/1

George Rankin or Rankins continued to assist the Indianapolis Police Department after his retirement from the force. He was placed on the pension list August 18, 1900 due to Bright's disease (kidney).[163] The first time he assisted IPD was in January 1901 when he agreed to meet William Alvord, a suspected burglar, on Rhode Island Street.

Two IPD detectives were hiding nearby. Rankins drew a revolver and the detectives stepped out to capture Alvord. In Alvord's pants were three gold watches and a valuable ring, which had been stolen recently at two crime scenes. Alvord confessed to both crimes.[164]
He was back on the force in 1902.

That year, Patrolmen Rankins and Wynn were making their rounds on W. 15th Street when they noticed a man trying to climb a porch at the residence of George Tobin.

---

[163] "Safety Board Meets", The Indianapolis Journal – August 18, 1900, 3, https://newspapers.library.in.gov/cgi-bin/indiana?a=d&d=IJ19000818.1.3&srpos=4&e=-------en-20--1--txt-txIN-%22george+rankins%22-----#

[164] "In a Hurry", The Indianapolis News – January 10, 1901, 11, http://indiamond6.ulib.iupui.edu/cdm/compoundobject/collection/IN/id/68650/rec/1

They began their pursuit but the man jumped to the ground and began running. The officers were in close pursuit for several minutes. The man ran across a vacant lot and while searching for him, Rankins ran against a post in the darkness, which caused injuries that would partially disable him from duty. They did arrest in capturing the suspect and took him to headquarters. The man had a reputation as a repeat burglar and received a sentence of 2-14 years.[165]

George Rankins again quit IPD in 1906. After two IPD officers were murdered that same year, George W. Rankins went to Tompkinsville, Kentucky with former officer Ben Lee, in search of the killer, Jesse Coe. From 1907-1909 he was serving as a Township Constable in Indianapolis.[166]

---

[165] 1904 Indianapolis Sentinel.
[166] 1907-1909 Indianapolis City Directories

Patrolman Gabriel L. Jones [167]

Patrolman Gabriel L. Jones
Born: September 1858 Gallatin, TN.
Died: February 20, 1915 Indianapolis, IN.
Date Appointed: August 6, 1898
Date of Separation:

Buried Crown Hill Cemetery, section 56, lot 328.

Gabriel Jones lived on the farm he was born on until 1875. He came to Indianapolis at

---

[167] "The Death of Gabriel Jones at One Time Member of the Indiana Legislature", The Freeman, February 27, 1915, 8, http://news.google.com/newspapers?nid=FIkAGs9z2eEC&dat=19150227&printsec=frontpage&hl=en

that time and worked as a railroader. He graduated with honors from normal college. He taught school for 10 years in Indianapolis and served six years as a clerk in City Hall. He served as Deputy County Recorder and Assessor for Marion County, Indiana.

In 1896 he was elected to a term in the Indiana General Assembly[168], one of four African-Americans to do this before 1900. When his term was up, he was appointed to the Indianapolis Police Department in 1898.

He was reappointed by the board of safety on December 10, 1901.[169] He was terminated for not patrolling his beat for 2 days in November, on November 23, 1904. He had served in the United States Revenue service under President Benjamin Harrison. "Gab" Jones was a watchman for the United States Custom House at the time of his death from pneumonia in 1915.[170]

---

[168] David J. Bodenhamer, et.al, The Encyclopedia of Indianapolis, 241
[169] "Fire Captains Dropped", The Indianapolis Journal, December 10, 1901, 10, https://newspapers.library.in.gov/cgi-bin/indiana?a=d&d=IJ19011210.1.10&srpos=7&e=-------en-20--1--txt-txIN-%22gabriel+jones%22-----#
[170] *The Indianapolis Star* – February 25, 1915 Death Notice,

Mr. Jones, described as one of the best known members of the African-American community in Indiana, was a member of Bethel A.M.E. Church, where he was one of the leading members. He also was a Mason, a Shriner, and a member of the Odd Fellows. He was survived by wife Addie and son Benjamin Jones, director of engineering at the A. & M. College, Normal, Alabama. He was buried in Crown Hill Cemetery. Details of his life come from his obituary in "The Freeman", February 27, 1915. [171]

---

http://www.newspapers.com/image/#7720377&terms=
[171] "The Death of Gabriel Jones At One Time Member of the Indiana Legislature", *The Freeman* – February 27, 1915, 8, http://news.google.com/newspapers?nid=2306&dat=19150227&id=iKknAAAAIBAJ&sjid=lAQGAAAAIBAJ&pg=6260%2c4239432

Patrolman Earl E. Titus

Born: May 14, 1867 Union City, PA.
Died: June 3, 1954 Indianapolis, IN.
Date Appointed: 1895
Date of Separation: February 22, 1900

Earl E. Titus served five years with the Indianapolis Police Department and had a high school education.[173] Serving as a

---

[172] Photograph from the F.B.I.
http://www.fbi.gov/news/stories/2011/february/history_021511
[173] Theodore Kornweibel, Seeing Red: Federal Campaigns against Black Militancy, 1919-1925, 150

patrolman in 1898-1899 according to Indianapolis City Directories. Dismissed February 22, 1900 from IPD for "indolence and neglect".[174] Titus opened up a barber shop which he operated for the next 20 years in Indianapolis.[175]

On January 9, 1922, Earl Titus joined the Bureau of Investigation (BOI), known after 1935 as the Federal Bureau of Investigation (FBI). He is recognized as the 3rd African-American agent in the agency's history. His assignments included undercover work in the investigation of Marcus Garvey, a black nationalist who was convicted of mail fraud in 1923. As part of his undercover investigation, Special Agent Titus filed frequent reports from Chicago, Illinois from August 10, 1923 to March 24, 1924. Titus retired in June 1924 at the age of 56.[176] In

---

http://books.google.com/books?id=rc-uwLkQmFAC&printsec=frontcover&dq=Theodore+Kornweibel,+Seeing+Red&hl=en&sa=X&ei=k81yU5jeHY2wyASukYHABQ&ved=0CC0Q6AEwAA#v=onepage&q=Theodore%20Kornweibel%2C%20Seeing%20Red&f=false

[174] "Crane is Reinstated", The Indianapolis Journal – February 22, 1900, 3, https://newspapers.library.in.gov/cgi-bin/indiana?a=d&d=IJ19000222.1.3&srpos=3&e=-------en-20--1--txt-txIN-%22earl+titus%22-----#

[175] Indianapolis City Directories

[176]

1954, aged "96", Earl was barbering fellow residents of the Marion County, Indiana Home for the aged.

Patrolman Carter Fredrick Payton Temple

Born: February 17, 1879 Indianapolis, IN.
Died: April 17, 1941, Indianapolis, IN.
Date Appointed: April 28, 1900
Date of Separation: August 18, 1900

---

http://www.fbi.gov/news/stories/2011/february/history_021511

[177] Photograph courtesy of Reginald Temple and Cecelia Boler.

Captain Carter F.P. Temple, Indiana Militia
Photograph courtesy of Reginald Temple

Carter Fredrick Payton Temple was born February 17, 1879 in Indianapolis, Indiana to Carter Temple Jr. and Martha A. Blackwell. Carter F.P. Temple was one of the best known men in the city of Indianapolis. His father was the first African-American police officer with the Indianapolis Police Department (1876). The son attended Purdue University until age 17, when he enlisted in the State Militia. On July 15, 1898 at age 19 he joined the Indiana National Guard and was appointed of Company A.

They then were stationed at Camp Mount, Indianapolis. On September 2, 1898, the two companies departed for Fort Thomas, Kentucky, where they were to be "attached" to the Eighth Infantry, an African-American regiment. They were stationed at Camp Capron on a hill which overlooked the Ohio River.

They spent a month at Fort Thomas, and then were sent with the Eighth Infantry to Chickamauga Park, Georgia, near Chattanooga, Tennessee. They took pride in their expertise on the parade ground, calling themselves the "Indiana Invincibles."

Despite being rated as good soldiers upon inspection, they were never given the opportunity they sought to go to Cuba to see action. They spent the next three months at Chickamauga, being discharged in January 1899.

They left for home on January 20, 1899, the day Carter received his honorable discharge. As described in "Indiana Negroes and the Spanish-American War" by Willard

B. Gatewood Jr., "Their return was celebrated at the Bethel A.M.E. Church in Indianapolis with a banquet sponsored by the Soldiers' Aid Society and attended by African-American citizens from throughout the state.

The ex-soldiers marched into the church while a large choir sang "John Brown's Body." Various speakers extolled their patriotism and predicted that their military service would inaugurate a new era in the quest for racial justice.

The week of his discharge, The Indianapolis Recorder said "First Sergeant Carter Temple of Company B has made a good record. As first sergeant of the Company he has been prompt, honest and strictly attentive to business. He deserves much praise for his quickness in forming the company and getting it ready for marching order on short notice. In this he greatly excelled. Sergt. Temple boasts of furnishing 61 orderlies to the commanding officers of the 8th regiment since the company has been attached. This he claims is more than any other company has furnished."

Upon the return of the regiment to Indianapolis, a large reception was held for them at the home of Carter's parents, Mr. & Mrs. Carter Temple Jr. Carter was a competitive bicycle rider. He and two other men made a "record time" in riding to Greenfield, Indiana, returning in 63 minutes.

On July 4, 1899, was one of 33 African-American members of the See-Saw Cycle Club, who participated in a race held at 26th and Meridian Streets. Carter finished with a time of 42:30 and won the time prize.

Carter joined the Indianapolis Police Department on April 28, 1900. He resigned August 18, 1900 to start a contracting business, which became very successful. In 1900 he was appointed Captain over two companies of Colored Militia, which were hoped, would be admitted into the Indiana National Guard. He became involved in politics in 1916 and became a powerful man whose support was welcomed.

It was said at his death that he secured more political jobs for African-Americans than any other man of color in Indiana.

Carter F.P. Temple worked throughout his life to support the rights of African-Americans. He was employed 25 years as a foreman in the Street Commissioner's Department. On April 17, 1941, after an afternoon of fishing, he died. He was found the next day by the White River and 10th St. Bridge. His engraved Bulova watch (which was given to him by a prominent white politician) was stopped at 4:50. They believed that to be the time of death. He was apparently struck by lightning.

Thank you to Reginald Temple and Cecelia Boler for the background information and for the vintage photographs of Carter F.P. Temple.

Rear seat: Retired IPD Officer Carter Temple Jr. and his wife; front seat, former IPD Officer Carter F.P. Temple and his wife. In the car are the children of Carter F.P. Temple. Photograph taken in 1915, courtesy of Reginald Temple.

Family home built by Carter Temple Jr. in 1872, which remained in his son Carter F.P. Temple's family until about 1979 when it was razed to make way for IUPUI. Located at 550 Minerva Street. Photograph courtesy of Reginald Temple.

BENJAMIN W. LEE, Patrolman

Patrolman Benjamin W. Lee

Born: April 1869 Cynthiana, Kentucky[178]
Date Appointed: May 1, 1900
Date of Separation/Retirement: 1906

Badge #62.

When he was aged 2, Benjamin Lee came to Indianapolis. He began working for an ice

---

[178] Year: 1900; Census Place: Indianapolis, Marion, Indiana; Roll: 388; Page: 5B; Enumeration District: 0053; FHL microfilm: 1240388.

company at age 11. He worked there until joining the police department. A few months after his appointment, Lee received information that Sam Baldwin and Ed McCarthy, known troublemakers, had entered Cox's drug store at 28th and Capitol Avenue. They brutally beat Edward Reese and left him on the floor, half dead. Lee started on the trail of the suspects and located Baldwin in a barn on Indianapolis Avenue and 29th Street. They fought for almost an hour before Lee subdued him.

After his prisoner was under control, Lee faced a problem. They were in the hay loft and if Lee went first down the stairs, the prisoner would not follow. If he let the prisoner go first, he would run away. He decided to slug the prisoner in the jaw and threw him down the hay chute and jumped on top of him. McCarthy was later caught and both were sent to the work house for two years.[179]

<u>December 4, 1903:</u> A gang of four burglars which Officer Benjamin W. Lee rounded up, were bound over to the grand jury. These

---

[179] 1904 Indianapolis Sentinel

men confessed to committing numerous crimes on the north side of Indianapolis.[180]

February 22, 1906: Chief of Police Metzger made verbal charges of conduct unbecoming an officer before the police board, which asked for specifics in writing. There's no evidence of what the specifics were, but Officer Lee left IPD around this time and became a court deputy along with his friend George Rankin.

March 2, 1904: Officer Benjamin W. Lee charged with conduct unbecoming an officer for becoming verbally abusive with a drug store owner after correcting the officer about a telephone number he was dialing which the druggist knew was incorrect.[181]

1906: Along with George Rankin, another former IPD officer, tried to track down Jesse Coe, killer of an IPD officer earlier that same year.

---

[180] "Members of a Gang", The Indianapolis Journal – December 4, 1903, 12, https://newspapers.library.in.gov/cgi-bin/indiana?a=d&d=IJ19031204.1.12&srpos=4&e=-------en-20--1--txt-txIN-%22ben+lee%22-----#

[181] "Patrolman in Trouble over Phone Number", The Indianapolis Journal – March 2, 1904, 12, https://newspapers.library.in.gov/cgi-bin/indiana?a=d&d=IJ19040302.1.12&srpos=3&e=-------en-20--1--txt-txIN-%22benjamin+w.++lee%22-----#

Patrolman Lewis Weaver Montgomery

Born: February 1867 Tennessee[182]
Date Appointed: Before 1900
Date of Separation: January 1, 1904

<u>August 3, 1900:</u> Dismissed from IPD by Police Board for being drunk on duty.[183]

<u>February 23, 1901:</u> Reappointed to IPD.[184]
<u>May 8, 1902:</u> Lewis Montgomery saw a man dive under the water in the canal while coming down 12th Street. He rescued Charles Wolf, who was intoxicated.[185]
<u>June 1, 1902:</u> Patrolman Lewis Montgomery was shocked while using a

---

[182] Year: 1900; Census Place: Indianapolis, Marion, Indiana; Roll: 388; Page: 4B; Enumeration District: 0064; FHL microfilm: 1240388.

[183] "Why he Lost Buttons", The Indianapolis Journal – August 4, 1900, 7, https://newspapers.library.in.gov/cgi-bin/indiana?a=d&d=IJ19000804.1.7&srpos=4&e=-------en-20--1--txt-txIN-%22l.+w.+montgomery%22-----#

[184] Twelve New Patrolmen", The Indianapolis Journal – February 21, 1901, 8, https://newspapers.library.in.gov/cgi-bin/indiana?a=d&d=IJ19010221.1.8&srpos=2&e=-------en-20--1--txt-txIN-%22louis+w.+montgomery%22-----#

[185] "Wanted a Mess of Fish", The Indianapolis Journal – May 9, 1902, 10, https://newspapers.library.in.gov/cgi-bin/indiana?a=d&d=IJ19020509.1.10&srpos=3&e=-------en-20--1--txt-txIN-%22lewis+montgomery%22-----#

Gamewell box to call headquarters and was knocked 10 feet. An electrical storm had been going on. His partner Officer Goens revived him.[186]

December 10, 1903: Submitted resignation, effective January 1st, to run a saloon.[187]

March 9, 1907: "Louis Montgomery, a saloon keeper at 2814 North Missouri street was arrested late Tuesday on a charge of insanity. Montgomery who is a Negro was formerly a member of the police department and is unusually powerful. The police had considerable difficulty to control him, but he quieted down after being locked in a cell at the Police Station. His mind has been failing for some time and last night it was feared that he might injure members of his family." [188]

---

[186] "Stunned by Lightning", The Indianapolis Journal – June 2, 1902, 8, https://newspapers.library.in.gov/cgi-bin/indiana?a=d&d=IJ19020602.1.8&srpos=4&e=-------en-20--1--txt-txIN-%22lewis+montgomery%22-----#

[187] "Policemen Ordered to do Work of Reporters", The Indianapolis Journal – December 10, 1903, 12, https://newspapers.library.in.gov/cgi-bin/indiana?a=d&d=IJ19031210.1.12&srpos=1&e=-------en-20--1--txt-txIN-%22lewis+montgomery%22-----#

[188] The *Indianapolis Recorder* – March 9, 1907, 4, http://indiamond6.ulib.iupui.edu/cdm/compoundobject/collection/IRecorder/id/13156/rec/1

November 22, 1927: Lewis W. Montgomery of Indianapolis received a U.S. Patent for a portable camper's stove.[189]

Patrolman George H. Goins

Born: March 1861 Indianapolis, IN.[190]
Died: April 30, 1930 Indianapolis, IN.

---

[189] U.S. Patent Office - https://www.google.com/patents/US1650529?dq=ininventor:%22Montgomery+Lewis+W%22&hl=en&sa=X&ei=I_9VU83JHs-lyATf74KgCg&ved=0CDgQ6wEwAA

[190] Year: 1900; Census Place: Indianapolis, Marion, Indiana; Roll: 388; Page: 1B; Enumeration District: 0069; FHL microfilm: 1240388.

Date Appointed: December 15, 1899
Date of Separation/Retirement: 1906

George Goins learned the barber's trade, which he performed until joining the police department. In 1901, George was credited with averting what would have been one of the worst accidents in Indiana history. While patrolling his district, he walked down the Big Four railroad tracks between Pratt and 10th Streets. He saw a large, heavy flagstone which was placed across the tracks. The midnight express loaded with passengers was due at that point in 15 minutes.

Officer Goins removed the stone and then did a careful search of the surrounding area and found an ex-convict named Togo, hiding in a box car. He admitted to leaving the stone in the track and was arrested.[191]

Still employed with IPD in 1905. Working as a barber, 1906-08.[192] Buried May 3, 1930 in section 71, lot 1066, in Crown Hill Cemetery.[193]

---

[191] 1904 Indianapolis Sentinel
[192] 1906, 1908 Indianapolis City Directories
[193] Findagrave.com

Patrolman John W. Cousins

Born: 1869 near Lexington, KY.
Died:
Date Appointed: March 1, 1901
Date of Separation/Retirement:

During his earlier years, John W. Cousins worked as a railroader, engineer and a butcher, until arriving in Indianapolis in 1896. He went into the railroading business here until joining the police force in 1901. After joining the force, he learned that there were three boys infatuated with dime novels about Jesse James and were buying weapons and ammunition. They were camped out on Fall Creek near College Avenue.

Cousins approached the camp and was immediately warned, "If you come any nearer you will be blown full of holes." He continued to approach and without drawing his weapons, got the boys to surrender. He found a quantity of guns and knives. The boys were fined and gave up their desire to be latter day "Robin Hoods."[194]

---

[194] 1904 Indianapolis Sentinel.

Detective Sergeant John M. Mosbey

Born: July 8, 1870 Harrodsburg, KY.
Died: July 7, 1935 Indianapolis, IN.
Date Appointed: March 21, 1906
Date of Retirement: December 1934

Badge #143, then #401, 5'10", 170 lbs., Republican.[196]

---

[195] IMPD Lichtenberger History Room.
[196] Public Safety Record, Indiana State Archives.

October 9, 1923: Promoted to Detective Sergeant.[197]

June 10, 1924: Reduced to Patrolman.[198]

July 22, 1924: Promoted to Traffic.[199]

December 12, 1929: Traffic Policeman John M. Mosbey was cut and bruised after Oliver Turner ran into his traffic semaphore at New York and Senate. Turner was arrested for driving recklessly and assault and battery.[200]

Buried in Crown Hill Cemetery, section 99, lot 663 as John M. Mosbey. [201]

---

[197] Ibid.
[198] Public Safety Record, Indiana State Archives.
[199] Ibid.
[200] The Indianapolis News – December 13, 1929, 16, http://www.newspapers.com/image/#37509590&terms=John+M.+Mosbey
[201] Findagrave.com

Detective Sergeant Edward Byron Trabue

Born: March 31, 1872 Kentucky
Died: February 17, 1927 Indianapolis, Indiana
Date Appointed: July 18, 1906
Date Separated: February 17, 1927 (death)
Badge #196, 5'10", 185 lbs., Republican.[203]

Buried in Crown Hill Cemetery, section 71, lot 338[204].

---

[202] IMPD Lichtenberger History Room.
[203] Public Safety Record, Indiana State Archives.

<u>January 8, 1914:</u> Patrolman Trabue arrested Bert Brant, 22, suspected of many robberies.

<u>May 28, 1919:</u> Promoted from Patrolman to Detective Sergeant. This was the first time an African-American was promoted to the rank of Sergeant. George Sneed & Joshua Spearis also reached this rank this date.[205]

His obituary described him as a currently serving Detective Sergeant with the Indianapolis Police Department. The Chief's office described him as one of the best men in the department. He and his "running mate" Detective Sneed "did commendable work in solving many mysteries for the department." Mayor Lewis Shank at one time called Trabue and Sneed "the best detectives in the department."[206] He was a Mason and a Shriner.

---

[204] Findagrave.com
[205] The Indianapolis News – May 28, 1919, http://www.newspapers.com/newspage/6887854/
[206] "Police Officer Dies", *Indianapolis Recorder* – February 19, 1927, 1, http://indiamond6.ulib.iupui.edu/cdm/compoundobject/collection/IRecorder/id/38696/rec/1

Edward Trabue died of a stroke.

Patrolman Ralph LaRue

Born: March 1, 1871 Kentucky[208]
Died: June 18, 1917 Indianapolis, IN.[209]
Date Appointed: September 24, 1907
Date of Separation: June 13, 1917 (death)

---

[207] IMPD Lichtenberger History Room.
[208] Year: 1900; Census Place: Indianapolis, Marion, Indiana; Roll: 388; Page: 8A; Enumeration District: 0089; FHL microfilm: 1240388.
[209] Findagrave.com

Badge #188, 6'1", 190 lbs., Republican.[210] Buried June 1917, Crown Hill Cemetery, section F, lot 5867.

November 29, 1914: While off duty, Patrolman LaRue who was with his son John LaRue, met Herbert Willis and a girl at West and Indiana Avenue. An altercation occurred, the father of Willis, C.M.C. Willis coming to the scene. John LaRue cut Herbert Willis on the face. John LaRue was later convicted and spent time at the Jeffersonville, Indiana, Reformatory.[211][212]

December 25, 1914: Patrolman LaRue is fined $25 in Criminal Court for assaulting George Glennending, reporter for *The Indianapolis News* in the IPD Roll Call Room for stories he wrote about LaRue which he objected to.[213]

---

[210] Public Safety Record, Indiana State Archives.
[211] The Indianapolis News – November 30, 1914, .16, http://www.newspapers.com/image/#35706903&terms=ralph+larue
[212] The Indianapolis News - December 3, 1914, 9, http://www.newspapers.com/image/#35721277&terms=ralph–larue
[213] The Indianapolis News – December 28, 1914, 10, http://www.newspapers.com/image/#35721746&terms=ralph+larue

<u>January 2, 1915:</u> Sentenced to 30 days and a fine of $1.
<u>July 7, 1915:</u> Returns to work after several months away from IPD. [214]

Patrolman Nelson Grandison [215]

---

[214] "Ralph LaRue Returns To Job As Policeman", The Indianapolis News – July 7, 1915, 1, http://www.newspapers.com/image/#37464775&terms=ralph+larue

[215] IMPD Lichtenberger History Room.

Born: October 7, 1874 Kentucky[216]
Died: July 1937 Indianapolis, Indiana (leukemia)
Date Appointed: April 27, 1910
Date of Separation: July 1937 (death)

Badge #281, then #165. 5'9", 180 lbs. Republican.[217]

<u>April 9, 1913:</u> Placed on Flood Roll of Honor by IPD, apparently having done heroic work during the great flood of March 1913.[218]

<u>July 10, 1915:</u> After sometime on the night force, Nelson Grandison changed to Day Force.

<u>October 7, 1919:</u> Submitted resignation after being accused in connection with janitors stealing confiscated whiskey at police headquarters.[219]

<u>November 28, 1919:</u> Nelson Grandison was arrested for assault & battery and gaming after a man complained of losing $130 in a dice game. He refused to give the dice to Grandison, who struck him. At this time

---

[216] Draft Card - Registration State: Indiana; Registration County: Marion; Roll: 1613156; Draft Board: 10.
[217] Public Safety Record, Indiana State Archives.
[218] Public Safety Record, Indiana State Archives.
[219] Public Safety Record, Indiana State Archives.

Grandison was a former IPD officer, having resigned after being caught taking confiscated whiskey from the basement of police headquarters.[220] He was working as a machinist, 1921 and confectioner, 1924[221].
July 1, 1924: Reinstated with IPD.[222]
February 1937:   Patrolman 1st Grade.
April 24, 1937: Recovering from serious injuries suffered while directing traffic at Attucks H.S.

---

[220] "Crap Game Ends", *The Indianapolis Star* – November 28, 1919, .19, http://www.newspapers.com/image/#6935529&terms=nelson+granderson
[221] 1921 and 1924 Indianapolis City Directories
[222] Public Safety Record, Indiana State Archives.

223

Patrolman William Whitfield

Born: June 2, 1885
Died: November 27, 1922 Indianapolis, Indiana
Date Appointed: April 27, 1910
Date of Separation/Retirement: November 27, 1922 (death)

"Officer William Whitfield succumbed to gunshot wounds suffered five months earlier while chasing a suspect.

---

223 Photographs from IMPD Historical Photograph Archives

The officer was in plainclothes on foot patrol when he entered an alley just west of 3500 North Collage Avenue and noticed a roughly-dressed man. He asked the man what he was doing there and the man suddenly turned and ran, with Officer Whitfield in pursuit.

During the chase the man suddenly turned and fired several shots from a revolver, striking Officer Whitfield once in the abdomen. He was able to stumble back to the street where he collapsed. Passers-by took him to a hospital where he lingered for five months before succumbing to his injuries. The suspect was never captured.

Officer Whitfield had served with the Indianapolis Police Department for 12 years. As he was initially buried in an unmarked grave, on November 30, 1998, he was given a full-honors funeral after members of the department contributed to the purchase of a headstone for his grave site.

Officer Whitfield is the first known African-American law enforcement officer killed in the line of duty in the state of Indiana, and the first of three unsolved police murders in Indianapolis." – From the "Officer Down Memorial Page."

Faces of IPD

IMPD Lichtenberger History Room.

Detective Sergeant Charles Mathew Carter

Born: April 30, 1883 Indiana[226]
Died: March 1934 Indianapolis, Indiana
Date Appointed: August 3, 1910
Date of Separation: March 1934 (death)

---

[225] IMPD Lichtenberger History Room.
[226] Draft card - Registration State: Indiana; Registration County: Marion; Roll: 1504021; Draft Board: 6.

Badge #29 (his father's badge), then #259, 6'0", 175 lbs., Republican.[227]

Buried in Crown Hill Cemetery.

<u>July 12, 1921:</u> Terminated for undetermined charges and reinstated in October 23, 1923.[228]
<u>December 11, 1923</u>: Promoted to Traffic man.[229]
<u>June 17, 1924:</u> Reduced to Patrolman.[230]
<u>July 20, 1925:</u> Suspended from duty for allegedly accepting a bribe from a bootlegger.[231]
<u>July 13, 1926</u>: Promoted to Traffic man.[232]
<u>By 1927:</u> Appointed to Detective Squad.
<u>By February 1934:</u> Promoted to Detective Sergeant.

He was son of former IPD Officer Daniel Carter and Mary Carter.

Indianapolis Recorder – March 24, 1934

---

[227] Public Safety Record, Indiana State Archives.
[228] Public Safety Record, Indiana State Archives.
[229] Public Safety Record, Indiana State Archives.
[230] Ibid.
[231] The Indianapolis News – July 22, 1925, 10, http://www.newspapers.com/image/#37408403&terms=
[232] Ibid.

RITES HELD FOR POLICE OFFICER CHARLES CARTER

"Glowing tributes befitting a worthy member of the Indianapolis police Department were paid Charles (Pete) Carter at funeral services were held Monday. Resolutions were read for the police department by Officer, Norville Bennett, and for the Policemen and Firemen's wives association by Mrs. George Sneed.

Solos were sung by Mrs. Starks and Hayes Wilson. Chief of Police Michael Morrissey, Chief of Detectives Fred Simons, and Capt. Rademacher headed the large escort of police officers who attended the funeral. Lieut. Roy Howard and firemen from Fire station No. 1, represented the Fire Department. Pallbearers were Officers Hopson, Jones, Bennett, Heater, Grandison and Kennedy. Survivors are: two brothers, William and Edward Carter, Chicago. Burial was in Crown Hill cemetery.

Carter died Thursday last week at the City hospital from an attack of pneumonia he suffered Tuesday. Friends say he told them at the time he had suffered a cold following a tramp through the slushy streets of Baltimore, Md., a few days earlier where he had gone to testify before a federal grand jury. Got pneumonia on Tuesday, died in hospital."[233]

---

[233] "Rites Held For Police Officer Charles Carter", *Indianapolis Recorder*, March 24, 1934, 1, http://indiamond6.ulib.iupui.edu/cdm/compoundobject/collection/IRecorder/id/17437/rec/1

Detective Sergeant Thomas W. Hopson

Born: August 1872 Goldsboro, N.C.
Died: July 18, 1947 Indianapolis, IN.[235]
Date Appointed: December 12, 1911
Date of Separation/Retirement: 1945

---

[234] IMPD Lichtenberger History Room.
[235] "Thos. W. Hopson's Funeral Rites Held", *Indianapolis Recorder* – July 26, 1947, 7,
http://indiamond6.ulib.iupui.edu/cdm/compoundobject/collection/IRecorder/id/90322/rec/1

Badge #165. 5'9 ½", 180 lbs., Republican.[236]

Buried Crown Hill Cemetery, Section 98, Lot 984.[237]

Tom Hopson, age 7, born North Carolina, was living in Indianapolis in 1880 with his parents. He settled in Indianapolis about that year.[238]

<u>June 10, 1924:</u> Promoted to Detective Sergeant.[239]

<u>January 4, 1926:</u> Reduced to rank of Patrolman.[240]

<u>March 24, 1934:</u> Patrolled beat until he became a plain clothes detective on this date.

<u>January 1, 1935:</u> Promoted to rank of Detective Sergeant, assigned to Burglary Division.

<u>February 1937:</u> Detective Sergeant.

---

[236] Public Safety Record, Indiana State Archives.
[237] Findagrave.com
[238] "United States Census, 1880," index and images, FamilySearch (https://familysearch.org/pal:/MM9.1.1/MH95-NGM : accessed 25 May 2014), Tom Hopson in household of Calfin Hopson, Indianapolis, Marion, Indiana, United States; citing sheet 781D, NARA microfilm publication T9.
[239] Public Safety Record, Indiana State Archives.
[240] Public Safety Record, Indiana State Archives.

December 1937: IPD Detectives Fred Simon, John Glenn, George Sneed, Claude White and Thomas Hopson receive a written letter of commendation from FBI agent Harold F. Rineicke in December 1937, for their part in assisting in the capture of Luther Benson on October 23, 1937, wanted for murder. [241]

January 2, 1940: Reduced in rank from Detective Sergeant to new position of Detective Investigator.

April 6, 1940: Police Begin New Type Work - a revision in the detective side at Police headquarters was announced here this week with the following appointments made known. Officers detailed to burglary cases with Detective Ferdinand Holt are Claude White and Thomas Hopson. Patrol Detailed to homicide with Detective George Sneed, Ples Jones and Eddie Butler, and Detective John Glenn, working as special investigator on larceny may expect an aide in that department soon, according to official sources.[242]

---

[241] "F.B.I. Cites Five Officers Here", *Indianapolis Recorder* – December 25, 1937, 1,
http://indiamond6.ulib.iupui.edu/cdm/compoundobject/collection/IRecorder/id/55787/rec/1

[242] "Police Begin New Type Work", *Indianapolis Recorder* – April 6,

March 13, 1943: Reduced from Detective Investigator to Patrolman First Class. Requested a Traffic post from Chief of Police Clarence Beeker, which was granted.

He spent most of his career enforcing vice and gambling laws. "No, I never did kill a man, but I did shoot two or three people. I am not glad that I did it". Interview with *Indianapolis Recorder*, May 15, 1937.

Profiled in *Indianapolis Recorder*, May 15, 1937.

1940, 1,
http://indiamond6.ulib.iupui.edu/cdm/compoundobject/collection/IRecorder/id/74290/rec/1

Patrolman John Coleman

Born: February 12, 1884 Indianapolis, Indiana[244]
Died: May 1952 Indianapolis, Indiana
Date Appointed: December 20, 1911
Date Retired: December 1944

---

[243] IMPD Lichtenberger History Room.
[244] Ancestry.com. U.S., World War II Draft Registration Cards, 1942 [database on-line]. Provo, UT, USA: Ancestry.com Operations, Inc., 2010.

Specialized in training rookie policemen the fundamentals.

John Coleman with a St. Louis police officer.[245]

February 1937: Patrolman 1st Grade.
1937: Directing traffic and New York and Capitol Avenue.
June 5, 1937: Profiled in *Indianapolis Recorder*.

---

[245] The Indianapolis Children's Museum.

May 24, 1952: Retired IPD Officer John Coleman, 70, found dead in basement while on duty as night watchman at School 26. Born here, he attended local public schools, Shortridge High, and early in life joined Allen Chapel AME Church in which he remained active until his death. He had been watchman at the Eastside School since 1950. When the city administration decided in 1923 to open other than patrolman and detective branches to Negro officers, he became one of the first of his group to serve in the traffic department, being stationed for years at New York and Capitol Avenue. Burial was in Crown Hill. Surviving are the stepson, Melvin Walker and a brother, Eli Coleman Jr., both of Indianapolis.[246]

---

[246] "Ex-Policeman's John Coleman's Last rites Held", *Indianapolis Recorder* – May 24, 1952, 2, http://indiamond6.ulib.iupui.edu/cdm/compoundobject/collection/IRecorder/id/87072/rec/1

Policewoman Mary Ena (Roberts) Mays

Born: January 3, 1856 Salem, Indiana[247]
Died: June 1, 1928 Los Angeles, CA.
Date Appointed: June 15, 1918
Date of Resignation/Separation: January 3, 1922

Mary Ena Roberts was born in Salem, Washington County, Indiana on January 3, 1856 to John Roberts and Mariah (Roberts) Roberts, Free Persons of Color. Her

---

[247] Public Safety Personnel Record – Indiana Historical Society

paternal grandmother was a Cherokee Indian, descended from Chief Red Bird.

The family moved to the Bedford, Indiana area in the 1860's, likely due to the rising race prejudice in Salem during the Civil War. Mary came to Indianapolis, Indiana with her mother and stepfather Thomas Crosson. On September 13, 1877 Mary wed Philip Mays. They had two children, Lucille (1878-1913) and Garrold E. Mays (1885-1960). The couple divorced in 1892.

Along with Emma Baker, Mary E. Mays has the distinction of being the first female police officer with IPD and the first African-American female. There were also 11 White women hired as officers on the same day in 1918.[248]

Mary E. Mays worked for a number of years for the Flower Mission of Indianapolis, an organization that existed to bring flowers to hospital patients but also to help the poor and unfortunate. As a mulatto woman, she

---

[248] "Mayor C.W. Jewett, Chief of Police Coffin and Women Chosen For the Police Department", *The Indianapolis Star* – June 15, 1918, 19,
http://indiamond6.ulib.iupui.edu/cdm/compoundobject/collection/IN/id/78082/rec/1

was not allowed to be a member of the organization, just an employee.

Mary was a district nurse for the organization and in 1885, the mission wanted to start a visiting nurse program and asked Mary to do the preliminary research for it. [249] For the next 20 years Mary served as a visiting nurse with the Flower Mission and became very familiar to the citizens of Indianapolis.[250] It was estimated that she visited 33,000 sick people in one year.

"Mary Mays has been appointed District Nurse for the Flower Mission, she being the only colored employed by the mission."
Indianapolis Recorder – August 2, 1902

---

[249] Thurman Brooks Rice, "History of the Medical Campus," 261.
[250] Amanda Jean Koch, "Not a Sentimental Charity" : A History of the Indianapolis Flower Mission, 1876-1993, 33, accessed May 25, 2014,
https://scholarworks.iupui.edu/bitstream/handle/1805/2191/K och%20Thesis.pdf?sequence=1

> **BRAVE RESCUE OF SIXTY PERSONS**
>
> A daring rescue was made yesterday afternoon by Mrs. Mary Mays, a Flower Mission nurse, with the help of her neice, Mrs. Claude Walker, and her daughter Lucile. In the water up to the hub, they bravely strove, and brought back William Lodback, colored, his wife and five children to terra firma. Lodback lives at 1500 Hiawatha street. With the assistance of Collins, a colored man, Mrs. Mays and her relatives rescued sixty persons.
>
> Four hundred persons were driven out of their homes in the neighborhood of Indiana avenue and Fall creek. Most of those sufferers from the flood were taken to the Flanner Guild.
>
> **Pennsylvania Street Suffered.**

The Indianapolis Journal – March 27, 1904

One of the most outstanding examples of a lifetime of service for Mary Mays came in March 1904 when Fall Creek flooded, going out of its banks and breaking a levee. Neighborhoods of the area now occupied by the IUPUI campus were flooded.

Mrs. Mary Mays and her son and daughter, Gerald and Miss Lucile will leave on the 20th, for a ten days outing at Benton Harbor, Mich. Recorder – August 13, 1910. Mary Mays vacationed annually at this resort, which was popular with African-Americans then.

The local papers were full of stories of Mary Mays, going by herself into homes with people suffering from deadly diseases, filled with all kinds of vermin. There are too many examples to recount here.

Despite her limitations, Mary put her daughter Lucille into Howard University, Washington, D.C. and after that she completed a course at the nurse's training school at the Freedman's Hospital in Washington. Lucille wed Dr. Walter T. Bailey and settled in Springfield, Tennessee. Tragically, she died of double pneumonia there in November 1913, age 32.

All the walking to and from the homes of sick people was taking its toll on Mary Mays. The local paper took up a collection in conjunction with the City to purchase a car for Mary Mays.

Plans were announced on November 18, 1916 to give the automobile to Mary Mays on Thanksgiving Day. John Shine, veteran Indianapolis Police Officer, attached to the Juvenile department, had the following to say about Mary Mays.

John Shine

"For more than twenty years this woman has trudged through snow and sleet, through rain and sunshine, to care for the sick poor. I have long been a police officer in Indianapolis and I have seen her. Why, man, I have seen that little woman enter homes that I would not enter on risk of losing my badge. All the filth that ever laid in human path was before her – yet in she went to battle for a baby's life.

Through the long hours of the night she fought it out, and the next day, she told me that she had walked home, a distance of three miles, through zero weather, in the hope of cleansing herself of the vermin that clung to her garments.

"Should a woman like that have an automobile in order to save her faltering feet? Should she? Why, man, she should have a dozen of them if the people of this community hoped, even in a measure, to repay her for the work she has done.

"Through alley and hovel she has gone at all hours of the night, a lone woman on a charitable mission. And yet there are people who cling to their dollars and dimes when her health is the stake. Mary Mays walks when she should be carried on the shoulders of grateful men."

At noon on November 29, 1916, friends of Mary Mays presented her with an automobile so she could better take care of the sick. Judge Frank J. Lahr, of the juvenile court, before a small group of friends on the east entrance to the court house, spoke of Mary's 20 years working for the Flower Mission. He thanked her for the assistance she had given to the Juvenile Court and other organizations. Representatives of the Flower Mission, the township trustee's office, the juvenile court and other institutions Mary had aided, were present.

So when the police department and the Mayor of Indianapolis decided to hire female police officers in 1918, Mary E. Mays was a good choice, because they wanted someone who would be able to deal with female juveniles for the most part. She had a little prior practice with police work, having chased a man making a young girl dance for change several blocks once. Officer Mays teamed up with fellow Salem native Emma Baker, being restricted to walking a beat in the African-American neighborhoods. They arrested drunken men, shoplifters and worked in dance halls, making sure women were protected from men who would prey on them.

In January 1920, Mary Mays was living in Los Angeles in her son Gerrold's home. The city requested her resignation and it was submitted on January 3, 1922. She was one of many police officers forced out by the incoming administration that day, possibly because they were of the wrong political party, which was traditional in

Indianapolis. The new administration and Chief of Police Herman Rickhoff had little use for policewomen as well. Mary Mays moved to Los Angeles immediately after resigning. She died there June 1, 1928. Her burial place isn't known.

251 IMPD Lichtenberger History Room.

Policewoman Emma (Christy) Baker

Born: February 10, 1865 Salem, IN.[252]
Died: September 23, 1955 Indianapolis, IN.
Date Appointed: June 15, 1918
Date of Retirement: March 15, 1939
June 17, 1918: First assignment for Indianapolis' first policewomen was to register German alien women across from the courthouse at Tomlinson Hall. Emma is pictured above at left.

July 2, 1918: Emma Baker and partner Mary Mays are assigned to patrol the "colored" neighborhoods. Their shift was from 1:30 p.m. to 11:30 p.m. She wore a badge and earned the same rate of pay as male officers.253 She was appreciated in the African-American community for her police work. Her primary duties were performing undercover shoplift and petty theft details.

---

[252] "Mrs. Emma Baker 1st Policewoman Here, Mourned", The *Indianapolis Recorder* – October 1, 1955, 1,
http://indiamond6.ulib.iupui.edu/cdm/compoundobject/collection/IRecorder/id/35217/rec/1

[253] "Mayor C.W. Jewett, Chief of Police Coffin and Women Chosen For the Police Department", The *Indianapolis Star* – June 15, 1918, 19,
http://indiamond6.ulib.iupui.edu/cdm/compoundobject/collection/IN/id/78082/rec/1

1922: Assigned to Juvenile Court. Here, Emma mentored the youths she worked with, trying to keep them from a life of crime.

March 31, 1922: Indianapolis policewomen were finally given the order to buy a gun. They had been expected to do their job since 1918 without one. They did and started taking target practice by June 1922. (The Indianapolis News, March 31, 1922 and June 29, 1922).

December 29, 1926: The City of Indianapolis informed 15 of their policewomen that the no longer had a job because there was no money in the budget in 1927 for them. Today this would be called RIF (Reduction in Funds). The women did not take it lying down and refused to go quietly. Officer Emma Baker and three other women working in Juvenile hired an attorney and on December 31st Judge Harry O. Chamberlin issued an injunction against the City and Chief of Claude F. Johnson. The women kept their jobs but worked without salaries until the next summer. Several sued for back pay. (The Indianapolis News, December 29 & 31, 1926).

March 28, 1930: Ohio Valley regional conference of the Child Welfare League of America was held at the Claypool Hotel. Mrs. Emma Baker of Juvenile Court attended these sessions on March 28-29th.[254]

July 18, 1931: Mrs. Emma Baker, only "colored" police officer assigned to Juvenile Court.[255]

October 18, 1932: Additional ranks were created for policewomen this date and Emma Baker and others were assigned the rank of fifth grade patrolman (the lowest) with a salary of $1,000. Third grade patrolman rank paid $1,500 by comparison. Considering Emma had the most seniority at this point, this appears to be a demotion and an attempt to urge her to retire.

1938: Assigned as a Matron by IPD. These female officers tended to female prisoners. Emma turned in her retirement papers in March 15, 1939. She was the only African-American women then working for IPD and

---

[254] "In Interest of Local Society", *Indianapolis Recorder* – April 5, 1930, 6, http://indiamond6.ulib.iupui.edu/cdm/compoundobject/collection/IRecorder/id/14943/rec/13

[255] "Marion County Juvenile Court Staff Meets – Issues Semi-Annual Report", *Indianapolis Recorder* – July 18, 1931, 1, http://indiamond6.ulib.iupui.edu/cdm/compoundobject/collection/IRecorder/id/15908/rec/30

this wouldn't change until a manpower shortage occurred during WWII (in 1943).

Emma Christy was born February 10, 1865 in the town of Salem, in Washington County, Indiana to William W. and Hester Christy,[256] Free African Americans who settled there in the 1830's from the Newberry District, South Carolina. Her family moved to the town of Indianapolis when she was an infant. Emma graduated from Public School No. 17 and Shortridge High School.[257] On May 12, 1876 her father was one of the first African-Americans who applied for the Indianapolis Police Department. He was not hired.[258]

On July 9, 1889[259], Emma married David M. Baker, born in 1870, Tennessee, who

---

[256] Year: 1870; Census Place: Indianapolis Ward 4 (2nd Enum), Marion, Indiana; Roll: M593_338; Page: 273A; Image: 549; Family History Library Film: 545837.

[257] "Emma C. Baker Policewoman Retired Here", *Indianapolis Recorder*, August 12, 1939, 1, http://indiamond6.ulib.iupui.edu/cdm/compoundobject/collection/IRecorder/id/72236/rec/1

[258] "Police Appointees", The Indianapolis News – May 12, 1876, 4, http://indiamond6.ulib.iupui.edu/cdm/compoundobject/collection/IN/id/9739/rec/1

worked as a barber. They had a child, John W.D. Baker, born January 22, 1892, who died July 1899. David M. Baker died in 1928. The William W. Christy family was well known in the African-American community of Indianapolis. W.W. Christy was one of 9 Directors and also was Treasurer of The Fidelity Savings and Loan Association in 1902. [260] He owned a successful laundry at 643 Blake Street.[261] His daughter Cora Christy was a long-time school teacher with IPS while Emma worked at the laundry for many years. She became well known in the community in that capacity.

She retired from the department on March 15, 1939. She was a member of the Bethel African Methodist Episcopal Church. On October 18, 1947, Emma Baker, one of 70 African-Americans representing civic, business, labor and professional groups,

---

[259] Marion County, Indiana; Index to Marriage Record 1886 - 1890 Inclusive Vol, Original Record Located: County Clerk's Office Ind; Book: 99.

[260] Ad for The Fidelity Savings and Loan Association", *Indianapolis Recorder* – September 6, 1902, 4, http://indiamond6.ulib.iupui.edu/cdm/compoundobject/collection/IRecorder/id/5110/rec/1

[261] 1891 Indianapolis City Directory

were assigned to a special committee to elect William H. Wemmer, Republican, to be Mayor. [262]

---

[262] "Citizens Group of 70 Back Wemmer Race", *Indianapolis Recorder* – October 18, 1947, 1, http://indiamond6.ulib.iupui.edu/cdm/compoundobject/collection/IRecorder/id/91092/rec/1

DEATHS AND FUNERALS

Policewoman Had an Eye for Shoplifters

Emma C. Baker, Indianapolis' first Negro policewoman, is dead.

Mrs. Baker was appointed to the force June 1, 1918. She retired March 15, 1939. Most of this time she was a patrolman assigned to the uniform division.

She worked mainly on shoplifting and petty theft details. For a year Mrs. Baker was assigned to Juvenile Aid Division.

Born at Salem, she came to Indianapolis in her infancy. Her home was at 512 N. West, where she died yesterday after an illness of a year.

Mrs. Baker was a member of Bethel AME Church, Old Settlers Social and Civic Club and the Loyal Legion.

Services will be Wednesday at 1:30 p.m. in the Dan Moore Mortuary. Burial will be in Crown Hill Cemetery.

Friends may call at the mortuary after 1 p.m. tomorrow.

Only immediate survivor is a sister, Cora C. Willis, Indianapolis.

EMMA BAKER ... 21 years on force

Dailey Burial in Holy Cross

Edward L. Dailey, 55, self-

Emma for most of her adult life was a member of numerous social and religious organizations including the Loyal Legion Club of the AME Bethel Church, The Old Settlers Social and Civic Club and the

Topaz Coral Club, of which she was elected club secretary in 1916. [263]

Emma died on September 23, 1955 and was buried in Crown Hill Cemetery with her son and husband. No headstone was provided for them because her last remaining immediate family member, sister Cora Willis died September 1, 1958, aged 91, before she could get it done.

On September 23, 2003, after the efforts of IPD Officer Marilyn Gurnell, 500 IPS school children, businesses, private individuals and members of the Indianapolis Police Department, an imposing headstone containing the names of David, Emma and John W.D. Baker was dedicated at her final resting place. Among those attending the dedication were IPD Chief of Police Jerry L. Barker, Marion County Sheriff Frank Anderson, State Police Superintendent Melvin Carroway and IPS School Superintendent Duncan P. Pritchett. The ceremony was carried on all media outlets in Indianapolis. Her grave site is now a stop on a tour conducted by Crown Hill Cemetery for Indianapolis Women of Note.

---

[263] Ibid

Marilyn Gurnell & husband Ed leave the dedication ceremony.

September 23, 2003: Police officials dedicate headstone of Officer Emma (Christy) Baker. [264] From Left: Assistant Chief Deborah L. Saunders, highest ranking African-American policewoman in IPD history, IPD Chaplain Philip Bacon, IPS School Commissioner Duncan P. Pritchett, ISP Superintendent Melvin Carroway, IPD Chief of Police Jerry Barker, Civilian Patrick R. Pearsey and current Assistant Chief Lloyd Crowe. Photo: David Dickens

---

[264] Photographs by David Dickens of IPD.

Lieutenant George William Sneed

Born: January 22, 1888 Indiana
Died: August 30, 1961 Indianapolis, IN.
Date Appointed: July 10, 1918
Date Retired: May 1, 1954

---

[265] The Indianapolis Children's Museum.

November 21, 1912: George Sneed was cut in a fight with James Powell at Senate and 13th Street. Powell was arrested and charged with assault and battery with intent to kill.[266]

May 28, 1919: Promoted to Detective Sergeant 6 months after being appointed due to his ability. He, along with Joshua Spearis and Edward Trabue became the first African-Americans to be promoted to the rank of Sergeant with the Indianapolis Police Department.[267] January 1926: Held rank of Lieutenant (First African-American on IPD to hold this rank).[268]

June 1928: Holds rank of Detective Sergeant.

February 22, 1929: Detective Sneed shoots and kills Matt Lee after attempting to serve warrants on him. Lee pointed a gun at Sneed and Det. Claude White.[269]

---

[266] *The Indianapolis Star* – November 21, 1912, 4, http://www.newspapers.com/image/#7745786&terms=george+sneed

[267] The Indianapolis News – May 28, 1919, http://www.newspapers.com/newspage/6887854/

[268] "Cleared Pal of Guilt, Guards Carry to Jail" – *Indianapolis Recorder* – January 23, 1926, 1, http://indiamond6.ulib.iupui.edu/cdm/compoundobject/collection/IRecorder/id/37480/rec/2

[269] Daniel Meadows, "Slain Man Threatened Two Women",

June 25, 1931: The man arrested in the nationally famous Edward Pierson murder case, George Washington, was exonerated by a grand jury. Detective Lt. George Sneed and Det. Claude White arrested Mr. Washington, which ignited a furor because he was a highly placed figure in the Indianapolis Baptist community. Mr. Pierson was likewise a respected auditor from Chicago.[270]

February 1937: Detective Sergeant.

September 17, 1937: A bit of police humor flashed across the wires, from Indianapolis, Indiana regarding Detective George Sneed. The story said Det. Sneed was on a midnight investigation and flashed a light on a figure lying on a basement floor. He whispered to Det. John Glenn, "It's a dead man, call the homicide squad." Glenn replied, "He's awfully dead, look at his glassy eyes." The two officers came closer. The figure turned out to be a ventriloquist's dummy.[271]

Indianapolis Recorder – February 23, 1929, 1, http://indiamond6.ulib.iupui.edu/cdm/compoundobject/collection/IRecorder/id/53949/rec/1

[270] "Famous Washington-Pierson Case Dismissed", *Indianapolis Recorder* – June 27, 1931, 1, http://indiamond6.ulib.iupui.edu/cdm/compoundobject/collection/IRecorder/id/15429/rec/1

December 1937: IPD Detectives Fred Simon, John Glenn, George Sneed, Claude White and Thomas Hopson receive a written letter of commendation from FBI agent Harold F. Rineicke in December 1937, for their part in assisting in the capture of Luther Benson on October 23, 1937, wanted for murder. [272]

April 6, 1940: Police Begin New Type Work - A revision in the detective side at Police headquarters was announced here this week with the following appointments made known. Officers detailed to burglary cases with Detective Ferdinand Holt are Claude White and Thomas Hopson. Patrol Detailed to homicide with Detective George Sneed, Ples Jones and Eddie Butler, and Detective John Glenn, working as special investigator on larceny may expect an aide in that department soon, according to official sources.[273]

---

[271] "Ventriloquist Dummy Was 'Murder' Victim", The Spokesman-Review, Spokane, Washington, – September 18, 1937, 3,
http://news.google.com/newspapers?nid=1314&dat=19370918&id=ym5WAAAAIBAJ&sjid=ueMDAAAAIBAJ&pg=7013,632933

[272] "F.B.I. Cites Five Officers Here", *Indianapolis Recorder* – December 25, 1937, 1,
http://indiamond6.ulib.iupui.edu/cdm/compoundobject/collection/IRecorder/id/55787/rec/1

[273] "Police Begin New Type Work", *Indianapolis Recorder* – April 6,

January 1943: Received a citation for Meritorious Service for efficient work in four specific cases and apprehending suspects in a series of robberies.
March 24, 1943: Commendation for Meritorious Service in the Line of Duty.[274]
April 1944: Commendation for Meritorious Service in the Line of Duty.
August 1945: Commendation for Meritorious Service in the Line of Duty.
September 1945: Commendation for Meritorious Service in the Line of Duty.
November 1945: Commendation for Meritorious Service in the Line of Duty.
October 1946: Commended by the Board of Safety "for excellent police work done in the arrest of William Porter Petty and John Collins, thus cleaning up a number of robberies and car thefts."
May 1947: Commendation for Meritorious Service in the Line of Duty.
May 28, 1947: Promoted to Lieutenant in the Uniform Division, making him the

---

1940, 1, http://indiamond6.ulib.iupui.edu/cdm/compoundobject/collection/IRecorder/id/74290/rec/1

[274] "Board Cites Sneed, Jones, Woodall, Bennett", *Indianapolis Recorder* – March 27, 1943, 1, http://indiamond6.ulib.iupui.edu/cdm/compoundobject/collection/IRecorder/id/95674/rec/1

highest ranking African-American on IPD. He was assigned to the Vice Squad. He replaced Preston Heater, who was retiring as the department's only African-American Lieutenant. He supervised a number of squads and walking officers. He conducted numerous vice raids as well.[275]

July 22, 1947: Commended by the Board of Safety for arrests which solved 17 robberies and a larceny.

October 7, 1947: Commended by the Board of Safety for the arrest of William Joyner, which cleared 235 burglary cases.

July 14, 1950: Commended by Chief of Police Edward Rouls.

June 16, 1951:
"RUMOR LT. SNEED TO STEP DOWN
Ranking Negro Officer May Take Reduction
Police circles are buzzing this week with a rumor, the persistency of which carries the suggestion it is well founded, that Police Lieutenant George Sneed will request to be returned to his former rank of detective sergeant. Queried regarding his reported

---

[275] "Det. Geo. Sneed Named Lieut.: Heater Retires", *Indianapolis Recorder* – May 31, 1947, 1, http://indiamond6.ulib.iupui.edu/cdm/compoundobject/collect ion/IRecorder/id/90866/rec/1

move, the widely admired and highly respected veteran officer replied, laconically. 'No comment.'

Lt. Sneed refused to affirm or deny the report that he would present his request to the Board' of Safety on his return from his vacation next week Speculation is that Lt. Sneed, who has spent many years treading graciously and courageously along the line of duty in an atmosphere marked by the clash of, personal ambitions natural to any, institution including police departments, has decided to seek a less turbulent role in view of his age.

This is not to suggest he will be any less vigorous and conscientious foe of all lawbreakers. "He is one of the finest officers we have on the department", J. Leroy Keach, president of the Safety Board, declares. "He can be depended upon always to do his duty to the full limit of his great capacity.

Chief Edward D. Rouls said there has been no pressure on him to maneuver Sneed's demotion. I although it is well known that many younger men cherish the; thought of a promotion to the lieutenancy. Rouls Pays Tribute "I will not recommend that Lt. Sneed be reduced. I am perfectly satisfied and proud of his long and distinguished record.

Lt. Sneed has been a member of the department for 31 years. His ability, personality and aggressiveness attracted such attention that after less than six months service he was promoted to detective sergeant, a rank he held until he was promoted in June 1947 to Lieutenant." [276]

May 1, 1954:
Lt. George Sneed Honored For His Service to City

"Lt. George Sneed, police officer 26 years who in January took a leave of absence from the force because of a serious illness, was honored by friends and city officials Wednesday in his home. The respected, well-liked officer was given a specially-built

---

[276] "Rumor Lt. Sneed to Step Down", *Indianapolis Recorder* – June 16, 1951, 1, http://indiamond6.ulib.iupui.edu/cdm/compoundobject/collection/IRecorder/id/85573/rec/1

electrical vibrating chair designed to stimulate blood circulation.

"This chair is a small tribute to the great service you have done our city," Mayor Alex M. Clark extolled. The city head said Lt. Sneed has been a "good citizen, a good father, and a good husband and has made tremendous inroads for his people."

MARCUS C. STEWART, editor of the *Recorder*, who has known Sneed throughout his police career, said "he has always fought for that in which he believed." He has an abundance of courage." Mr. Stewart, while heralding Mayor Clark as "the finest mayor as regards to Negroes since 1918," pointed out that a Columbus, O., Negro took a Chief of Police test last week. "We want another Negro lieutenant in Indianapolis. We should have a captain," the Recorder editor directed to the mayor.

CHIEF OF POLICE John E. Ambuhl told the gathering he and Lt. Sneed went on the force the same year and have enjoyed a "very pleasant association." He said "I appreciate his friendship."

STEPHEN NOLAND, Republican candidate for county clerk, was introduced. He praised Sneed as a "credit to the police force." "He is Indianapolis' first Negro lieutenant, and he made it on merit." Noland, former editor of the Indianapolis News, said he had followed the outstanding officer's career very closely and added that Lt. Sneed has brought national renown to the Indianapolis force.

RUFUS C. KUYKENDALL, as-assistant city attorney, called Sneed "the ablest officer on the force." In acceptance of the gift, Lt. Sneed said "I've never felt this happy before in my life." He introduced his wife, Mrs. Addie Sneed, who thanked the group for the honor.

HENRY FLEMING was chairman of a committee responsible for receiving donations from police officers to purchase the gift. SGT. ALEXANDER POSEY was vice chairman, and Mr. Stewart served as treasurer. SGT. CLARENCE LEWIS, Sgt. Thomas Williams and Patrolman William Lee were members of the committee."[277]

---

[277] "Lt. George Sneed Honored For His Service to The City", *Indianapolis Recorder* – May 1, 1954, 1, http://indiamond6.ulib.iupui.edu/cdm/compoundobject/collect

May 22, 1954: *Indianapolis Recorder* Editorial

Lieut. Sneed Retires
"The retirement from the Indianapolis police force of Lieut. George W. Sneed is an occasion for both eulogy and regret. Regret, because this fine, intelligent, level-headed veteran officer will be sorely missed from police activities and civic life. As for eulogy, any spoken or written effort will be vain in comparison with Lieutenant Sneed's unmatched record. His reputation and renown are deeply etched in the hearts and minds of his fellow men. For courage in the line of duty, who can surpass the episode of "Hellcat" Thomas? The two-gun desperado had sent a murder threat to Sneed, but the officer closed in on him and Sneed's life was spared when the bandit's weapon, aimed pointblank, failed to fire.

For intelligent detective work, the team of Sneed and (Edward) Trabue was nationally famed. Detective Sneed's name became a byword, like that of Sherlock Holmes. "Don't do a George Sneed on me" was a common expression of persons jokingly wishing to avoid exposure. In the field of human relations, Lieutenant Sneed was a model of what every police officer should be—kind and understanding toward the ordinary citizen who got into difficulty; of disciplined but manly bearing toward his superiors.

There was nothing of the bully about him, and his aim was to prevent trouble rather than persecute minor lawbreakers. Above all, his honesty stands unquestioned as a shining beacon amidst surrounding darkness. He should have been a Captain long ago; but he was more than a Captain— 'He was a man, take him for all in all; we shall not look upon his like again.'" [278]

---

[278] "Lieut. George Sneed Retires", *Indianapolis Recorder* – May 22, 1954, 10, http://indiamond6.ulib.iupui.edu/cdm/compoundobject/collection/IRecorder/id/33441/rec/1

A FINAL SALUTE: Fellow officers stand in ranks in front of the Indianapolis Police Department to render a final salute to deceased Police Lt. George W. Sneed during the funeral precession to Crown Hill Cemetery last Saturday. Lt. Sneed, who died Aug. 30, was the first Negro to attain the rank of Lieutenant in the police department. After 36 years on the force, he retired in 1954. He was known as "The Father Of Negro Police Officers." (Recorder photo by Jim Burres)

Indianapolis Recorder – September 9, 1961[279]

---

[279] "A Final Salute", *Indianapolis Recorder* – September 9, 1961, 1, http://indiamond6.ulib.iupui.edu/cdm/compoundobject/collection/IRecorder/id/39706/rec/1

FELLOW OFFICERS LEAVE RITES: Fellow police officers (most of whom are no longer with the force) of Lt. George W. Sneed are shown leaving Corinthian Baptist Church following funeral services last Saturday the noted lawman who died Aug. 30 in his home. Identifiable in the picture are ex-Detective Sgts. Alexander Posey, Jack Hadley, Claude White, Fred Starks, Edward Butler and Patrolman Colion Chaney, (Recorder photo by Jim Burres) [280]

---

[280] "Fellow Officers Leave Rites", *Indianapolis Recorder* – September 9, 1961, 1, http://indiamond6.ulib.iupui.edu/cdm/compoundobject/collection/IRecorder/id/39706/rec/1

THE AVENOO September 9, 1961
"Working with Sneed when he headed a vice squad were Chester Coates and Garland Jones, both now detective sergeants and former Sgt. Clarence Lewis . . . He 'broke' in several young officers, all of whom made good in the department. Other officers who worked with Sneed, according to years, and prior to that time our info, include Slim Brown, Grandison and Admiral Harris in the 1920's, when the Lieutenant headed a special vice squad.

He also worked with Detective Butler. ONE of the most outstanding and hair-raising events in his career was the time many years ago, when he was part of a detail sent to arrest a man known as 'Hell-Cat', a very dangerous character. Mr. Sneed said as they walked down an alley, 'Hell-Cat' opened fire point blank at him . . . and he fell flat on his stomach .... escaping death by an eyelash. AMONG the hundreds who attended the funeral were: Mr. and Mrs. Oscar (Oscar's Loan Co.) Tavel, Mr. and Mrs. Bud Shirley, Mrs. Rubina Winston, Marcus C. Stewart, Recorder publisher; Bubber Mitchell, Officer James Mitchell, Jack Hadley, Opal Tandy, Detectives'

Garland Jones, Thomas Bryant, Chester Coates, Mr. and Mrs. Leroy Johnson (Sarah, ex- policewoman), Roy Kennedy, Guy Lester, John Glenn, Mr. and Mrs. Edward Weathers, Lieutenant Oscar Donahue, Captain Anthony Watkins, Officer Colion Chaney, Alexander Posey (former sgt.), Lieutenant Spurgeon Davenport and many, many others." [281]

---

[281] "The Avenoo", The *Indianapolis Recorder* – September 9, 1961, 12,
http://indiamond6.ulib.iupui.edu/cdm/compoundobject/collection/IRecorder/id/39706/rec/1

Detective Sergeant Claude C. White

Born: January 25, 1890 Kentucky
Died: January 1974 Indianapolis, IN.[283]
Date Appointed: July 15, 1918
Date Retired: September 1957.

Buried Crown Hill Cemetery, Section 100, Lot 309.
Census records say Claude was born in Kentucky[284] but he stated on his 1942 draft

---

[282] IMPD Lichtenberger History Room.
[283] Birth & Death data from SSDI: 306-42-5563; Issue State: Indiana; Issue Date: 1957-1958.

registration card that he was born in Evansville, Indiana.[285] Claude did grow up near Evansville, living in 1900 in Pigeon, Vanderburgh County, Indiana.[286]

Claude White played with George Sneed when they were boys. They later went to school together and eventually worked together on the IPD Detective Squad where they made a great team.

December 17, 1922 – Involved in an incident in which he himself was shot and badly wounded and then returned fire, killing his assailant. Near Senate and 11th Avenue, a shot rang out from a saloon.

Officer White, who was off duty, charged through the saloon door as a 2nd shot was

---

[284] Year: 1900; Census Place: Pigeon, Vanderburgh, Indiana; Roll: 407; Page: 1A; Enumeration District: 0108; FHL microfilm: 1240407.

[285] Ancestry.com. U.S., World War II Draft Registration Cards, 1942 [database on-line]. Provo, UT, USA: Ancestry.com Operations, Inc., 2010.

[286] "United States Census, 1900," index and images, FamilySearch (https://familysearch.org/pal:/MM9.1.1/M99Z-1F1 : accessed 25 May 2014), Claude White in household of Robert White, Pigeon Township Evansville city Ward 5, Vanderburgh, Indiana, United States; citing sheet 1A, family 11, NARA microfilm publication T623, FHL microfilm 1240407.

fired, which struck him in the right arm. White returned fire until his assailant fell to the floor. Then from behind, the dead man's brother attacked White with a knife. He slashed at White's throat repeatedly but White was saved by a scarf he had put on that morning due to the cold weather.

White's gun was almost empty but he managed to get a shot off which struck the man as he ran from the scene. The suspect managed to get back up and run, being chased by Officer White for several blocks. White stopped the chase and returned to the saloon due to heavy loss of blood. [287]

<u>March 27, 1923:</u> First African-American assigned to the Traffic Division along with three other African-Americans.[288]
<u>May 15, 1925:</u> Detective Claude White shoots and kills James Cloyd.[289]
<u>August 1927:</u> Working in the Detective Bureau.

---

[287] Opal Tandy, "The Human Side of the Law" *Indianapolis Recorder* - January 8, 1938, 2, http://indiamond6.ulib.iupui.edu/cdm/compoundobject/collection/IRecorder/id/60319/rec/1

[288] Ibid

[289] The Kokomo Tribune – September 6, 1929, 10, http://www.newspapers.com/newspage/41813108/

May 22, 1928: Promoted to rank of Detective Sergeant.

June 25, 1931: The man arrested in the nationally famous Edward Pierson murder case, George Washington, was exonerated by a grand jury. Detective Lt. George Sneed and Det. Claude White arrested Mr. Washington, which ignited a furor because he was a highly placed figure in the Baptist community. Mr. Pierson was likewise a respected auditor from Chicago.[290]

About 1933: Appointed Acting Lieutenant by special order.

February 1937: Detective Sergeant.

December 1937: IPD Detectives Fred Simon, John Glenn, George Sneed, Claude White and Thomas Hopson receive a written letter of commendation from FBI agent Harold F. Rineicke in December 1937, for their part in assisting in the capture of Luther Benson on October 23, 1937, wanted for murder. [291]

---

[290] "Famous Washington-Pierson Case Dismissed", *Indianapolis Recorder* – June 27, 1931, 1, http://indiamond6.ulib.iupui.edu/cdm/compoundobject/collection/IRecorder/id/15429/rec/1

[291] "F.B.I. Cites Five Officers Here", *Indianapolis Recorder* – December 25, 1937, 1, http://indiamond6.ulib.iupui.edu/cdm/compoundobject/collection/IRecorder/id/55787/rec/1

January 2, 1940: Reduced in rank from Detective Sergeant to Detective Investigator.

April 6, 1940: Police Begin New Type Work - A revision in the detective side at Police headquarters was announced here this week with the following appointments made known. Officers detailed to burglary cases with Detective Ferdinand Holt are Claude White and Thomas Hopson. Patrol Detailed to homicide with Detective George Sneed, Ples Jones and Eddie Butler, and Detective John Glenn, working as special investigator on larceny may expect an aide in that department soon, according to official sources.[292]

Numerous citations including one in 1945 for solving 3 armed robberies.

December 12, 1953: Almost hit in the face with shotgun blast while on scene of a double murder at 535 Indiana Avenue.
June 9, 1954: Promoted to merit rank of Sergeant.[293]

---

[292] "Police Begin New Type Work", *Indianapolis Recorder* – April 6, 1940, 1, http://indiamond6.ulib.iupui.edu/cdm/compoundobject/collection/IRecorder/id/74290/rec/1

[293] "Police Sgts. Given Permanent Rank", *Indianapolis Recorder*

September 21, 1957:
Det. Claude White Slated To Retire
"Detective Sergeant Claude White, veteran police officer, was slated to retire after 38 years on the Indianapolis Police force. For many years, he teamed with George Sneed, retired, to form a detective team that won universal recognition far and wide for their bravery, devotion to duty, and skill in tracking down criminals, and especially those reputed to be "bad men."

Appointed to the department July 15, 1919, he served as patrolman and was promoted to the traffic department March 27, 1923. He shortly thereafter was appointed detective sergeant and except for several short periods, remained on the acting detective sergeant status until his permanent to that rank in 1954." [294]

– June 12, 1954, 1, http://indiamond6.ulib.iupui.edu/cdm/compoundobject/collection/IRecorder/id/33492/rec/1

[294] "Det. Claude White Slated to Retire", *Indianapolis Recorder* – September 21, 1957, 1, http://indiamond6.ulib.iupui.edu/cdm/compoundobject/collection/IRecorder/id/31508/rec/1

Patrolman James S. Vincent

Born: October 18, 1879 Indiana
Died: November 1, 1947 Indianapolis, Indiana[296]

---

[295] IMPD Lichtenberger History Room.
[296] "Rites Held for James Vincent", *Indianapolis Recorder* - November 8, 1947, 1,
http://indiamond6.ulib.iupui.edu/cdm/compoundobject/collection/IRecorder/id/91147/rec/1

Date Appointed: July 12, 1916
Date of Separation/Retirement: 1937
Buried in Crown Hill Cemetery section 99, lot 2089.[297]

<u>1899:</u> Was a bicycle racer along with Carter F.B. Temple.[298]

<u>October 7, 1919:</u> Turned in his resignation after being accused in connection with janitors stealing confiscated whiskey at police headquarters.

<u>February 24,1925:</u> Reinstated as a police officer by Police Board.

---

[297] Findagrave.com
[298] *Indianapolis Recorder* – June 17, 1899, 2, http://indiamond6.ulib.iupui.edu/cdm/compoundobject/collection/IRecorder/id/779/rec/2

Detective Sergeant Clarence "Plez" Jones

Born: March 27, 1885 Nashville, TN.[300]
Died May 9, 1955 Indianapolis, IN.[301]

---

[299] IMPD Lichtenberger History Room.
[300] Draft Card - Registration State: Indiana; Registration County: Marion; Roll: 1504020; Draft Board: 5.
[301] "Plez C. Jones, Retired Detective Sergeant, Buried", *Indianapolis Recorder* – May 14, 1955, 1, http://indiamond6.ulib.iupui.edu/cdm/compoundobject/collect

Date Appointed: September 30, 1919
Date Retired: December 22, 1954

Plez Jones, age 59, married on September 24, 1948 in Davidson County, Tennessee to Sara Alice Mize, 35, who was a policewoman with the Indianapolis Police Department. [302] Buried Crown Hill Cemetery, Section 99, Lot 2767.[303]

January 4, 1926: Promoted to Detective Sergeant.
May 22, 1928: Demoted to Patrolman.
March 1930: Assigned to Detective Bureau.
February 1937: Patrolman 1st Grade.
April 6, 1940: Police Begin New Type Work - A revision in the detective side at Police headquarters was announced here this week with the following appointments made known. Officers detailed to burglary cases with Detective Ferdinand Holt are Claude White and Thomas Hopson. Patrol Detailed

---

ion/IRecorder/id/36827/rec/1

[302] "Tennessee, County Marriages, 1790-1950," index and images, FamilySearch (https://familysearch.org/pal:/MM9.1.1/KZW9-SQJ : accessed 25 May 2014), Plez Jones and Sara Alice Mize, 24 Sep 1948; citing Davidson, Tennessee, United States, ; FHL microfilm 1994120.

[303] Findagrave.com

to homicide with Detective George Sneed, Ples Jones and Eddie Butler, and Detective John Glenn, working as special investigator on larceny may expect an aide in that department soon, according to official sources.[304]

1943: Detective.

March 24, 1943:
BOARD CITES SNEED,JONES, WOODALL,BENNETT
"Sergeant George Sneed, Officers Plez Jones, Osa Woodall and Norvell Bennett were cited by the board of safety Tuesday for Outstanding and meritorious service.[305]

1952: Detective Sergeant.

June 12, 1954: Promoted to the rank of Merit Sergeant.

December 22, 1954: After being on sick leave for several months due to ill health, was retired by the Board of Safety this date.

---

[304] "Police Begin New Type Work", *Indianapolis Recorder* – April 6, 1940, 1,
http://indiamond6.ulib.iupui.edu/cdm/compoundobject/collection/IRecorder/id/74290/rec/1

[305] "Board Cites Sneed, Jones, Woodall, Bennett", *Indianapolis Recorder* – March 27, 1943, 1,
http://indiamond6.ulib.iupui.edu/cdm/compoundobject/collection/IRecorder/id/95674/rec/1

Plez Jones had received 6 commendations for bravery and meritorious service during his career. 30 of his 35 years were spent as a detective. Chief John E. Ambuhl said at his retirement, "there is not a bad mark on his record. He was a fine officer."[306]

May 14, 1955:

Plez C. Jones, Retired Detective Sergeant, Buried

"Some fine work as a courageous, loyal detective was written into local police records during the 35 years Plez Jones served the city as a member of the police department. His death Monday at his residence. 3536 Graceland was deeply mourned by official representatives, family and many friends gathered at Corinthian Baptist Church Thursday afternoon. He was 70 years old and had retired in December. 1954. During the more than 35 years of his service, 30 of which were spent as a detective, he received six commendations

---

[306] "Sgt. Plez Jones Leaves Force", *Indianapolis Recorder* – December 25, 1954, 1, http://indiamond6.ulib.iupui.edu/cdm/compoundobject/collection/IRecorder/id/34843/rec/1

for bravery and meritorious service. Early in his career he won wide respect for his high devotion to duty, his fearlessness evidenced many times in his bold capture of hardened criminals and his fair treatment of his fellow man." [307]

---

[307] "Plez C. Jones, Retired Detective Sergeant, Buried", *Indianapolis Recorder* – May 14, 1955, 1, http://indiamond6.ulib.iupui.edu/cdm/compoundobject/collection/IRecorder/id/36827/rec/1

Detective Sergeant Roy Sonnie Kennedy

Born: July 26, 1888 Nashville, TN.
Died: January 5, 1969 Indianapolis, IN.
Date Appointed: November 11, 1919
Date Retired: October 1946

Buried Crown Hill Cemetery, Section 99, Lot 4346.

---

[308] IMPD Lichtenberger History Room.

Roy Kennedy wearing his traffic cap. [309]

January 16, 1923: Promoted to Traffic Officer. Along with Claude White, he was the first African-American in IPD history to work in the Traffic Branch.
January 4, 1926: Demoted to Patrolman 2nd Grade.
March 23, 1926: Promoted to Patrolman 1st Grade.
August 22, 1931: Appointed Detective Sergeant.[310]

---

[309] The Indianapolis Children's Museum.

<u>June 1934:</u> The Chief of Police had three men who were eligible for Promotion to Sergeant, all African American. Roy S. Kennedy and the other two men, Plez Jones and Thomas Hopson drew slips of paper from a hat and the one with "Sergeant" on it was drawn by Kennedy. The promotion was approved by the Board of Safety. He had held the rank previously.[311]

<u>January 1, 1935:</u> Reduced to Patrolman 1st Grade in shakeup.

<u>February 1937:</u> Patrolman 1st Grade.

<u>November 18, 1944:</u> In an interview with the *Indianapolis Recorder*, 25 year IPD officer Roy Kennedy reflects on how things were when he was hired in 1919. Among his observations:

"At that time it was the practice to assign colored officers to the Northeast section of the city from 23rd street to the city limits at 42nd St., from College ave., east. Kennedy recalls that a few of Negro patrolmen were assigned to the old 34th district, which

---

[310] "In Shakeup", *Indianapolis Recorder* – August 22, 1931, 1, http://indiamond6.ulib.iupui.edu/cdm/compoundobject/collection/IRecorder/id/15944/rec/1

[311] "Lucky Sergeant" – *Indianapolis Recorder* – June 9, 1934, 1, http://indiamond6.ulib.iupui.edu/cdm/compoundobject/collection/IRecorder/id/16457/rec/18

contained a miniature of hell known as 'Pat Ward's bottoms'".

"I have long looked for the day when colored officers would be given the opportunity to serve under colored superiors who know the sufferings of my people and have the answers to the problems in their conduct. It was one of the proudest days of my life when I saw Officers Preston Heater appointed a uniformed lieutenant and Jack Hadley and Norvel Bennett made sergeants. Their high efficiency in performance of their duties has reflected credit upon all of us and their historic promotions serve as an inspiration and worthy goal for the young officer of today, a prospect which I did not face a quarter century ago". [312]

"Roy S. Kennedy, ex-policeman, rites observed Roy S. Kennedy, age 80, 2161 Boulevard Place, a former member of the city policeman department, and later active in Republican politics and on the civic front died Monday, Jan.5, in St. Vincent's Hospital. The funeral was held in St. Bridget's Roman Catholic

---

[312] Roy Kennedy, "Roy Kennedy Completes 25 Years on Force", *Indianapolis Recorder* – November 18, 1944, 1-2, http://indiamond6.ulib.iupui.edu/cdm/compoundobject/collection/IRecorder/id/95357/rec/1

Church, Thursday, Jan. 9. After 27 years of service he retired from the city police department in 1946. He was a native of Nashville, Tenn. and had lived here most of his adult life. He was an organizer of the "colorful" Bohemian Club of the days when Indiana Ave. was "in flower." He was a Republican precinct committeeman of the 15th precinct of the Seventh Ward for 25 years, the Fraternal Order of Police and the retired Police Protective Association. Survivors include, his wife, Mrs. Fannie Kennedy and three daughters, Mrs. Florence Goode, Mrs. Thelma Cosby, Mrs. Barbara Sharpe and Mrs. Carrie Robinson."[313]

---

[313] "Roy S. Kennedy, ex-policeman, rites observed", *Indianapolis Recorder* – January 25, 1969, 13, http://indiamond6.ulib.iupui.edu/cdm/compoundobject/collection/IRecorder/id/48117/rec/1

Detective Sergeant Frederick "Fred" Harrison Starks

Born: March 6, 1889 Franklin, IN.[315]
Died: February 15, 1968 Detroit, MI.
Date Appointed: April 20, 1920
Date Separated/Retired: March 6, 1959

---

[314] The Indianapolis Childrens Museum.
[315] Draft Card - Registration State: Indiana; Registration County: Marion; Roll: 1504016; Draft Board: 2.

Buried Crown Hill Cemetery, section 98, lot 1560. [316]

Broken in by Officer John Coleman.

<u>1926:</u> Assigned to Traffic. Shown the ropes by Roy S. Kennedy. Spent 18 years in Traffic.

<u>August 1, 1931:</u> While directing traffic at Indiana Avenue and New York Street, Patrolman Starks heard gunfire coming from a pawn shop at 234 Indiana Avenue. As Starks neared the pawn shop, the owner of the store Jack Warren, exchanged gunfire with Roy Love, who was in the street. Starks was between them and grabbed the barrel of Love's gun and wrenched it from his hand, which badly burned Stark's hand as it was hot from the rapid fire. Love had robbed Warren and shot him in the stomach, killing him.

<u>February 1937:</u> Patrolman 1st Grade.

<u>May 1937:</u> Stationed at New York St. and Senate Ave. as Traffic officer.

<u>January 27, 1943:</u> Promoted to Detective Investigator from the Traffic Division. Described at that time as "probably the most popular traffic officer on the force."[317]

---

[316] Findagrave.com

May 29, 1937: Profiled in *Indianapolis Recorder*.

June 12, 1954: Promoted to rank of Merit Sergeant.

1955-56: Assigned to Detective Division, general cases on foot.

Earned 7 commendations during his career.

March 7, 1959:
Fred Starks Retires as Policeman after 35 Years

" Veteran Policeman Fred Starks has announced his retirement from the force after more than 35 years of service. His retirement with pensions was to become effective Friday, his 70th birthday. Appointed April 21, 1920, Starks, 2220 Martindale was a patrolman for four years, a traffic officer 18 years until his appointment in January, 1944, to the rank of sergeant in the Detective Division. Except for two years following his resignation in 1924, his service has been continuous.

---

[317] "Raise Starks, Send Woodall to Traffic Post", *Indianapolis Recorder* – January 30, 1943, 1, http://indiamond6.ulib.iupui.edu/cdm/compoundobject/collection/IRecorder/id/95540/rec/1

Sgt. Starks was commended seven times for outstanding police work, including apprehension of three bandits involved in 17 robberies and a larceny; arrest of two murderers and other citations for meritorious service in the line of duty.

THE COMMENDATIONS came from several different police chiefs, including Jesse McMurtry, C. F. Beaker and Edward Rouls.

Despite the glamor attached to Sgt. FRED STARKS detective work, Sgt. Starks said he enjoyed most his work on traffic details. "I especially liked my old post down at Market and Capitol where I saw four governors come and go," he recalls. He rates as his most frightening experience the time in the early 30's when he broke up a gun duel during which Pawn Broker Jack Warner was killed. "When I grabbed the gun away from the killer," he remembers, "it was so hot it blistered my fingers." He said that was the only time he was ever hurt while on duty.

ALTHOUGH HE BELIEVES opportunities for Negro officers are much greater now than during his early day on the force, Sgt. Starks says he has had "a mighty nice career." His plans include "a whole lot of fishing" and more time at home with his wife, Sadie, an active worker with The Recorder's Women Sponsors." [318]

March 7, 1959
A GOOD OFFICER RETIRES
". . . The retirement of Det. Sgt. Fred Starks after 39 grueling years on the force, will leave a void hard to fill in the department ... He was a conscientious officer, well disciplined, and enjoyed the respect and friendship of people in all walks of life ... It would be a good idea for some of the younger officers to pattern their careers along the path of this friendly officer, who served the citizens of this community well ... It is a joy unrestrained to pay this tribute to Fred Starks . . A gentleman . . .A good citizen . . . And a good COP!" [319]

---

[318] "Fred Starks Retires as Policeman after 35 Years", *Indianapolis Recorder* – March 7, 1959,.1, http://indiamond6.ulib.iupui.edu/cdm/compoundobject/collection/IRecorder/id/37101/rec/1

[319] The Saint, "A Good Officer Retires", *Indianapolis Recorder* –

Faces of IPD

Officer James A. Johnson [320]

March 7, 1959, 12,
http://indiamond6.ulib.iupui.edu/cdm/compoundobject/collection/IRecorder/id/37101/rec/1
[320] IMPD Lichtenberger History Room

Lieutenant James "Preston" Heater

Born: February 4, 1882 Scottsville, KY.[322]
Died: June 11, 1949 Indianapolis, IN.[323]

---

[321] IMPD Lichtenberger History Room.
[322] Draft Card -. Ancestry.com. U.S., World War II Draft Registration Cards, 1942 [database on-line]. Provo, UT, USA: Ancestry.com Operations, Inc., 2010. Original data:
[323] "Retired Police Officer's Rites Held June 14", *Indianapolis Recorder* – June 18, 1949, 1,

Date Appointed: August 13, 1920
Date Retired: June 9, 1947

Buried Crown Hill Cemetery, Section 98, Lot 1297.[324]

May 28, 1928: Appointed Detective Sergeant.
August 22, 1931: Demoted to Patrolman 2nd Grade.[325]
March 26, 1935: Promoted to Patrolman 1st Grade.
January 23, 1943: Promoted to Uniform Sergeant, which is a rank an African-American hadn't held on IPD in about a decade.   Assigned to head a 3-man Vice Squad team. [326]
October 26, 1943: Promoted to Lieutenant in the uniformed division, becoming the highest ranked African-American on IPD.

---

http://indiamond6.ulib.iupui.edu/cdm/compoundobject/collection/IRecorder/id/88026/rec/1
[324] Findagrave.com
[325] "In Shakeup", *Indianapolis Recorder* – August 22, 1931, 1, http://indiamond6.ulib.iupui.edu/cdm/compoundobject/collection/IRecorder/id/15944/rec/1
[326] Opal Tandy, "Bennett Made Detective, Colored in Car 31 Feb 1", *Indianapolis Recorder* – January 23, 1943, 1, http://indiamond6.ulib.iupui.edu/cdm/compoundobject/collection/IRecorder/id/95523/rec/1

He is the first African-American promoted to Lieutenant since George Sneed in 1925.[327]
June 17, 1944: Credited by *Indianapolis Recorder* with reducing crime along Indiana Avenue.
May 28, 1947: Retired with rank of Lieutenant due to ill health. It became effective June 9th. [328]
(Promotion dates recounted in *Indianapolis Recorder*, January 23, 1943)[329]

June 7, 1947:
A GOOD POLICE OFFICER RETIRES
"The retirement of Lieutenant Preston Heater from the Indianapolis Police Department effective as of June 10 marks another milestone in the trend of changing things in community civic affairs. While he was not the first of his racial group to hold

---

[327] "Men Won Promotions – Chief Says", *Indianapolis Recorder* – November 6, 1943, 1,
http://indiamond6.ulib.iupui.edu/cdm/compoundobject/collection/IRecorder/id/96214/rec/1
[328] "Det. Geo. Sneed Named Lieut.: Heater Retires", *Indianapolis Recorder* – May 31, 1947, 1,
http://indiamond6.ulib.iupui.edu/cdm/compoundobject/collection/IRecorder/id/90866/rec/1
[329] Opal Tandy, "Bennett Made Detective, Colored in Car 31 Feb 1", *Indianapolis Recorder* – January 23, 1943, 1,
http://indiamond6.ulib.iupui.edu/cdm/compoundobject/collection/IRecorder/id/95523/rec/1

such a rank, he was the first to be appointed regularly to such rank.

Lieutenant Heater entered the department in September of 1920. He observed that there has been nothing spectacular about his service record, but he has always tried to do police duty and do what was right. Along the way his service record or work has been associated with that of George Sneed, Edward Trabue, Claude White and Plez Jones and others who made history in the police department. He was sincere, honest and unassuming, members of the department and people who really know him observe. He did not like the limelight and the individual who shuns the limelight when it is favorable is sometimes at a disadvantage when it is unfavorable. Along with some of his associates he received several commendations from superior officers through the years.

Always he sought to inspire younger men entering the department to do their duties and meet rightly their obligations to the department and as public servants. His record in the department has been good, and he leaves the department with no regrets except he observes that young men of today on entering the department can look forward to bigger promises if they shall prove equal to their opportunities."[330]

Sergeant Jesse "Jack" Hadley

Born: January 18, 1894 Indianapolis, IN.[332]

---

[330] *Indianapolis Recorder* – June 7, 1947
[331] IMPD Lichtenberger History Room.
[332] Birth and Death dates from SSDI, Number: 306-48-0157;

Died: September 15, 1969 Indianapolis, IN.
Date Appointed: September 5, 1920
Date Retired: March 22, 1960
Buried Crown Hill Cemetery, section 98, lot 1593.[333]

WWI veteran, serving one year overseas. [334]

1920: Patrolman Jack Hadley's first assignment was "old District 35", an area between 9th and 16th Streets and West Street and Capitol Avenue. Other beats he patrolled were known as "Pat Ward's Bottoms (West 11th Street) and the "badlands" of the Eastside.[335]

"One Man Squad"
On one occasion when in Pat Ward's Bottoms, Jack Hadley arrested over 12 hardened gamblers, confiscated their money

---

Issue State: Indiana; Issue Date: 1962.

[333] Findagrave.com

[334] "Sgt. Hadley In Local Police Dept. 25 Years", *Indianapolis Recorder* – September 15, 1945, 1, http://indiamond6.ulib.iupui.edu/cdm/compoundobject/collection/IRecorder/id/26491/rec/1

[335] "Sgt. Hadley In Local Police Dept. 25 Years", *Indianapolis Recorder* – September 15, 1945, 1, http://indiamond6.ulib.iupui.edu/cdm/compoundobject/collection/IRecorder/id/26491/rec/1

and dice and loaded them in the paddy wagon for transport to jail, single handedly.[336]

July 9, 1926: Had a hand in the capture of Gene Alger, who had just murdered Officer John F. Buchanan in the Beyer Hotel. He exchanged shots downtown with Alger, who fired a shot that passed an inch over Hadley's head.[337] [338]

February 18, 1929: Officer Jesse Hadley shoots and kills a man in the line of duty.[339]

August 19, 1933: BRASS BUTTONS and a six shooter does not make a policeman, but Jack Hadley (Jackie Boy) as called by his sister, and the above combination plus a blue uniform and puttees, make one of the best policemen that ever patrolled the Indiana Avenue beat. Kind, courteous, considerate, but not lax or afraid in the performance of his duty.[340]

---

[336] Ibid.
[337] "Gunman Runs Amock: Kills Policeman", *Indianapolis Recorder* – July 17, 1926, 1,
http://indiamond6.ulib.iupui.edu/cdm/compoundobject/collection/IRecorder/id/37687/rec/1
[338] "Sgt. Hadley In Local Police Dept. 25 Years", *Indianapolis Recorder* – September 15, 1945, 1,
http://indiamond6.ulib.iupui.edu/cdm/compoundobject/collection/IRecorder/id/26491/rec/1
[339] "Man Killed", *Indianapolis Recorder* – February 23, 1929, 1,
http://indiamond6.ulib.iupui.edu/cdm/compoundobject/collection/IRecorder/id/53949/rec/1

February 1937: Patrolman 1st Grade.
March 13, 1943: At his request, transfers out of the Vice Branch and assigned to a district after 2 weeks, because he wasn't sure what was expected of him.
September 11, 1943: Becomes 2nd man to hold the rank of Uniform Sergeant in 1943. He was assigned to Indiana Avenue.   "Highly rated for his efficiency and getting the job done."

SERGT. JACK HADLEY "One of the best liked officers and one of the most efficiency Jack Hadley, has been promoted to the rank of uniform sergeant in charge of a squad, effective September 11, it was disclosed here Tuesday. Chief of Police Clifford Beeker made the announcement and it was approved by the Board of Safety. A member of the police department 23 years, Sgt. Hadley has made a fine record and the announcement of his promotion drew city-wide enthusiasm." [341]

---

[340] *Indianapolis Recorder* – August 19, 1933, 4, http://indiamond6.ulib.iupui.edu/cdm/compoundobject/collection/IRecorder/id/17247/rec/1

[341] "Hadley Made Serg't; Given Cruiser Squad", *Indianapolis Recorder* – September 11, 1943, 1, http://indiamond6.ulib.iupui.edu/cdm/compoundobject/collection/IRecorder/id/96078/rec/1

September 15, 1945: Profiled by the *Indianapolis Recorder* on the occasion of marking 25 years with the Indianapolis Police Department, he was described as a "cleanup man" and a "trouble shooter", who preferred not to speak of his numerous adventures. [342]

1948 – Reduced to Patrolman under new administration.

Jack Hadley built a reputation as an excellent police officer in his 40-year career. He was never suspended. On the occasion of his retirement, he said of his time with IPD, "I enjoyed every minute of it." He also said as a child he always envisioned himself as a police officer. "If I were to choose a career again it would definitely be with the department." So great was the respect he earned that there was a time when the tougher elements of the east side neighborhood he patrolled would salute his empty patrol car and say "be careful because Jack is in the neighborhood." [343]

---

[342] "Sgt. Hadley In Local Police Dept. 25 Years", *Indianapolis Recorder* – September 15, 1945, 1,
http://indiamond6.ulib.iupui.edu/cdm/compoundobject/collection/IRecorder/id/26491/rec/1

[343] "Second Oldest Officer Retires from Force", *Indianapolis*

"When they call my name at roll call, it's "MR. Officer Hadley" – Jack Hadley, as remembered by Clarence White. One time when they didn't use that title, Jack said loudly, "My name is MISTER. Remember that."

Jack Hadley with members of the Attucks H.S. Safety Patrol, 1941.

Recorder – April 9, 1960, 2,
http://indiamond6.ulib.iupui.edu/cdm/compoundobject/collect ion/IRecorder/id/38540/rec/21

Policewoman Mayme E.(Pettiford) Shelton

Born: April 1872 Franklin, Indiana[345]
Died: October 9, 1922 Indianapolis, Indiana[346]
Date Appointed: January 2, 1922
Date Separated: October 9, 1922 (her death)

---

[344] IMPD Lichenberger History Room.
[345] Year: 1900; Census Place: Indianapolis, Marion, Indiana; Roll: 388; Page: 6A; Enumeration District: 0074; FHL microfilm: 1240388.
[346] Findagrave.com

Buried in Crown Hill Cemetery, section 53, lot 675.[347]

Badge #424, 5'3", 130 lbs., Republican.[348]
<u>1880:</u> Mary Pettiford, age 8 and parents John W. and Sarah Pettiford, "black", reside in town of Franklin, in Johnson County, Indiana. [349]
<u>November 28, 1894:</u> James N. Shelton marries Mayme Pettiford of Franklin, Indiana. He was a prominent funeral director in Indianapolis from 1914 until his death in 1921. He served as Deputy Assessor in Marion County, Indiana for 12 years.[350]
<u>March 6, 1898:</u> Mayme (Pettiford) Shelton and husband James have a daughter Zelda Marion born in Johnson County, Indiana. [351]

---

[347] Ibid.
[348] Public Safety Record, Indiana State Archives.
[349] Year: 1880; Census Place: Franklin, Johnson, Indiana; Roll: 289; Family History Film: 1254289; Page: 131B; Enumeration District: 155; Image: 0043.
[350] Franklin Lincoln Mather, Who's Who in the Colored Race (1915), .241
http://books.google.com/books?id=tWTXAAAAMAAJ&pg=PA10 8&dq=Franklin+Lincoln+Mather,+Who%E2%80%99s+Who+in+t he+Colored+Race&hl=en&sa=X&ei=HdFyU-DjAYGeyAToOYCwAw&ved=0CEEQ6AEwAA#v=onepage&q=Frar klin%20Lincoln%20Mather%2C%20Who%E2%80%99s%20Who %20in%20the%20Colored%20Race&f=false

1910: Mayme Shelton, 32, wife of James Shelton, proprietor of undertaker's shop. [352] He died on June 7, 1921.

May 23, 1922: While pursuing a thief, fires a warning shot into the air and arrests him. She was the first IPD policewoman to fire her gun in the line of duty.

August 25, 1922: Along with African-American Patrolwoman "Anna" Brewer (below), is assigned to the "colored" district. [353]

October 9, 1922: Dies while on duty of "paralysis", apparently having had a stroke. She is buried October 13, 1922 in Crown Hill Cemetery.

POLICEWOMAN DEAD. "Mrs. Mayme Shelton was on duty Monday and patrolled the district to which she had been assigned. She was taken ill suddenly Monday night number and died in a short time." [354]

---

[351] Johnson County, Indiana Index to Birth Records 1882 - 1920 Inclusive Volume I Letters A - Mac Inclusive
    Johnson County, Indiana Index to Birth Records 1882 – 1920 Volume II Mac - Z Book: CH-2 Page: 10
[352] 1910; Census Place: Indianapolis Ward 5, Marion, Indiana; Roll: T624_367; Page: 10B; Enumeration District: 0099; FHL microfilm: 1374380.
[353] The Indianapolis News – August 25, 1922, 7, http://www.newspapers.com/image/#37381723&terms=mayme
[354] "Policewoman Dead", The Indianapolis News – October

Officer Hester H. "Hettie" (Johnson) Brewer Vaulx

Born: March 7, 1875 Kentucky[355]
Died: August 9, 1943 Indianapolis, IN.
Date Appointed: January 2, 1922
Date Separated: September 9, 1926

In 1880, she and her family resided in Terre Haute, Indiana. Her parents were Major

---

10, 1922, 5,
http://www.newspapers.com/image/#39567010&terms=sheltcn

[355] Marion County, Indiana; Index to Marriage Record 1906 - 1910 Inclusive Vol, Original Record Located: County Clerk's Office Ind; Book: 49; Page: 392.

Johnson and Anna Jones.[356] She came to Indianapolis from Danville, Illinois in 1898. Hettie Johnson wed on June 15, 1908 in Indianapolis to Robert L. Brewer, born about 1872 in Georgia.[357] From 1915-1916, Hettie Brewer owned and operated "Brewer's Café", 422 Indiana Avenue. [358]

<u>August 25, 1922:</u> Along with African-American Patrolwoman Mayme Shelton, is assigned to the "colored" district. [359]
<u>January 13, 1923:</u> Hettie Brewer is assigned to a newly created division of Housing & Sanitation, assigned to inspect sanitary conditions, along with 4 other policewomen. Previously she had been

---

[356] "United States Census, 1880," index and images, FamilySearch https://familysearch.org/pal:/MM9.1.1/MHSP-SXB : accessed 26 May 2014), Anna Johnson in household of Major Johnson, Terre Haute, Vigo, Indiana, United States; citing sheet 473B, NARA microfilm publication T9.
[357] 1910; Census Place: Indianapolis Ward 5, Marion, Indiana; Roll: T624_367; Page: 7B; Enumeration District: 0096; FHL microfilm: 1374380.
[358] *Indianapolis Recorder* – February 13, 1915, 3, http://indiamond6.ulib.iupui.edu/cdm/compoundobject/collection/IRecorder/id/29783/rec/4
[359] The Indianapolis News – August 25, 1922, 7, The Indianapolis News – August 25, 1922, 7, http://www.newspapers.com/image/#37381723&terms=mayme

assigned to the traffic division, basically a "meter maid". [360]

February 22, 1923: Policewoman Hettie Brewer was again reassigned, this time to temporary duty in the office of the City Clerk, to assist in collection of delinquent fines. [361] This had nothing to do with Officer Brewer's ability. Throughout 1922-1923, Chief of Police Herman Rikkoff was doing everything he could to run the policewomen out of the Indianapolis Police Department, whom he publicly stated he had no use for.

March 9, 1923: Officer Hettie Brewer becomes the second IPD policewoman to fire her gun in the line of duty (above).

On June 22, 1927, Thomas H. Vaulx married Hettie A. Brewer. [362] They had a religious ceremony in Noblesville, Indiana, June 29th.

---

[360] *The Indianapolis Star* – January 13, 1923, 1, http://www.newspapers.com/search/#ymd=1923-01-13&lnd=1&query=hettie&t=384

[361] *The Indianapolis Star* – February 22, 1923, p.11

[362] . "Indiana, Marriages, 1780-1992," index, FamilySearch (https://familysearch.org/pal:/MM9.1.1/XFX6-W5Q : accessed 27 Apr 2014), Thomas H. Vaulx and Hettie A Brewer, 22 Jun 1927; citing reference ; FHL microfilm 1940146.

Hettie Brewer, 2nd from left, 1924.

A past president of the Old Settlers Club, Hettie Brewer was very involved in local women's and religious groups. She was very ill the last 5 years of her life, before passing away August 9, 1943.[363]

Buried in Crown Hill Cemetery, section 99, lot 1650.[364]

---

[363] "Former Policewoman Mrs. Hettie B. Vaulx Dies; Ill for 5 Years", *Indianapolis Recorder* – August 14, 1943, 2, http://indiamond6.ulib.iupui.edu/cdm/compoundobject/collection/IRecorder/id/96010/rec/1

[364] Findagrave.com

Patrolman Admiral D. Harris

Born: July 4, 1894 Louisville, KY.
Died: June 20, 1926 Indianapolis, IN.
Date Appointed: May 24, 1922
Date Separated: December 8, 1925
(terminated)

---

[365] IMPD Lichtenberger History Room.

<u>February 4, 1923:</u> Involved in a fatal police action shooting which began on Indiana Avenue when Officer Harris observed four men he suspected of being bootleggers, enter a vehicle. Harris approached to talk to the driver, identified later as Gene Cortier. Cortier drove off, dragging Officer Harris who had grabbed onto the car. Harris managed to get on the running board and tried to get control of the vehicle. Cortier kicked Harris in the head and face while the car drove on.

Cortier eventually jumped from the vehicle while holding onto Harris' belt, pulling him onto him. Cortier got up and ran northwest on Indiana Avenue. As he was 10 feet away, Officer Harris fired once, hitting Cortier, who later died in the hospital. [366] Charged with murder, Harris was tried in criminal court in November 1924 and was acquitted.

<u>July 20, 1925:</u> Officers Charles Carter and Admiral Harris were suspended from duty in an alleged shakedown of a suspected bootlegger.   Police had obtained a

---

[366] *The Indianapolis Star*, February 6, 1923, 4, http://www.newspapers.com/image/#7075142&terms=admiral+harris

statement from Cornelius Jorman, who stated Carter and Harris caught him in possession of 10 gallons of alcohol. They allegedly said they would "square" it with Jorman if he gave them $3200. He said he handed Harris $3132. They met the next night where they received the remainder of the $3200.[367]

December 8, 1925: Terminated by Police Board after he was tried for assaulting a man over a woman named Lovie Thomas.

Buried Crown Hill Cemetery, section 9, lot 1658. [368]

World War I veteran, serving in the 158th Depot Brigade. Arrested at one time for allegedly accepting a bribe from bootleggers[369].

After leaving IPD, was shot and killed in 1926, allegedly by Mrs. Lovie Thomas.

---

[367] The Indianapolis News, July 21, 1925, 12, The Indianapolis News, July 21, 1925, 12, http://www.newspapers.com/image/#37408377&terms=admiral

[368] Findagrave.com

[369] Richard Crenshaw, Black Police Officers 1876-2005

Patrolman George Thomas "Slim" Brown

Born: August 1, 1888 Millersburg, KY.[371]
Died: July 1, 1939 Indianapolis, IN.[372]
Date Appointed: November 14, 1922
Date Separated/Resigned: 1935

---

[370] IMPD Lichtenberger History Room.
[371]   Registration State: Indiana; Registration County: Marion; Roll: 1504018; Draft Board: 4.
[372]   "Bury Slim Brown Here", *Indianapolis Recorder* – July 8, 1939, 1,
http://indiamond6.ulib.iupui.edu/cdm/compoundobject/collection/IRecorder/id/72155/rec/1

Inducted into the U.S. Army August 22, 1918 and served in the 109th Pioneer Infantry. He was honorably discharged July 23, 1919.[373] Known as "Slim", he was well known and liked among those who met him on the Avenue or within the police department.

[374]

---

[373] Ibid

Patrolman George Blunt Paxton

Born: July 4, 1876 North Carolina[375]
Died: Buried October 25, 1933 Indianapolis, Indiana[376]
Date of appointment: May 1925
Date Separated/Retired: July 1931

Buried in Crown Hill Cemetery.

George B. Paxton enlisted at Portsmouth, Virginia, June 15, 1898 in the U.S. Navy as a mess attendant on the U.S.S. Franklin. He was discharged at Norfolk, Virginia, October 17, 1898. He arrived in Indianapolis, 1912.

<u>January 27, 1931</u>: Suffered a stroke at 10th and Indiana Avenue.
<u>July 18, 1931</u>: Was granted a 6 months medical leave.

He was admitted May 27, 1932 at the Danville, Illinois home for disabled soldiers, due to hardening of his arteries.[377]

---

[374] IMPD Lichtenberger History Room.
[375] Registration State: Indiana; Registration County: Marion; Roll: 1504020; Draft Board: 5.
[376] *Indianapolis Recorder* – October 28, 1933, p.1
[377] "Police Officer George Paxton Buried Tuesday",

378

Indianapolis Recorder October 28, 1933, 1, http://indiamond6.ulib.iupui.edu/cdm/compoundobject/collection/IRecorder/id/16259/rec/1

Patrolman George W. Helm

Born: 1872 Kentucky
Died: December 1914 Indianapolis, IN.
Appointed: December 22, 1909
Separated: 1914

June 12, 1907: Elected Town Marshal of the suburb of Norwood, near the southeast of Indianapolis.
September 22, 1907: Shot and wounded Gus Evans, who was causing trouble and pulled a revolver on Marshal Helm. Helm was doing a good job to this point, having arrested 62 people since getting the job.[379]
March 20, 1909: It was reported in the Indianapolis News that due to his efficiency, Helm had "dutied himself out of a job". Since he was paid with subscriptions by the 800 residents of Norwood, an African-American community, each time he arrested a resident, his salary was reduced by that amount. He was looking for something else to do. He gained the nickname "Walk Heavy Helm."

---

[378] IMPD Lichtenberger History Room.
[379] The Indianapolis News – September 23, 1907, p.14

December 22, 1909: Appointed an officer with the City of Indianapolis. Assigned to patrol Indiana Avenue.

September 14, 1913: After interrupting a dice game in Lovetown, a suburb near Norwood, Officer Helm fired his gun to halt the fleeing gamblers. One shot hit Alvin Harrison, seriously wounding him. Helm maintained this was an accidental shooting as he was warning them and thought a shot had been deflected off something.

Patrolman Harry B. Manuel

Born: September 6, 1886 Vigo Co. IN.
Died: September 1930 Indianapolis, IN.
Appointed: June 7, 1922
Separated: May 1923

Harry Manuel was a resident of Terre Haute, Indiana in 1905 when he married

---

[380] IMPD Lichtenberger History Room.

and relocated to Indianapolis. He died of cancer in 1930.

Patrolman Turner "Rail" Robinson

Born: May 29, 1898 Nashville, TN.
Died:
Appointed: November 30, 1925
Separated: January 1929

---

[381] IMPD Lichtenberger History Room.

January 21, 1928: Appointed to temporary duty in the Traffic Division.[382] This assignment became permanent in November 1928.[383] The *Recorder* at that time said this young policeman had made a good record.

March 19, 1929: Suspended after Captain Lester Jones found Robinson drunk at an Indiana Avenue address.

December 22, 1929: Turner Robinson was suspended and arrested after being found with a white woman in a room on California Street. Captain Jesse McMurtry and Lieutenant Victor Houston had kicked the door in and found the couple. Both were charged with immorality.[384]

---

[382] Indianapolis Recorder, January 21, 1928, p.2
[383] Ibid, December 1, 1928, p.2
[384] The Indianapolis Recorder, December 24, 1929, p.1

JESSE McMURTRY.

In April 1950, Turner Robinson was admitted to Bellevue Hospital in New York City for a serious operation.[385]

---

[385] The Indianapolis Recorder, April 8, 1950, p.7

Patrolman George W. Spinks

Born: December 15, 1888 Alabama
Died:
Appointed: December 29, 1925
Separated: By 1930

George Spinks left IPD under unknown circumstances and opened up a pool room which sold liquor during the prohibition era. In September 1930 he was indicted along with five other civilians and six IPD officers for prohibition law violations. Spinks pleaded guilty on September 26, 1930. This was part of a major scandal for the police department where 18 officers were indicted.[387]

Sergeant Norvel Bennett

Born: February 26, 1892 Princeton, KY.[389]

---

[387] The Indianapolis Star, September 27, 1930, p.1
[388] IMPD Lichtenberger History Room.
[389] "Sgt. Bennett of City's Police Dept. Dies", *Indianapolis Recorder* – September 22, 1945, 1,

Died: September 17, 1945 Indianapolis, Indiana -in hospital, where he'd been since July 4th.
Date Appointed: October 27, 1925
Date Separated: September 17, 1945 (death)

Buried Crown Hill Cemetery, Section 9, Lot 1954. Birth and death dates come from his tombstone. [390]
Served WWI 1918-1919, serving 14 months, including duty in France as a Corporal with the 436th Engineers.

1929: Received two citations this year, the 2nd from Chief Worley in March, for helping to capture a burglar found after hours in a Kroger store.[391]
March 20, 1933: Promoted to Patrolman 1st Grade.
1943: Received citation for helping to solve several cases late in 1942.

---

http://indiamond6.ulib.iupui.edu/cdm/ref/collection/IRecorder/id/26508/rec/12

[390] Ancestry.com. Indianapolis, Indiana, Crown Hill National Cemetery, 1866-1999 [database on-line]. Provo, UT, USA: Ancestry.com Operations, Inc., 2011.

[391] "Chief Worley Commends Officer Norvel Bennett", *Indianapolis Recorder* – March 9, 1929, 1, http://indiamond6.ulib.iupui.edu/cdm/compoundobject/collection/IRecorder/id/53967/rec/1

January 23, 1943: Promoted to Detective Investigator. He is the 7th African-American in the Detective Division, an all-time high.[392]

March 24, 1943:
BOARD CITES SNEED, JONES, WOODALL, BENNETT
"Sergeant George Sneed, Officers Plez Jones, Osa Woodall and Norvell Bennett were cited by the board of safety Tuesday for Outstanding and meritorious service."[393]
Shot it out with a racketeer, killing him on the north side several years before 1943.[394] Received citations for bravery and meritorious service.

April 17, 1943: Passed a new detective sergeant's examination at police school. This entitled him to be promoted to the

---

[392] Opal Tandy, "Bennett Made Detective, Colored in Car 31 Feb 1", *Indianapolis Recorder* – January 23, 1943, 1, http://indiamond6.ulib.iupui.edu/cdm/compoundobject/collection/IRecorder/id/95523/rec/1

[393] "Board Cites Sneed, Jones, Woodall, Bennett", *Indianapolis Recorder* – March 27, 1943, 1, http://indiamond6.ulib.iupui.edu/cdm/compoundobject/collection/IRecorder/id/95674/rec/1

[394] Opal Tandy, "Bennett Made Detective; Colored in Car 31 Feb 1", *Indianapolis Recorder* – January 23, 1943, http://indiamond6.ulib.iupui.edu/cdm/compoundobject/collection/IRecorder/id/95523/rec/1

rank of Detective Sergeant to fill existing vacancies. [395]

January 1944: Promoted to Sergeant in Uniform Division.

Promotion history of Norvel Bennett recounted in *Indianapolis Recorder*, January 23, 1943. [396]

---

[395] "Bennett, Butler, Woodall, Pass Detective Exam", *Indianapolis Recorder* – April 17, 1943, 2, http://indiamond6.ulib.iupui.edu/cdm/compoundobject/collection/IRecorder/id/95725/rec/1

[396] Opal Tandy, "Bennett Made Detective, Colored in Car 31 Feb 1", *Indianapolis Recorder* – January 23, 1943, 1, http://indiamond6.ulib.iupui.edu/cdm/compoundobject/collection/IRecorder/id/95523/rec/1

397

Det. Sgt. Ferdinand Desoto Holt

Born: June 6, 1895 Pierce Station, TN.
Died: June 30, 1949 Indianapolis, IN.[398]
Date Appointed: February 13, 1930
Date Separated/Resigned: October 1946

---

[397] IMPD Lichtenberger History Room.
[398] "Police Officer's Rites Are Held on Wednesday", *Indianapolis Recorder* – July 9, 1949, 3,
http://indiamond6.ulib.iupui.edu/cdm/compoundobject/collection/IRecorder/id/88077/rec/1

Born in Pierce Station, Tennessee, he arrived in Indianapolis, 1911. He was a member of St. Rita's Catholic Church.[399]

<u>August 22, 1931:</u> Promoted to Patrolman 1st Grade.[400]

<u>April 1933:</u> Assigned as Traffic Officer.

<u>February 1937:</u> Detective Sergeant.

<u>April 6, 1940:</u> "Police Begin New Type Work - a revision in the detective side at Police headquarters was announced here this week with the following appointments made known. Officers detailed to burglary cases with Detective Ferdinand Holt are Claude White and Thomas Hopson. Patrol Detailed to homicide with Detective George Sneed, Ples Jones and Eddie Butler, and Detective John Glenn, working as special investigator on larceny may expect an aide in that department soon, according to official sources."[401]

---

[399] Ibid

[400] "In Shakeup", *Indianapolis Recorder* – August 22, 1931, 1, http://indiamond6.ulib.iupui.edu/cdm/compoundobject/collection/IRecorder/id/15944/rec/1

[401] "Police Begin New Type Work", *Indianapolis Recorder* – April 6, 1940, 1,

http://indiamond6.ulib.iupui.edu/cdm/compoundobject/collection/IR

402

Patrolman John Frank Buchanan

Born: November 9, 1895 Williamson Co. TN.[403]

---

ecorder/id/74290/rec/1

[402] IMPD Lichtenberger History Room.

[403] Indianapolis Metropolitan Police Department webpage, accessed April 9, 2014, http://www.indy.gov/eGov/City/DPS/IMPD/About/Memoriam/Pages/jbuchanan.aspx

Died: July 9, 1926 Indianapolis, IN.
Date Appointed: November 11, 1919
Date Separated/Retired: July 9, 1926 (death)

Buried in Crown Hill Cemetery.

John F. Buchanan was hired in 1919 and in 1923 was one of four African-American officers appointed to the IPD Traffic Division, a first.[404] He was well known at his station located at Capitol and Indiana Avenues.

"Officer John Buchanan was shot and killed through a closet door by a suspect the officers were chasing. As Officer Buchanan stood outside the door and ordered the man out the suspect opened fire. The suspect was found guilty of manslaughter and sentenced to two to 21 years in prison. The man died in 1971. Officer Buchanan had served with the Indianapolis Police Department for six years. He was survived by his wife." – From the "Officer Down Memorial Page."

---

[404] Gunman Runs Amock, Kills Policeman, *Indianapolis Recorder* – July 17, 1926, 1,
http://indiamond6.ulib.iupui.edu/cdm/compoundobject/collection/IRecorder/id/37687/rec/1

Sergeant John R. Glenn

Born: October 16, 1897 Gallatin, TN.[406]
Died: May 30, 1977 Indianapolis, IN.[407]

---

[405] IMPD Lichtenberger History Room.
[406] Registration State: Indiana; Registration County: Marion; Roll: 1504015; Draft Board: 2.
[407] "John R. Glenn, retired policeman, dead at 79", *Indianapolis Recorder* – June 4, 1977, 1,

Date Appointed: January 15, 1934
Date Separated/Resigned: August 10, 1958

1917: Employed as an iron molder at the American Foundry on south Warman Avenue.
1934: Assigned to detective squad.
February 1937: Patrolman 1st Grade.
December 1937: IPD Detectives Fred Simon, John Glenn, George Sneed, Claude White and Thomas Hopson receive a written letter of commendation from FBI agent Harold F. Rineicke in December 1937, for their part in assisting in the capture of Luther Benson on October 23, 1937, wanted for murder. [408]
January 2, 1940: Reduced in rank from Detective Sergeant to Detective Investigator.
April 6, 1940: Police Begin New Type Work - A revision in the detective side at Police headquarters was announced here this week with the following appointments made known. Officers detailed to burglary cases

---

http://indiamond6.ulib.iupui.edu/cdm/compoundobject/collection/IRecorder/id/22519/rec/1

[408] "F.B.I. Cites Five Officers Here", *Indianapolis Recorder* – December 25, 1937, 1, http://indiamond6.ulib.iupui.edu/cdm/compoundobject/collection/IRecorder/id/55787/rec/1

with Detective Ferdinand Holt are Claude White and Thomas Hopson. Patrol Detailed to homicide with Detective George Sneed, Ples Jones and Eddie Butler, and Detective John Glenn, working as special investigator on larceny may expect an aide in that department soon, according to official sources.[409]

May 11, 1940: Detective John Glenn arrested John Hancock, who was charged with stealing 18 purses.

April 16, 1938: Profiled in the *Indianapolis Recorder*.

October 26, 1943: Becomes the 3rd man in 1943 to hold the rank of Uniform Sergeant.[410]

May 6, 1953: Promoted to Merit Detective Sergeant. [411]

---

[409] "Police Begin New Type Work", *Indianapolis Recorder* – April 6, 1940, 1,

http://indiamond6.ulib.iupui.edu/cdm/compoundobject/collection/IRecorder/id/74290/rec/1

[410] "Men Won Promotions – Chief Says", *Indianapolis Recorder* – November 6, 1943, 1,
http://indiamond6.ulib.iupui.edu/cdm/compoundobject/collection/IRecorder/id/96214/rec/1

[411] "Four Police Get Permanent Rank", *Indianapolis Recorder* – May 9, 1953, 1,
http://indiamond6.ulib.iupui.edu/cdm/compoundobject/collection/IR

August 2, 1958:
Sgt. John Glenn Ends 24 Years
"John R. Glenn, 57, of 2947 Highland place, detective sergeant will retire from the Indianapolis Department effective as of Aug. 10. His plan or desire to retire from the department was approved by the Board of Safety on Tuesday of this week. Sgt. Glenn joined the department January 15, 1934 and became a member of the Detective division in 1940. He has received several commendations for helping to solve three murders and many burglaries or robberies during his 24 years of service in the department. Sgt. Glenn stated that he is retiring to accept employment in a private capacity. It is widely reported that his new work will be a post with the Indianapolis School Board."[412]

Sgt. Glenn had 9 commendations by the end of his career.

---

ecorder/id/31774/rec/1

[412] "Sgt. John Glenn Ends 24 Years", *Indianapolis Recorder* – August 2, 1958, 1,
http://indiamond6.ulib.iupui.edu/cdm/compoundobject/collection/IRecorder/id/32857/rec/1

Patrolman Guy Luster

Born: July 13, 1898 Columbia, KY.[414]
Died: November 5, 1970 Indianapolis, IN.
Date Appointed: June 27, 1934
Date Separated/Retired: 1945

---

[413] IMPD Lichtenberger History Room.
[414] Birth and Death information: Ancestry.com. U.S., Department of Veterans Affairs BIRLS Death File, 1850-2010 [database on-line]. Provo, UT, USA: Ancestry.com Operations, Inc., 2011.
Original data: Beneficiary Identification Records Locator Subsystem (BIRLS) Death File. Washington, D.C.: U.S. Department of Veterans Affairs.

Guy Luster moved from Columbia, Kentucky to Richmond, Indiana by 1910.[415] He moved to Indianapolis, Indiana by 1915.[416]

WWII Veteran.

<u>December 25, 1936:</u> Without being dispatched on the run, Luster and Spurgeon Davenport, captured James Girton for the murder of Dan Smith, before white officers knew who had committed the crime.[417]
<u>February 1937:</u> Patrolman 1st Grade
<u>May 1, 1939:</u> First African-American in IPD history to be assigned to a motorcycle post, along Indiana Avenue and adjoining area. [418]

---

[415] Year: 1910; Census Place: Richmond Ward 4, Wayne, Indiana; Roll: T624_388; Page: 6B; Enumeration District: 0194; FHL microfilm: 1374401.

[416] 1915 Indianapolis City Directory

[417] "Dice, Whiskey Held Causes in Yule Slaying", *Indianapolis Recorder* - January 2, 1937, 1, http://indiamond6.ulib.iupui.edu/cdm/compoundobject/collection/IRecorder/id/54360/rec/1

[418] "Morrissey Names First 'Cycle Traffic Man", *Indianapolis Recorder* – May 6, 1939, 1,

http://indiamond6.ulib.iupui.edu/cdm/compoundobject/collection/IRecorder/id/72019/rec/1

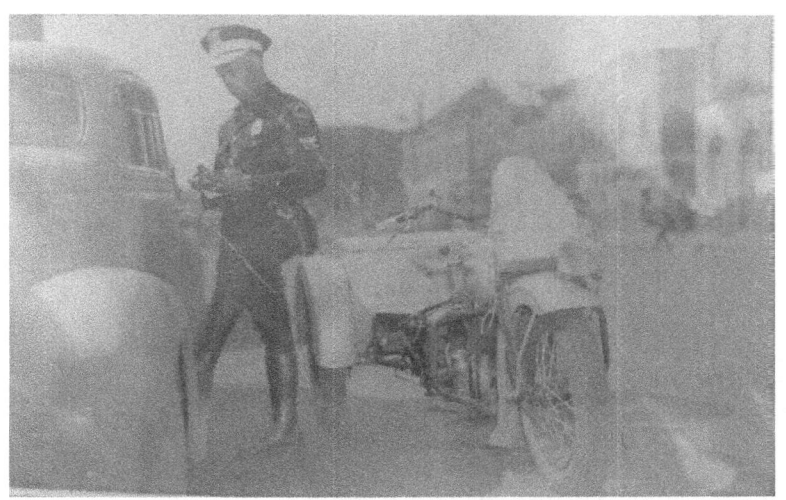
Guy Luster making a traffic stop, 1936.

<u>March 13, 1943:</u> Assigned to foot patrol.

Patrolman Robert Edward "Eddie" Butler

Born: December 2, 1901 Munfordville, KY.[420]
Died: September 4, 1963 Indianapolis, IN.[421]

---

[419] IMPD Lichtenberger History Room.
[420] "Rites Set Saturday For Retired City Police Officer", *Indianapolis Recorder* – September 7, 1963, 2, http://indiamond6.ulib.iupui.edu/cdm/compoundobject/collection/IRecorder/id/41631/rec/1
[421] Ibid.

Date Appointed: June 27, 1934
Date Separated/Resigned: 1962

February 1937: Patrolman 1st Grade.
September 4, 1937: Profiled in *Indianapolis Recorder*.
March 12, 1938: Partnered with Osa Woodall, Officer Butler left his car having answered a call of a service station robbery at 9th and Capitol Avenue. They saw two suspects run from the door of the station. Butler joined in a lengthy foot pursuit, calling for the suspect to stop. He refused and as the suspect went to jump a fence, Officer Butler fired, striking the suspect. It turned out it was 15-year old Tommy Lee Brown, who Butler thought was a full grown man in the dark.[422]
April 6, 1940: Police Begin New Type Work - A revision in the detective side at Police headquarters was announced here this week with the following appointments made known. Officers detailed to burglary cases with Detective Ferdinand Holt are Claude White and Thomas Hopson. Patrol Detailed to homicide with Detective George Sneed,

---

[422] Opal Tandy, "Officer Fires One Shot To Stop Robbery Suspect" *Indianapolis Recorder* – March 12, 1938, 1, http://indiamond6.ulib.iupui.edu/cdm/compoundobject/collection/IRecorder/id/60453/rec/1

Ples Jones and Eddie Butler, and Detective John Glenn, working as special investigator on larceny may expect an aide in that department soon, according to official sources.[423]

April 17, 1943: Passed a new detective sergeant's examination at police school. This entitled him to be promoted to the rank of Detective Sergeant to fill existing vacancies. [424]

December 29, 1945: "Two Win Promotions Detectives Robert Butler and Osa Woodall, veterans of the Indianapolis department have been promoted to the rank of detective sergeants in the detective department. Jesse McMurtry, chief of police announced last week following a meeting Thursday of the board of safety. The promotions were made purely on a merit basis and in

---

[423] "Police Begin New Type Work", *Indianapolis Recorder* –

April 6, 1940, 1,

http://indiamond6.ulib.iupui.edu/cdm/compoundobject/collection/IR

ecorder/id/74290/rec/1

[424] "Bennett, Butler, Woodall, Pass Detective Exam", *Indianapolis Recorder* – April 17, 1943, 2,
http://indiamond6.ulib.iupui.edu/cdm/compoundobject/collection/IR
ecorder/id/95725/rec/1

recognition of the fine records made by these men, the chief explained. Woodall is active in Elks circles and is exulted ruler of Indiana lodge No. 104." [425]

June 9, 1954: Promoted to rank of merit Sergeant.[426]

1955-1956: Teamed with Patrolman Albert Booth in detective division assigned to general cases, east side.

July 6, 1957: "Because of the alertness of Sgt. Robert Butler, a young gunman, believed to be the terrorist who last week made assault attempts upon three couples, has been apprehended. Fletcher Foster, 20, 2405 N. Arsenal, was picked up last Friday after Sgt. Robert Butler of the Indianapolis Police department recalled that the youth had been a suspect in an earlier case involving a missing shotgun.

Sherriff's deputies said Foster admitted he was the man who terrorized the three couples as they sat along the bank of Fall

---

[425] "Two Win Promotions", *Indianapolis Recorder* – December 29, 1945, 3, http://indiamond6.ulib.iupui.edu/cdm/compoundobject/collection/IRecorder/id/27523/rec/1

[426] "Police Sgts. Given Permanent Rank", *Indianapolis Recorder* – June 12, 1954, 1, http://indiamond6.ulib.iupui.edu/cdm/compoundobject/collection/IRecorder/id/33492/rec/1

Creek on the city's North Side, Sunday night, a week ago. Foster said he had borrowed the gun and a car from his brother, McKinley. It was the brother who reported the missing weapon. Foster was ordered held under $7,500 bond and was slated to appear in Lawrence Magistrate's Court Monday to answer preliminary charges of robbery." [427]

September 7, 1963: Rites Set Saturday for Retired City Police Officer - Detective Sgt. Robert E. Butler, veteran of the Indianapolis Police Department, 28 years prior to retiring in 1962, died Sept. 4 at Methodist Hospital. Funeral services will be held Sept. 7 at 11 a.m., at Bethany Baptist Church, Madeira and Prospect, with Rev. C. A. Hunt, pastor, delivering the eulogy. A native of Munfordville, Ky., Sgt. Butler had lived in this city since 1922 and was a member of the Bethany Church. He also was a member of Elks Lodge No. 104. Survivors include his wife, Mrs. Marie Butler; a brother, Carl Butler.[428]

---

[427] "Cop's Alertness Traps Attacker", *Indianapolis Recorder* – July 6, 1957, 1,
http://indiamond6.ulib.iupui.edu/cdm/compoundobject/collection/IRecorder/id/31339/rec/1

Deputy Chief Spurgeon Dewitt Davenport

Born: May 4, 1911 Georgia
Died: December 21, 2003 Indianapolis, Indiana
Date Appointed: December 11, 1934
Date Retired: November 1, 1973

---

[428] "Rites Set Saturday For Retired City Police Officer", *Indianapolis Recorder* – September 7, 1963, 2, http://indiamond6.ulib.iupui.edu/cdm/compoundobject/collection/IRecorder/id/41631/rec/1

In Attucks High School, Spurgeon Davenport was a letterman in athletics. He received a scholarship to Wilberforce University due to his scholastic abilities. Spurgeon's greatest desire was to become a police officer however. For some time he had wanted to be an astronomer, dreaming of looking through telescopes. Due to the need for another bread winner in the home, those hopes were put aside and he drove a grocery truck until he entered politics.

At the earliest age anyone could remember to hold the position, Spurgeon was elected precinct committeeman of his district. He served as master of ceremonies during political events. His work in politics helped in part to get him a job with the Indianapolis Police Department.

Davenport grew up in an area where thievery, murder and bootlegging were commonplace and during his early years on the force he had occasion to arrest people who he was acquainted with. This occurred in December of 1935 when he made his first big arrest. He and Officer Robert "Eddie" Butler, another new officer, were sitting in a cold car. Suddenly a call came out to break the monotony: "Car fifty-two, at 14th and Muskingum Streets, a holdup. Make that run snappy!"

The two officers sped to the scene and before they could jump out, they saw a small, stocky man with a gun in his hand. They called on him to halt but he ran, only to slip on the snow. Both officers jumped on him and when they pulled him to his feet, Davenport recognized the face of Bummie Horton, who he had known for years. It hurt Davenport deeply to make this arrest. Horton had robbed a milkman of $9 and was sentenced to 10-20 years in prison.

On December 25, 1936, James Girton murdered William Smith with a shotgun after an argument erupted over allegedly crooked dice being used. The department tended to ignore African-American officers on homicide runs, but Spurgeon Davenport and his partner Guy Luster decided to do their own investigating. Davenport had played baseball with Girton as children and he went to his apartment, finding him in a sweat. Girton calmly said, "Well, I did it." IPD didn't even have a suspect at this time.

Girton was sentenced from 2-14 years.[429]: (Much of the details of Spurgeon Davenport's early years comes from an excellent profile published by Opal Tandy in the *Indianapolis Recorder*, July 24, 1937 in his series "The Other Side of the Law.") [430]

He and Officer Gilbert Jones received a commendation from the Chief of Police, March 10, 1937 for their capture of a taxi cab bandit, who had fired shots at them.[431] For the first 11 years of his career, Officer Davenport patrolled the near west side and made a name for himself as an excellent officer. He was a crack shot and made a good impression on the witness stand in court. He was assigned to Car 31 in 1943, partnered with Roy S. Kennedy. One humorous story he related many years later was when he walked into a numbers

---

[429] "Dice, Whiskey Held Causes in Yule Slaying", *Indianapolis Recorder* - January 2, 1937, 1, http://indiamond6.ulib.iupui.edu/cdm/compoundobject/collection/IRecorder/id/54360/rec/1

[430] Opal Tandy "The Other Side of the Law" - *Indianapolis Recorder* – July 24, 1937, 1, http://indiamond6.ulib.iupui.edu/cdm/compoundobject/collection/IRecorder/id/55434/rec/1

[431] "Cites Alert Cop Whose Coolness Traps Killer", *Indianapolis Recorder* – May 22, 1937, 1, http://indiamond6.ulib.iupui.edu/cdm/compoundobject/collection/IRecorder/id/54700/rec/1

operation and arrested a big time gambler. This got him banished to a walking beat. (For years, IPD Vice had a quasi-relationship with gamblers, particularly Isaac "Tuffy" Mitchell).

Detectives Spurgeon Davenport & James Rogers, 1954.

On August 30, 1946, Spurgeon Davenport was assigned to the Detective Division. In 1946, he teamed up with Officer James Rogers and together, these two men built a record of arrests and convictions which has been described as unsurpassed. When IPD formed a Homicide Division for the first time, in March 1948, Davenport and Rogers were two of the men selected to join it.[432]

April 7, 1948: The newly formed IPD

[432] "Homicide Bureau Organized in City Police Department",

Indianapolis Recorder - April 3, 1948, 1,

http://indiamond6.ulib.iupui.edu/cdm/compoundobject/collection/IRecorder/id/90016/rec/1

Homicide Division. Spurgeon Davenport and James Rogers sitting on either side of Forrest McKeighan (with ink dot on his chest).[433]

In 1949, Davenport was promoted to the rank of Detective Sergeant. Probably due to his scholastic history, Davenport always studied and went to all the promotional schools. He finished first in his division in the officer's school in July 1952.

He was appointed to the rank of Acting Detective Lieutenant on March 11, 1953.[434] He was promoted to the full rank of Merit Detective Lieutenant, May 6, 1953.[435] Lieutenant Davenport said at the time of his promotion he expected to enter the next school in July 1953 to qualify for the rank of Captain. At this point he was second in command of the Homicide Division.

---

[433] Photograph courtesy of Laura (Gilyeat) Callahan, granddaughter of Forrest McKeighan.
[434] "Sgt. Davenport Made Lieutenant by Safety Board", *Indianapolis Recorder* – March 14, 1953, 1, http://indiamond6.ulib.iupui.edu/cdm/compoundobject/collection/IRecorder/id/31003/rec/1
[435] "Four Police Get Permanent Rank", *Indianapolis Recorder* – May 9, 1953, 1, http://indiamond6.ulib.iupui.edu/cdm/compoundobject/collection/IRecorder/id/31774/rec/1

In 1963 he was named head of the Homicide Division, after a change in the manning table which changed this position from one filled by a Captain, to one of Lieutenant rank.[436]

---

[436] "The Avenoo", *Indianapolis Recorder* - October 5, 1963, 12, http://indiamond6.ulib.iupui.edu/cdm/compoundobject/collection/IRecorder/id/41695/rec/1

1958: Lt. Spurgeon Davenport reads letters written by Connie Nichols, accused of murdering Eli Lilly executive Forrest Teal.[437]

By 1965, Lieutenant Davenport was frustrated at the lack of opportunity to advance and stay within the detective area as he desired. He had been offered a

---

[437] IMPD Lichtenberger History Room.

Captaincy more than once but it would have meant a transfer elsewhere. He was also not making enough money to support his family. He announced his retirement, which would take place October 1, 1965. He had been courted by outside agencies for some time and was going to take a post as head of security for a large local corporation.[438]

As events developed, he chose to stay with the Indianapolis Police Department. The Mayor of Indianapolis John J. Barton, highly respected the abilities of Spurgeon Davenport. It was announced in early February 1966 that Spurgeon Davenport was being promoted to Captain and being placed in charge of the Burglary-Larceny Division.[439] He was the second African-American man in IPD history to achieve this rank. The shift from Homicide was a

[438] "Davenport retires from police dept.", *Indianapolis Recorder* – August 28, 1965, 1, http://indiamond6.ulib.iupui.edu/cdm/compoundobject/collection/IRecorder/id/43305/rec/1

[439] "Davenport Promoted to Captain", *Indianapolis Recorder* - February 5, 1966, 1,

http://indiamond6.ulib.iupui.edu/cdm/compoundobject/collection/IRecorder/id/43671/rec/1

surprise to observers, since Davenport had built a national reputation as a homicide detective.

On January 3, 1967, Mayor John J. Barton announced that he was appointing Captain Davenport to the position of Inspector, one of the highest ranks you could hold in the police department. There were four Inspector positions.[440] Chief of Police Noel Jones objected to this and the resulting feud ended in Mayor Barton firing the chief. In 1968 Davenport was named Deputy Chief of Inspection & Training (another first).[441] While in this position, he modified the entrance examination for the police department, making it fairer for all applicants. He held this position he held until his retirement, which took place November 1, 1973. He was taking a position as head of security for I.U.P.U.I.

---

[440] "Growing Support for Davenport to Fill New Deputy Chief Vacancy", *Indianapolis Recorder* - January 7, 1967, 1, http://indiamond6.ulib.iupui.edu/cdm/compoundobject/collection/IRecorder/id/44460/rec/1

[441] IPD Monthly Slate – October 1968

A three time recipient of the Robinson-Ragsdale Post Award of the American Legion, in March of 1963 he earned another high honor, the Judge Jerome Frank Memorial Award, administered by New York University. It was presented annually to an officer who contributed the most to preserving and guarding the rights of individuals charged with felony crimes. He earned this award by spending five years trying to find evidence clearing a man serving 10-25 year term in Michigan City Prison of a crime he did not commit.[442]

During his police career, Mr. Davenport furthered his education in criminology by attending the Homicide Institute, the "University of Cincinnati, Law Enforcement University, the Illinois Institute of Technology, and several seminars conducted by the FBI (Federal Bureau of Investigation).[443]

---

[442] "Gets High Award For Clearing Innocent Man", *Indianapolis Recorder* – March 16, 1963, 1,
http://indiamond6.ulib.iupui.edu/cdm/compoundobject/collection/IRecorder/id/41224/rec/1

[443] Henry Hedgepath, "Who's Who In the Community", *Indianapolis Recorder* – April 6, 1968, 14,
http://indiamond6.ulib.iupui.edu/cdm/compoundobject/collection/IRecorder/id/45335/rec/1

Career Highlights:

March 10, 1937: Patrolman Gilbert Jones and Patrolman Spurgeon Davenport received a commendation from the Chief of Police for their capture of a taxi cab bandit in the act. Several shots were exchanged.[444]
August 30, 1946: Assigned to Detective Division.
January 2, 1947: Promoted to Detective Sergeant.
April 1948: Assigned to the newly created Robbery & Homicide Division.
March 11, 1953: Appointed Acting Lieutenant of Detectives.
May 6, 1953: Promoted to Merit Detective Lieutenant. Was 2nd in command of Homicide Division from this point.[445]
February 8, 1962: Received the Robinson-Ragsdale American Legion Post Award for solving 4 major crimes. This was his 3rd time earning this award.[446]

---

[444] "Cites Alert Cop Whose Coolness Traps Killer", *Indianapolis Recorder* – May 22, 1937, 1,
http://indiamond6.ulib.iupui.edu/cdm/compoundobject/collection/IRecorder/id/54700/rec/1

[445] "Four Police Get Permanent Rank", *Indianapolis Recorder* – May 9, 1953, 1,
http://indiamond6.ulib.iupui.edu/cdm/compoundobject/collection/IRecorder/id/31774/rec/1

<u>October 1963:</u> Becomes head of Homicide Division with Lieutenant rank. At this point he had received 9 commendations and 3 merit citations.[447]

<u>April 7, 1963:</u> Lt. Spurgeon Davenport presented with a plaque by the Defiants Club, who honored him for his civic duty. Davenport was guest speaker. [448]

<u>August 28, 1965:</u> Lt. Spurgeon Davenport announces his retirement which will take place October 1st. He will accept a post as head of security for a large local corporation. He rescinded this within a short while.[449]

<u>February 1966:</u>   Became 2nd African-American to be promoted to rank of

---

[446] "Firemen, Police Cited by Legion", *Indianapolis Recorder* – February 10, 1962, 1, http://indiamond6.ulib.iupui.edu/cdm/compoundobject/collection/IRecorder/id/40317/rec/4

[447] "The Avenoo", *Indianapolis Recorder* - October 5, 1963, 12, http://indiamond6.ulib.iupui.edu/cdm/compoundobject/collection/IRecorder/id/41695/rec/1

[448] "Detective Honored", *Indianapolis Recorder* – April 13, 1963, 15, http://indiamond6.ulib.iupui.edu/cdm/compoundobject/collection/IRecorder/id/41292/rec/1

[449] "Lt. Davenport retires from police dept.", *Indianapolis Recorder* – August 28, 1965, 1, http://indiamond6.ulib.iupui.edu/cdm/compoundobject/collection/IRecorder/id/43305/rec/1

Captain. Assigned to the Burglary and Larceny Division.[450]

January 3, 1967: Appointed Inspector of Police. First African-American to hold this rank.[451]

February 23, 1968: Appointed as Deputy Chief of Inspection and Training.

October 1968: Serving as Deputy Chief of Investigations.

Earned the Robinson-Ragsdale American Legion Post award 3 times, the only African-American and one of five men to achieve this feat.

Profiled in *Indianapolis Recorder* July 24, 1937.

October 20, 1973: *Indianapolis Recorder* Davenport writes finis to Police Dept. career Highest black officer resigns after 39 years

"Deputy Police Chief Spurgeon D. Davenport, thought by many to be one of the most capable police administrators in

---

[450] "Davenport Promoted to Captain", *Indianapolis Recorder* - February 5, 1966, 1,
http://indiamond6.ulib.iupui.edu/cdm/compoundobject/collection/IRecorder/id/43671/rec/1

[451] "Growing Support for Davenport to Fill New Deputy Chief Vacancy", *Indianapolis Recorder* - January 7, 1967, 1,
http://indiamond6.ulib.iupui.edu/cdm/compoundobject/collection/IRecorder/id/44460/rec/1

the nation, ends an illustrious 39-year career with the Indianapolis Police Department Nov. 1 when he assumes the position of security director of Indiana University-Purdue University, Indianapolis.

In announcing Davenport's appointment to head the university's 62-man campus police department, IUPUI Chancellor Glenn W. Irwin Jr. said that the appointment, 'coming after an intensive series of interviews with several candidates, will capably and successfully fill a s sensitive administrative post on the IUPUI campus.' He said that Davenport will serve as the equivalent of a chief of police in a city of more than 30,000 population.

The Indiana University system director of safety, Irvin K. Owen, said there had been several candidates with experience in city, state and federal police work and that Davenport emerged as the best candidate for the job. Davenport, who joined the department in 1934, has compiled a number of 'firsts' during his distinguished police care. He became the first black officer to head the police department's homicide and robbery branch when he was named to that position as a detective lieutenant in 1963, became the department's first black captain three years later, the first black inspector (now major) in 1967, and the department's only deputy chief when he was promoted to his present job in 1968.

Presently in charge of the department's inspection and training division, Davenport has received numerous commendations and national recognition for his outstanding police work. A three-time recipient of the Robinson-Ragsdale Post Award of the American Legion, he is also the recipient of the Judge Frank Memorial Award. The award, administered by New York University, is presently annually to an officer who has contributed most to preserving and guarding the rights of individuals charged with felony crimes. Davenport received the award for his part in determining the innocence of man who had been sentenced to prison for a crime he did not commit.

In 1968, he was named to the Crispus Attucks (High School) Hall of Fame. Although long recognized as a 'no nonsense' policeman, Davenport is both admired and respected by many men he has sent to prison because he has always held to the belief that every individual, even the most harden criminal, is entitled to be treated with respect and dignity." [452]

Lieutenant Osa Garland Woodall

Born: March 28, 1906 Burnett, IN.[453]

---

[452] *Indianapolis Recorder* – October, 1973
[453] SSDI Number: 306-52-2135; Issue State: Indiana; Issue

Died: February 24, 1972 Indianapolis, IN.
Date Appointed: December 1, 1936
Date Retired: April 3, 1964

Buried Crown Hill Cemetery, section 98, lot 1469.[454]

<u>1936-1942:</u> Patrolled the streets.
<u>April 1942:</u> Assigned to the Homicide Division under Sergeant George Sneed.[455]
<u>1942:</u> Promoted to Detective Sergeant in the Burglary Division.
<u>January 27, 1943</u>: Demoted from Acting Detective Investigator to Patrolman 1st Grade. He replaces Fred Starks as a traffic patrolman.[456]
<u>March 13, 1943:</u> Appointed to Detective Investigator (he had held that position two months earlier). He was assigned to the Burglary Division.

Date: 1964.

[454] Findagrave.com

[455] "Raise Starks, Send Woodall to Traffic Post", *Indianapolis Recorder* – January 30, 1943, 1, http://indiamond6.ulib.iupui.edu/cdm/compoundobject/collection/IRecorder/id/95540/rec/1

[456] "Raise Starks, Send Woodall to Traffic Post", *Indianapolis Recorder* – January 30, 1943, 1, http://indiamond6.ulib.iupui.edu/cdm/compoundobject/collection/IRecorder/id/95540/rec/1

March 24, 1943: Received commendation for apprehending two holdup men.[457]

April 17, 1943: Passed a new detective sergeant's examination at police school. This entitled him to be promoted to the rank of Detective Sergeant to fill existing vacancies. [458]

December 29, 1945: "Two Win Promotions Detectives Robert Butler and Osa Woodall, veterans of the Indianapolis department have been promoted to the rank of detective sergeants in the detective department. Jesse McMurtry, chief of police announced last week following a meeting Thursday of the board of safety. The promotions were made purely on a merit basis and in recognition of the fine records made by these men, the chief explained. Woodall is active in Elks circles and is exulted ruler of Indiana lodge No. 104." [459]

---

[457] "Board Cites Sneed, Jones, Woodall, Bennett", *Indianapolis Recorder* – March 27, 1943, 1, http://indiamond6.ulib.iupui.edu/cdm/compoundobject/collection/IRecorder/id/95674/rec/1

[458] "Bennett, Butler, Woodall, Pass Detective Exam", *Indianapolis Recorder* – April 17, 1943, 2, http://indiamond6.ulib.iupui.edu/cdm/compoundobject/collection/IRecorder/id/95725/rec/1

[459] "Two Win Promotions", *Indianapolis Recorder* – December 29, 1945, 3, http://indiamond6.ulib.iupui.edu/cdm/compoundobject/collection/IRecorder/id/27523/rec/1

August 14, 1937: Profiled in *Indianapolis Recorder*.

June 9, 1954: Promoted to rank of merit Sergeant.[460]

January 1958: Detective Sergeant Osa Woodall promoted to rank of uniformed Lieutenant.

March 4, 1972: Retired police Lieutenant Osa Woodall dead
Retired police lieutenant Osa Garland Woodall, died Feb.24 in Winona Memorial Hospital. Funeral services were held Feb. 28 in Mount Zion Baptist Church, where he was a member, with burial in Crown HIU Cemetery. Born at Burnett, Ind., but later moving to Brazil, Mr. Woodall, 65, 321 Congress, retired from the department in 1964 and since that time had been employed by the Indianapolis Public Schools in the Security Division, serving at Crispus Attucks High School. He was a lover of the outdoor sports, particularly hunting and fishing and invariably spent his vacations enjoying these activities. He dedication to fraternal affiliations was most evident in the Elks Lodge, IBPOE of W.

---

[460] "Police Sgts. Given Permanent Rank", *Indianapolis Recorder* – June 12, 1954, 1,
http://indiamond6.ulib.iupui.edu/cdm/compoundobject/collection/IRecorder/id/33492/rec/1

He was exalted ruler of Lodge No. 104 for 13 years and served at national sessions with the Grand Lodge Police Commissioner. He was serving his 12th consecutive term as district grand deputy for Indiana. He served as chief antler of Hoosier Council No. 44 for 26 years. Survivors include his wife, Mrs. Stella B. Woodall; a stepson, Richard Walker of this city, three sisters, Mrs. Helen Gordon, Mrs. Kathryn Dunbar of Brazil, Ind., and Mrs. Vivian Hall of Gary, and a brother, Harley Woodall of Brazil. [461]

---

[461] "Retired police lieutenant Osa Woodall dead", *Indianapolis Recorder* – March 4, 1972, 1, http://indiamond6.ulib.iupui.edu/cdm/compoundobject/collection/IRecorder/id/50630/rec/1

Patrolman Gilbert Jones

Born: About 1910 Indianapolis, Indiana
Died August 4, 1940 – Accidently shot with own gun.[463]
Date Appointed: December 1, 1936
Date Separated: August 4, 1940 (death)

<u>March 10, 1937</u>: Jones and Patrolman Spurgeon Davenport received a commendation from the Chief of Police for

---

[462] A History of the Indianapolis Police Department's Black Police Officers by Captain Richard Crenshaw

[463] "Hundreds Grieve Officer Jones Death Here", *Indianapolis Recorder* – August 10, 1940, 1,
http://indiamond6.ulib.iupui.edu/cdm/compoundobject/collection/IRecorder/id/88666/rec/1

their capture of a taxi cab bandit n the act. Several shots were exchanged.[464]

April 5, 1937:   Cited for bravery in the capture of Frank Clark, later convicted of robbery.

May 17, 1937:   Engaged in a shootout with Carl Scroggs. While off duty, Jones heard screams and shots at the corner of East and Vermont. Scroggs passed him, having just murdered his wife and son. After an initial struggle, a gun battle ensued in which Jones shot Scroggs twice, who fell dead. The coroner determined the fatal wound was self-inflicted. [465]

April 9, 1938: Partnered with Clyde Ashby.

September 3, 1938: On Police Ambulance Squad with Clyde Ashby.

January 6, 1940: Officers Gilbert Jones, Alexander Posey, David Clark and Clyde Ashby were nominated for the 6th Annual Bruce P. Robinson American Legion Post

[464] "Cites Alert Cop Whose Coolness Traps Killer", *Indianapolis Recorder* – May 22, 1937, 1, http://indiamond6.ulib.iupui.edu/cdm/compoundobject/collection/IRecorder/id/54700/rec/1

[465] "Cites Alert Cop Whose Coolness Traps Killer", *Indianapolis Recorder* – May 22, 1937, 1,

http://indiamond6.ulib.iupui.edu/cdm/compoundobject/collection/IRecorder/id/54700/rec/1

Award. They were the first African-Americans to get nominated for this prestigious award. [466]

August 10, 1940:

Hundreds Grieve Officer Jones Death Here Accidently wounded By Own Service Pistol

"Funeral services for Gilbert Jones, 30, 033 Leon Street, Apartment 3, a city police officer whom everybody loved, were held Wednesday at 1:30 pm., at the Corinthian Baptist with Rev. David C. Venerable officiating. Hundreds were grieved at the death of the well-known policeman who was fatally wounded Sunday afternoon when his wife. Mrs. Stella Jones, accidentally discharged his service pistol while attempting to place it in the bolster. Ferdinand Holt, who was recently switched to the rank of first grade patrolman following an automobile accident in which he was driving a car belonging to Joe Mitchell, was teamed with Spurgeon

[466] "Editor Nominates Five for Legion Merit Awards",

Indianapolis Recorder – January 6, 1940, 1,

http://indiamond6.ulib.iupui.edu/cdm/compoundobject/collection/IRecorder/id/74075/rec/1

Davenport the night the officer was fatally wounded. Immediately following the accident Jones was rushed to City hospital where his wife donated blood for a transfusion. The injured policeman died about six hours later, however.

Mr. and Mrs. Jones were sitting in an automobile waiting for friends at 1061 North Belmont Avenue when the accident occurred. At the request of her husband. Mrs. Jones picked up the gun lying on the seat between them and was attempting to place it in the holster which had fallen on the floor of the car when the gun discharged. The bullet tore through Jones' right arm at the elbow and penetrated his right side." [467]

---

[467] "Hundreds Grieve Officer Jones Death Here", *Indianapolis Recorder* – August 10, 1940, 1, http://indiamond6.ulib.iupui.edu/cdm/compoundobject/collection/IRecorder/id/88666/rec/1

468

Detective Sergeant David N. Clark Jr.

Born: About 1914 Newport, Arkansas [469]
Died: January 1, 1974 Indianapolis, IN[470]
Date Appointed: September 26, 1938
Date Separated: February 19, 1954

Buried in Crown Hill Cemetery, section 99, lot 4775.[471]

---

[468] A History of the Indianapolis Police Department's Black Police Officers by Captain Richard Crenshaw
[469] "David N. Clark, retired police detective, dies", *Indianapolis Recorder* – January 12, 1974, 8,
http://indiamond6.ulib.iupui.edu/cdm/compoundobject/collection/IRecorder/id/2644/rec/1
[470] Ibid.
[471] Findagrave.com

<u>1939-1940:</u> Paired with Clyde Ashby in Car 31.

<u>January 6, 1940:</u> Officers Gilbert Jones, Alexander Posey, David Clark and Clyde Ashby were nominated for the 6th Annual Bruce P. Robinson American Legion Post Award. They were the first African-Americans to get nominated for this prestigious award.[472]

<u>March 1942:</u> Assigned to Sgt. Preston Heater's Vice Squad.

<u>April 17, 1943:</u> Promoted to Acting Corporal and assigned to the Juvenile Aid Division.[473]

<u>July 1947:</u> Promoted to Detective Investigator.

<u>July 1947:</u> Received Commendation from Board of Public Safety for his efficient

---

[472] "Editor Nominates Five for Legion Merit Awards", *Indianapolis Recorder* – January 6, 1940, 1, http://indiamond6.ulib.iupui.edu/cdm/compoundobject/collection/IRecorder/id/74075/rec/1

[473] "Bennett, Butler, Woodall, Pass Detective Exam", *Indianapolis Recorder* – April 17, 1943, 2, http://indiamond6.ulib.iupui.edu/cdm/compoundobject/collection/IRecorder/id/95725/rec/1

handling of an investigation which resulted in the capture of three wanted men.
<u>January 1948:</u> Promoted to Acting Detective Sergeant.
<u>January 8, 1952:</u> Demoted to Patrolman First Grade.

A graduate of Attucks H.S. and an accomplished musician and sideman. In November of 1936, was a member of Frank Reynolds & His Orchestra, playing second tenor sax.

January 12, 1974:

DAVID CLARK JR.
"Dave died at 12:01 a.m. Tuesday (New Year's Morning) at the Marlon County General Hospital. He was born at Newport, Ark., and lived here more than 56 years. Clark was a 1931 graduate of Attacks High School and studied music under J. Harold Brown, then director of the Musical Dept. He also attended the Lewis Business College. During the late 1920s, and early 1930s, Dave was an ace-sideman with the Brown Buddies and the Frank Reynolds large orchestras respectively. My friend

wailed much tenor sax and he could have made it to the top, on the national musical scene. However, he; wanted to become a "fuzz" (policeman).

In 1937, he was appointed to the Indianapolis Police Dept. Clark was a member of Naptown's Finest for 16-years during which time, he attained the rank of Detective Sergeant. He retired in 1953. Dave was one of first Soul Brother's Pal Officers at the Douglas Park Community Center, located on the Eastside of this city. Also, he was a member of The Southern Cross Lodge (F&AM) ...It is true, my OL' Buddy is gone, but; he will never be forgotten ..Believe Me ... When I Tell You These Things!" [474]

---

[474] Bob Womack Sr., "Believe Me When I Tell You", *Indianapolis Recorder* – January 12, 1974, 10, http://indiamond6.ulib.iupui.edu/cdm/compoundobject/collection/IRecorder/id/2644/rec/1

Patrolman Clyde L. Ashby

Born: September 14, 1913
Died: June 27, 1978 Indianapolis, IN.[475]
Date Appointed: January 11, 1938
Date Separated: February 9, 1951

---

[475] *Indianapolis Recorder* – July 15, 1978, 9, http://indiamond6.ulib.iupui.edu/cdm/compoundobject/collection/IRecorder/id/24991/rec/1

<u>1938-1939:</u> Officer Clyde Ashby, partnered with Gilbert Jones.

<u>1939-1940:</u> Partnered with Officer Dave Clark in Car #31.

<u>January 6, 1940:</u> Officers Gilbert Jones, Alexander Posey, David Clark and Clyde Ashby were nominated for the 6th Annual Bruce P. Robinson American Legion Post Award. They were the first African-Americans to get nominated for this prestigious award.[476]

<u>December 8, 1945:</u> Assigned to Squad Car #12 with Officer Clarence Lewis.

<u>November 26, 1949:</u> Partnered with Officer James Dabner in Squad 29, when they arrested Fred Bean, charged with 20 robberies.

---

[476] "Editor Nominates Five for Legion Merit Awards", *Indianapolis Recorder* – January 6, 1940, 1, http://indiamond6.ulib.iupui.edu/cdm/compoundobject/collection/IRecorder/id/74075/rec/1

Sergeant Alexander H. Posey

Born: June 24, 1907 Indianapolis, IN.
Died: January 9, 1964 Indianapolis, IN.
Date Appointed: September 26, 1938
Date Separated/Retired: September 1959
Graduate of the University of Michigan.[477]

<u>January 6, 1940:</u> Officers Gilbert Jones, Alexander Posey, David Clark and Clyde Ashby were nominated for the 6th Annual Bruce P. Robinson American Legion Post Award. They were the first African-

---

[477]   The Saint, "The Avenoo", *Indianapolis Recorder* – September 25, 1954, 12,
http://indiamond6.ulib.iupui.edu/cdm/compoundobject/collection/IRecorder/id/33747/rec/1

Americans to get nominated for this prestigious award.[478]

March 1942: Promoted to Corporal, remaining in the Juvenile Aid Division. Posey had already established several Pal Clubs at this point.

October 11, 1945: Promoted from Corporal to Acting Sergeant in Uniform Division.[479]

November 10, 1945: Sergeant Posey is currently assigned to the Pal Club, for which he received an honor this date. The occasion was his replacement in the Pal Club by Cpl. Albert Booth.

1950: Attended the Police Training School and was certified by the Promotion Board in 1951.[480]

September 2, 1953: Promoted to Merit rank of Sergeant.

---

[478] "Editor Nominates Five for Legion Merit Awards", *Indianapolis Recorder* – January 6, 1940, 1, http://indiamond6.ulib.iupui.edu/cdm/compoundobject/collection/IRecorder/id/74075/rec/1

[479] "Sgt. Posey Given Permanent Rank", *Indianapolis Recorder* – September 5, 1953, 2, http://indiamond6.ulib.iupui.edu/cdm/compoundobject/collection/IRecorder/id/32151/rec/1

[480] Ibid.

September 5, 1953:
Sgt. Posey Given Permanent Rank Sergeant

"Alexander Posey, for many years regarded as one of the top officers of the local police force, Wednesday was promoted to the permanent rank of sergeant. An acting sergeant since October 11, 1945, Sgt. Posey was appointed to the force September 26, 1938. His outstanding record includes several commendations from superiors, including one for the apprehension of a notorious "wanted" person. He attended the Police Training School in 1950 and was certified by the Promotion Board in 1951." [481]

January 11, 1964:
"The scion of an old family of the community. Alexander H. Posey, 55, R.R. 1, Clayton. Ind. died in St. Vincent's Hospital Thursday, Jan. 9. He was a veteran of more than twenty-one years' service in the Indianapolis Police department. Mr. Posey held the rank of sergeant at the time of his retirement in September, 1959. Recently he was employed as an investigator for the Marion County Welfare department. Preceding his association with the

---

[481]   Ibid.

Welfare Department he had been, for a short time, a supervisor at the Indiana Boys' School. He was the son of the late Mr. and Mrs. Clarence Posey. He attended local public schools and was a graduate of the University of Michigan. His father was widely known as the operator of two or more downtown barbershops including one in the Central YMCA and one in the now First Federal Building. The late Clarence Posey was a native of Pennsylvania and the brother of the late "Cum"- Posey, nationally famous longer than two decades as the mentor of the widely heralded Homestead Grays baseball team. Sgt. Posey was a member of Omega Psi Phi Fraternity, the Fraternal Order of Police and St. Bridget's Roman Catholic Church. Funeral services will be held Monday, Jan. 13 at St. Bridget's. The burial will be in Holy Cross Cemetery. The Rosary will be in the Patton Funeral Home Sunday at 8:00 p.m. and Last Prayers Monday at 9:30 a.m. in the funeral home. He is survived by his wife, Mrs. Juanita Posey, and one sister, Mrs. Hortense Shelton of this city." [482]

---

[482] "Rites Set Monday for Alexander Posey, Retired Police Sergeant", *Indianapolis Recorder* - January 11, 1964, 1, http://indiamond6.ulib.iupui.edu/cdm/compoundobject/collection/IRecorder/id/41919/rec/1

Patrolman Grant William Hawkins

Born: May 5, 1911 Lexington, Fayette County, Kentucky[483]
Died: September 24, 2003 Indianapolis, IN.
Date Appointed: October 19, 1940
Date Separated/Retired: 1955

Buried in Crown Hill Cemetery, section 98, lot 1251.[484]
Graduate of Manuel H.S. & Indiana University, B.A., 1933.[485] In 1973 he

---

[483] SSDI: Number: 314-28-7699; Issue State: Indiana; Issue Date: Before 1951.,
Kentucky Department for Libraries and Archives. Kentucky Birth, Marriage, and Death Databases: Births 1911-1999. Frankfort, Kentucky: Kentucky Department for Libraries and Archives.
[484] Findagrave.com

received the Distinguished Alumni Service Award from I.U.[486]

October 1955: First African-American member of the Indianapolis School Board. January 1964: Appointed to the Board of Public Works by Mayor John J. Barton, the first African-American in Indianapolis history to hold this position.

Grant W. Hawkins accomplished a lot in his lifetime and working for the Indianapolis Police Department is not among the most significant achievements. After graduating from Manuel H.S. and Indiana University, he was appointed to the department in 1940. In 1955 he had left IPD and had been elected a member of the Indianapolis Board of School Commissioners, a first for an African-American.[487] He achieved another first for an African-American here in 1964,

---

[485] "Grant Hawkins, businessman, in 6th District Council Race", *Indianapolis Recorder* – April 10, 1971, 1, http://indiamond6.ulib.iupui.edu/cdm/compoundobject/collection/IRecorder/id/50948/rec/1

[486] http://www.iu.edu/~uha/search-awards/honoree.shtml?honoreeID=2276

[487] "Get Grant Hawkins on City School Board", *Indianapolis Recorder* – October 29, 1955, 1, http://indiamond6.ulib.iupui.edu/cdm/compoundobject/collection/IRecorder/id/35285/rec/1

when Mayor John J. Barton appointed him to the Board of Public Works.

He also was a successful local businessman, operating Hawkins Janitor Supply, the Hawkins Realty Co., among others. He at one time served as a deputy state fire marshal and field director of the American Red Cross. Mr. Hawkins also served on the Metropolitan Planning Commission. In April 1971 he ran for the 6th District City-Council seat. [488]

Grant Hawkins served on the board of governors of the Boy Scouts of America, the Indiana University Alumni Association and the 500 Festival Committee. Hawkins was a member of Alpha Phi Alpha Fraternity, the I. U. Varsity Club and the Indiana University Varsity Club.[489]

Faces of IPD

---

[488] "Grant Hawkins, businessman, in 6th District Council Race", *Indianapolis Recorder* – April 10, 1971, 1, http://indiamond6.ulib.iupui.edu/cdm/compoundobject/collection/IRecorder/id/50948/rec/1

[489] Ibid.

Officer Charles Jewell

Detective Sergeant Clarence W. Lewis

Born: 1910 Indianapolis, Indiana
Died: March 25, 1964 Indianapolis, IN.[491]
Date Appointed: August 11, 1941
Date Separated/Retired: April 24, 1963

---

[490] IMPD Lichtenberger History Room.
[491] "Rites for C.L. Lewis, Retired Police Officer Sat. at Witherspoon", *Indianapolis Recorder* – March 28, 1964, 1, http://indiamond6.ulib.iupui.edu/cdm/ref/collection/IRecorder/id/42094/rec/1

Buried in Crown Hill Cemetery, section 98, lot 1515. [492]

<u>1945-1954:</u> Assigned to Vice Branch.
<u>September 1942:</u> Member of a special vice squad led by Sergeant George Sneed with Patrolman Norval Bennett.
<u>November 25, 1943:</u> Took a run to 528 Minerva after getting a tip that a deserter was there. The man resisted Officers Oscar Donahue and Lewis and fled. Officer Lewis shot the suspect in the shoulder, who survived.
<u>December 8, 1945:</u> Patrolling in Squad Car #12 with Officer Clyde Ashby and Lt. Preston Heater.
<u>September 15, 1948:</u> Promoted to Acting Sergeant.
<u>September 1948:</u> Appointed Acting Sergeant.
<u>December 1948:</u> Sergeant Lewis is a member of Vice Squad led by Lt. George Sneed and rookie Clarence Snorden.
<u>January 1952:</u> Promoted to full Merit rank of Sergeant.
<u>June 30, 1952:</u> Lt. Sneed and Sgt. Lewis led raids on three drug houses on Saturday night, arresting nine people.

---

[492] Source for birth & death dates, Findagrave.com

July 27, 1954: Transferred to the Detective Division from his beat on Indiana Avenue (switching with Sgt. Chester Coates). He became partners with newly promoted James Dabner in June 1955.

August 1, 1955: Demoted to Patrolman.

1957-1963: Working in the Traffic Division.

After his retirement in April 1963, Clarence Lewis took a job as an officer at Crispus Attucks High School. He died later that year.

[493]

Policewoman Sara Alice Mize Jones

Born: About 1913
Died:
Date Appointed: May 11, 1943
Date Separated/Retired: March 9, 1956 (resigned)

Sara Alice Mize married September 24, 1948 in Davidson County, Tennessee to Plez Jones, a Sergeant with the Indianapolis Police Department.[494]

---

[493] A History of the Indianapolis Police Department's Black Police Officers by Captain Richard Crenshaw

[494] "Tennessee, County Marriages, 1790-1950," index and images, FamilySearch (https://familysearch.org/pal:/MM9.1.1/KZW9-SQJ : accessed 25 May 2014), Plez Jones and Sara Alice Mize, 24 Sep 1948; citing Davidson, Tennessee, United States, ; FHL microfilm 1994120.

<u>August 22, 1953:</u> Patrolwomen Georgia Rogers and Sarah Mize of the Juvenile Aid Division question three 17-year olds who admitted their involvement in shooting a 20-year old during a disturbance.[495]

She resigned in March 1956 to accept more lucrative employment. She had been assigned to the Juvenile Aid Division since 1950.[496]

---

[495] "1 Shot, 2 Cut in Teen Gang Battle", *Indianapolis Recorder* – August 22, 1953, 1,
http://indiamond6.ulib.iupui.edu/cdm/compoundobject/collection/IRecorder/id/32117/rec/1

[496] "Policewoman Retires", *Indianapolis Recorder* – March 17, 1956, 1,
http://indiamond6.ulib.iupui.edu/cdm/compoundobject/collection/IRecorder/id/29007/rec/1

Policewoman Georgia M. (Broach) Rogers

Born: July 5, 1915 Paris, Tennessee
Died: June 12, 1985 Indianapolis, IN.
Date Appointed: May 11, 1943
Date Retired: September 1977

Buried Crown Hill Cemetery, section 224, lot 226. [498]

<u>August 22, 1953</u>: Patrolwomen Georgia Rogers and Sarah Mize of the Juvenile Aid Division question three 17-year olds who

---

[497] A History of the Indianapolis Police Department's Black Police Officers by Captain Richard Crenshaw
[498] Birth date from Findagrave.com

admitted their involvement in shooting a 20-year old during a disturbance. She spent 30 years in Juvenile.[499]

1968-1969: Assigned to Teletype Office.[500]

1969-77: Assigned to Police Public Affairs Branch where citizens could go to file a complaint.

Married Officer James Rogers, February 14, 1944. [501]

October 29, 1977: Police Department retiree had very fulfilling career
By WILLA THOMAS
"What do you do upon retirement after being with the Indianapolis Police Department 34 years? Well, if you're Georgia Rogers you reflect on a lengthy career just ended, make future plans and

---

[499] "1 Shot, 2 Cut in Teen Gang Battle", *Indianapolis Recorder* – August 22, 1953, 1,

http://indiamond6.ulib.iupui.edu/cdm/compoundobject/collection/IR

ecorder/id/32117/rec/1

[500] Personnel records of IPD Teletype Unit, 1966-1974.
[501] Original data: Marriage Record Search. Marion County, Indiana, Circuit Court.
http://www.biz.indygov.org/apps/civil/marriage/search.

think about a vacation. "I'm really enjoying myself," the fresh civilian says, "and plan to take off for Atlanta in a few days." With her retirement last month of badge 659, a valuable worker and a goodwill ambassador of the rare type. She joined the force in 1943, worked for a number of years in Juvenile Court and seven years in the Citizens Police Complaints office. In both, Officer Rogers was decidedly effective. But it was in the complaints office that she exhibited a "special knack."

Often upset citizens coming to gripe about some police action were surprised to be confronted by such a warm, friendly female with such an understanding and soothing voice.
If this was not shock enough, there was the decor. Officer Rogers' office was filled with eye-catching, exotic souvenirs from around the world given her by various friends. She herself especially admires a miniature ceramic elephant received from a police officer.

The Complaints Office charm however, does not take away from her commendable work with youths. She made countless contacts through Juvenile Court and says she hopes she helped some of the young people along the way "to get a better start and something worthwhile out of life." She has standing advice for all young people: "Pick yourself up, hang onto your wishes, hopes and dreams. Education and learning are essentials needed for a successful life."

At a reception in her honor, Officer Rogers was presented a plaque by Mayor William Hudnut shaped like a police badge and inscribed with 659. Earlier, she had received a letter of commendation from him. Another letter of congratulations was from Former Mayor and now U.S. Senator Richard Lugar: "I join with your family and all Hoosiers in thanking you for your outstanding contributions and in wishing you continued happiness in the years to come." Now that she's out of uniform, Mrs. Rogers says she really enjoyed her work especially that with young people, she served with the Job Corps and prizes a China doll made by hand and given her by a corpsman from the Virgin Islands." [502]

---

[502] "Police Department retiree had very fulfilling career", *Indianapolis Recorder* – October 29, 1977, 6, http://indiamond6.ulib.iupui.edu/cdm/compoundobject/collection/IRecorder/id/22938/rec/1

Sergeant Thelma M.(Evans) Graves

Born: April 7, 1911 Rockford, Illinois
Died: May 3, 1990 Indianapolis, IN.[503]
Date Appointed: May 11, 1943
Date Retired: March 13, 1969

Wife of Richard Graves.
<u>1955-1956</u>: Teamed with Policewoman Ella Coleman assigned to patrol downtown

---

[503] Birth & Death Information: Source Information: Ancestry.com. U.S., Social Security Death Index, 1935-Current [database on-line]. Provo, UT, USA: Ancestry.com Operations Inc, 2011.

stores as part of the "Center Detail", between 8:30 a.m. and 4:30 p.m.

July 1967-October 1968: Assigned to Community Relations Unit.

April 18, 1968:

PRESENTED PEN: "Mrs. Thelma Graves was presented a diamond studded pencil as an award for her Human Relations Report in the Dorothy Carnegie School for Women at the Marot Hotel. Mrs. Graves is shown receiving the pen from Lt. Chester Coates, who is in charge of the internal affairs human relations unit." [504]

November 1968: Became first African-American female in IPD history to be promoted to rank of Sergeant (along with Thelma Sansbury).[505]

---

[504] "Mrs. Graves completes 25 years as policewoman", *Indianapolis Recorder* – May 18, 1968, 2, http://indiamond6.ulib.iupui.edu/cdm/compoundobject/collection/IRecorder/id/45437/rec/1

[505] *Indianapolis Recorder* – November 16, 1968, 4,

http://indiamond6.ulib.iupui.edu/cdm/compoundobject/collection/IRecorder/id/47850/rec/4

Newly promoted Thelma Graves[506]

November 16, 1968:

"In describing her reason for having joined the Indianapolis Police Department 'Sergeant' Thelma Graves of 5211 Hines ley, who was recently promoted to that rank,

---

[506] IMPD Lichtenberger History Room.

said her inspiration was one of the first Negro women on the force, - the late Mrs. Mary Baker. Sgt. Graves noted that she 'always' wanted to join the department since she knew of the great work Mrs. Baker did and the kind of lady she was. 'I would call her a police lady,' the charming Sgt. Graves said.

Sgt. Graves and Sgt. Thelma Sansbury were the first two Negro women to be promoted to their present rank. In her 25 years of service, Sgt. Graves has scored a number of 'firsts' for Negroes. She was the first Negro woman to serve as a secretary to any official in the police department meaning her present job with Inspector James Langford in n personnel and training. She was the first Negro woman to be assigned to the downtown shoplifting detail - a post she held for 13 years. She was the first Negro woman to be In charge of the pawn records in the detective division. She was the first Negro woman to be assigned to the community relations unit headed by Lt. Chester Coates.

Her post with Lt. Coates was held until her recent promotion to secretary to Inspector

Langford. 'I was very much surprised and honored at getting the promotion. 1 won't do anything to tarnish that (gold) badge,' Sgt. Graves said.

She attended the sergeant's school during the year and the police department sent her during the spring to the Dale Carnegie School for Women. Off and on in her present position, Sgt. Graves will be wearing navy blue police uniform and black shoes. 'I would advise Negro women to go into police work because it gives them a chance to do something for someone else, because all police have a heart. We are doctors, lawyers, mothers, fathers, brothers and sisters to the general public. We are there when everyone else is sleeping' Sgt. Graves said emphatically.

Her official working hours are from 8 a.m. to 4 p.m. but she admits to working 'overtime' when it is necessary. 'I would like to thank those who were responsible and thought I was worthy of being a sergeant,?' she asserted, adding: 'I plan to stay with the police department. I am very happy in my present position and I have wonderful memories all through the department, along with some sadness.'

A native of Rockford, Illinois, Sgt. Graves has lived in Indianapolis many years. She does a lot of civic work and helps the needy - anybody in need - through her church, St. John Missionary Baptist, or through the appropriate agencies. Sgt. Graves is a member of St. John's missionary circle and is president of the lady's guild of the Eastside Christian Center. She is affiliated with Citizens Forum. Her spouse, Richard Graves, is a retired government employee. They have one daughter, Mrs. Beatrice Jenkins of 2525 Springfield." [507]

May 12, 1990:
"Services were held for THELMA M EVANS GRAVES, 79, Indianapolis, who died May 3. Services were held a Mount Paran Baptist Church, May 8th. She had been a policewoman with the Indianapolis Police Department 26 years, retiring in 1968. She was a deaconess and taught Sunday school at the church. She was the widow of Richard Graves. Survivors include: daughter, Beatrice M. Jenkins; brothers,

---

[507] Ibid.

Carl Lee and Samuel Evans; seven grandchildren; 18 great grandchildren; and a great-great grandchild." [508]

Sergeant William W. DeJarnette

Born: April 14, 1914 Muncie, IN.
Died: July 9, 1965 Indianapolis, IN.
Date Appointed: June 4, 1943
Date Separated: July 9, 1965 (his death)

<u>May 1946:</u> Assigned to Car 27, he was stabbed by a woman while on patrol.
<u>November 1947:</u> Assigned to the PAL Club.

---

[508]   *Indianapolis Recorder* – May 12, 1990, B12, http://indiamond6.ulib.iupui.edu/cdm/compoundobject/collection/IRecorder/id/82230/rec/1

<u>1955-1956:</u> Supervisor of PAL Club #2 at Northwestern.

In 1961 as assistant supervisor of the city's PAL Clubs, directly supervising 5 clubs.[509] He served in Juvenile Aid and PAL during his last years, in which he had the rank of Sergeant. He received 5 commendations while serving IPD.

510

Detective Sergeant James W. Rogers

Born: September 13, 1913 Indiana

---

[509] "City's PAL Clubs Seek Funds During PAL Booster Week", *Indianapolis Recorder* – April 15, 1961, 1, 3, http://indiamond6.ulib.iupui.edu/cdm/ref/collection/IRecorder/id/39642/rec/19

[510] James P. Pearsey photograph collection.

Died: November 11, 1995 Indianapolis, IN.[511]
Date Appointed: June 4, 1943
Date Separated/Retired: 1966

July 13, 1946: Rumored to be soon changed from Car 27 to the Detective Bureau.
March 1948: One of first men assigned to the newly created Homicide Division.[512]
August 25, 1948: Appointed as Acting Detective Sergeant.
March 8, 1952: Given rank of Merit Detective Sergeant.
June 30, 1956: Under the skillful interrogation of Det. Sgt. James Rogers, Samuel W. Woodson and Ivo Harding confessed to shooting IPD Detective Sergeants Fred Whisler and John T. Morris the previous day. Both officers were in fair condition. [513]
November 11, 1956: One of four detectives who solved the Lt. Phillip Glessner murder

---

[511] SSDI: Number: 304-03-0753; Issue State: Indiana; Issue Date: Before 1951.
[512] "Homicide Bureau Organized in City Police Department", *Indianapolis Recorder* - April 3, 1948, 1, http://indiamond6.ulib.iupui.edu/cdm/compoundobject/collection/IRecorder/id/90016/rec/1
[513] "Hold 2 Ex-Convicts in Shooting of Detectives", *Indianapolis Recorder* – June 30, 1956, 1, http://indiamond6.ulib.iupui.edu/cdm/compoundobject/collection/IRecorder/id/29500/rec/1

case and were commended by the Mayor and the Board of Public Safety.[514]

<u>February 7, 1957:</u> Earned Robinson-Ragsdale American Legion Award.

<u>February 10, 1962:</u> Detective Sergeants James Rogers and James V. Dabner arrest Fred W. Hardin, 34, for robbing a Marion County Treasurer of $32,000 in tax money as it was being transported to a car. [515]

Detective Sergeant James Rogers was a longtime partner of Spurgeon Davenport and the two collected numerous commendations for solving high level cases.

---

[514] "Ace Detectives Solve Murder of U.S. Army Officer",

Indianapolis Recorder – November 24, 1956, 1,

http://indiamond6.ulib.iupui.edu/cdm/compoundobject/collection/IRecorder/id/30421/rec/1

[515] "Parolee Is Prime Suspect In Daring Daylight Robbery", 1, http://indiamond6.ulib.iupui.edu/cdm/compoundobject/collection/IRecorder/id/40317/rec/4

Detective Sergeant Albert R. Booth

Born: April 12, 1918 Indianapolis, IN.[517]
Died: July 9, 1998 Indianapolis, IN.
Date Appointed: June 4, 1943
Date Separated/Retired: July 31, 1965
Buried in Crown Hill Cemetery, section 98, lot 1224.[518]

---

[516] Albert Booth scrapbook, IMPD Lichtenberger History Room
[517] Birth and death dates from SSDI: Number: 315-01-3438; Issue State: Indiana; Issue Date: Before 1951.
[518] Findagrave.com

As a PAL Club officer, Albert Booth led the Northwestern PAL Junior Basketball team to the 1946-47 championship.

1946-   As the officer assigned to supervise the Northwestern PAL Club, the teams he coached won numerous trophies in basketball, football, baseball and boxing.

---

519 Albert Booth scrapbook, IMPD Lichtenberger History Room

December 1946: The Police PAL Club football team of the Northwestern Center won the city football championship of city grade schools in a thrilling game at Riverside Park last Saturday. The Police PAL's club defeated the Ray Street Center with a score of 25-0. Albert Booth was coach.

---

[520] Albert Booth scrapbook, IMPD Lichtenberger History Room

April 1947:
Albert Booth notes: "Northwestern PAL Club boxing team winning the most state championships in all divisions and also the team trophy. Half of the team was sent to Boston to represent the state in the national tournament.- Willie Clemmons winning the heavyweight national AAU-boxing championship (April 9, 1947).[521]

---

[521] Albert Booth scrapbook, IMPD Lichtenberger History Room.

<u>March 12, 1948:</u> Albert Booth shot and killed a robbery suspect. [522]
<u>1952:</u> Commended highly by the Marion County Grand Jury for his testimony.

Patrolman Albert Booth

---

[522] Opal L. Tandy, "Recorder Newsman Cites Feats of Local Police & Firemen", *Indianapolis Recorder* - April 2, 1949, 7, http://indiamond6.ulib.iupui.edu/cdm/compoundobject/collection/IRecorder/id/87839/rec/1

[523] Albert Booth scrapbook, IMPD Lichtenberger History Room.

1953: Promoted to Detective Sergeant.

SGT. ALBERT BOOTH
Albert R. Booth, a member of the police force since 1943, has been promoted to the rank of detective sergeant and will be assigned to larceny and burglary investigations, Chief Frank Mueller
Continued on Page 2

March 2, 1956: Commended for recapturing two ex-convicts who had escaped from the Marion County Jail after overpowering two deputies. After one of the most intense

---

[524] Albert Booth scrapbook, IMPD Lichtenberger History Room.

manhunts in city history, Booth and Anthony Watkins spotted them. Both officers fired at one of the fleeing men who although he escaped, turned himself in with bullet wounds. The other man was captured.[525]

March 1956: One of the two African-American officers selected to join the newly formed Narcotics Unit.[526]

October 1956: Selected along with Detective Sergeant William Pond to attend the Federal Bureau of Narcotics Training School for two weeks in October.

November 1957: Promoted to Detective Sergeant and assigned to Burglary & Larceny Division.[527]

October 29, 1960: Detective Sergeant Albert Booth helps crack a theft ring at RCA. This ended a nine month investigation where IPD plain clothes

---

[525] Commend Officers in Recapture of Ex-Convicts", *Indianapolis Recorder* – March 10, 1956, 1,
http://indiamond6.ulib.iupui.edu/cdm/compoundobject/collection/IRecorder/id/28990/rec/2

[526] Jim Cummings, "New Dope Law Works Magic", *Indianapolis Recorder* - March 10, 1956, 1,
http://indiamond6.ulib.iupui.edu/cdm/compoundobject/collection/IRecorder/id/28990/rec/2

[527] "Albert Booth 'Upped" in Police Dept.", *Indianapolis Recorder* – November 23, 1957, 1-2,
http://indiamond6.ulib.iupui.edu/cdm/compoundobject/collection/IRecorder/id/31657/rec/18

detectives went undercover as workers at RCA. Booth made the arrest.[528]

Officer Albert Booth was the first Black man to be Indiana State Pistol Champion. Albert Booth was perennial pistol marksman champion of IPD. He set records that had not been bettered at the time of his retirement, such as when he scored 300 out of a possible 300.[529] Sgt.

---

[528] "Det. Sgt. Albert Booth Helps Crack Record Theft Ring at RCA", *Indianapolis Recorder*, October 29, 1960, 1, http://indiamond6.ulib.iupui.edu/cdm/compoundobject/collection/IRecorder/id/39597/rec/1

[529] "Ace Marksman retires from police dept.", *Indianapolis Recorder* – August 7, 1965, 1, http://indiamond6.ulib.iupui.edu/cdm/compoundobject/collection/IRecorder/id/43254/rec/1

Booth received commendations from each of the chiefs he served under during his 22-year career. He was a 1939 graduate of Attucks H.S., where he was all-state football star.[530] He began his own Realty Company after retirement.

---

[530] "Albert Booth 'Upped" in Police Dept.", *Indianapolis Recorder* – November 23, 1957, 1-2, http://indiamond6.ulib.iupui.edu/cdm/compoundobject/collection/IRecorder/id/31657/rec/18

Lieutenant Oscar B. Donahue

Born: March 20, 1919 Indianapolis, IN.[531]
Died: January 12, 2005 Indianapolis, IN.
Date Appointed: June 4, 1943
Date Separated/Retired:

Buried Crown Hill Cemetery.[532]

Appointed to IPD on June 2, 1942, during WWII, Oscar Donahue took leave from the department, January 15, 1945 to serve with the U.S. Army, being assigned to G-2. Army

---

[531] Birth & death records: SSDI - Issue State: Indiana; Issue Date: Before 1951.
[532] Findagrave.com

Intelligence). Upon being discharged December 5, 1945, Chief of Police Michael Morrissey requested his rehiring.[533]

1944: Survived a brush with death when an escaped mental patient fired a gun twice in Donahue's face, the gun not going off. After he was subdued, another officer tried to fire the gun and it went off. [534]

1955-1956: Assigned to Car 27.

July 12, 1956: Promoted to Sergeant.

From his 1956 promotion announcement: "DONAHUE, whose unusual ability to be on the scene of holdups and capture holdup men made him one of the most highly publicized officers on the force, became a policeman June 4, 1943. In little more than a year, 1954-55, Donahue and his partner, Jimmy Gaines, captured 15 holdup men. Of this number, 13 were convicted and are serving 10-to- 25-year sentences, one was dismissed but later convicted on another felony, and one is still awaiting trial. He

---

[533] "War Vet Rejoins Police Dept.", *Indianapolis Recorder* – December 15, 1945, 1, http://indiamond6.ulib.iupui.edu/cdm/compoundobject/collection/IRecorder/id/27485/rec/3

[534] "Officers' Promotions Climax Behind the Scenes Struggle", *Indianapolis Recorder* – February 20, 1960, 1, http://indiamond6.ulib.iupui.edu/cdm/compoundobject/collection/IRecorder/id/38495/rec/1

was a hero last year when he disarmed a bandit who had his loaded gun leveled on Patrolman Thomas Hodges, after a holdup at 21st and Boulevard place. Donahue personally disarmed two other holdup men. The outstanding officer earned a commendation in 1954 for his part in the apprehension of five strong-armed holdup men and was awarded the Robinson - Ragsdale merit award in 1953. Described by superiors as "an officer who does his job well but never toots his own horn," Donahue also received a number of departmental citations." [535]

April 1959: Sergeant Oscar Donahue almost single handled captured Edgar "The Slasher" Alexander, responsible for two rape-butcher attacks around 19th and College. [536]

February 20, 1960: Appointed to Acting Lieutenant, becoming IPD's 3rd African-American to hold this rank at that time

---

[535] "Records Support Promotions of Three Officers", *Indianapolis Recorder* – July 14, 1956, 1-2, http://indiamond6.ulib.iupui.edu/cdm/compoundobject/collection/IRecorder/id/29075/rec/1

[536] "Officers' Promotions Climax Behind the Scenes Struggle", *Indianapolis Recorder* – February 20, 1960, 1, http://indiamond6.ulib.iupui.edu/cdm/compoundobject/collection/IRecorder/id/38495/rec/1

(joining Spurgeon Davenport & Osa Woodall). [537]

January 7, 1963: Promoted to Merit rank of Lieutenant.

[538]

Lieutenant Garland Jones Sr.

Born: June 24, 1912 Illinois[539]
Died: December 27, 1989 Indianapolis, Indiana
Date Appointed: June 16, 1946

---

[537] Ibid.
[538] A History of the Indianapolis Police Department's Black Police Officers by Captain Richard Crenshaw
[539] Birth & death dates – SSDI, Number: 332-03-3218; Issue State: Illinois; Issue Date: Before 1951.

Date Separated/Retired: September 15, 1975

Buried in Crown Hill Cemetery, section 96, lot 583. [540]

January 1950: Promoted to Acting Sergeant.
May 6, 1953: Promoted to Detective Sergeant. [541]
November 16, 1956: One of a team of four detectives who solved the shocking murder of U.S. Army Lt. Phillip Glessner. They were commended by the Board of Public Safety for their fine work. [542]
December 21, 1963: Proudly pinned the IPD badge on his son, Garland Jones Jr. in a ceremony at the City-County Building as he became an officer. Both men served together for 13 years. [543]
June 1969-July 1971: Sergeant, Auto Desk.

---

[540] Findagrave.com
[541] "Four Police Get Permanent Rank", *Indianapolis Recorder* – May 9, 1953, 1, http://indiamond6.ulib.iupui.edu/cdm/compoundobject/collection/IRecorder/id/31774/rec/1
[542] "Ace Detectives Solve Murder of U.S. Army Officer", *Indianapolis Recorder* – November 24, 1956, 1,
http://indiamond6.ulib.iupui.edu/cdm/compoundobject/collection/IRecorder/id/30421/rec/1

"The Rev. GARLAND JONES Sr., 77, Indianapolis, died December 27. Summers Capitol Avenue Funeral Chapel arranged services which were held December 30 in Corinthian Baptist Church, where he was assistant pastor. He had been an officer with the Indianapolis Police Department for 32 years, retiring in 1976. Survivors include: wife, Rebecca Jones; sons, Garland Jr. and Herman Jones; daughter, Ernestine Wells; six grandchildren and three great-grandchildren."[544]

---

[543] "Two of a Kind", *Indianapolis Recorder* – December 28, 1963, 1, http://indiamond6.ulib.iupui.edu/cdm/compoundobject/collection/IRecorder/id/41872/rec/1

[544] *Indianapolis Recorder* – January 6, 1990, .B8, http://indiamond6.ulib.iupui.edu/cdm/compoundobject/collection/IRecorder/id/82790/rec/1

Patrolman John T. Bailey

Born: May 15, 1915 Rockfield, Warren County, Kentucky[545]
Died: December 18, 1972 Indianapolis, Indiana
Date Appointed: April 26, 1944
Date Separated/Retired: 1965

Buried Crown Hill Cemetery, section 212, lot 399.[546]

---

[545] Kentucky Department for Libraries and Archives. Kentucky Birth, Marriage, and Death Databases: Births 1911-1999. Frankfort, Kentucky: Kentucky Department for Libraries and Archives.
[546] Findagrave.com

October 9, 1953: Along with Officer Hardison Buckner, Officer Bailey arrests a man for refusing to serve them at a local deli, believed to be the first time the Indiana Civil Rights Law had been enforced. [547]

December 23, 1972:
"A former city policeman, John T. Bailey and his wife, Katherine, started the J. Bailey Company, which manufactures Jay's Hair Rel and Rix beauty products, as a part-time business venture 25 years ago. He operated the firm full time when he retired from the force in 1965. A native of Rockfield, Ky., Mr. Bailey, 5403 Michigan Rd. had lived here 32 years and was a policeman 23 years. He studied chemistry at the Chicago Institute of Technology and Butler University. His temporary funds company distributed products in seven states. He was a member of the Beauty and Barber Institute, Beauty Manufactures

---

[547] "Jimcrowed Cops Jail Café Owner", *Indianapolis Recorder* – October 17, 1953, 1,
http://indiamond6.ulib.iupui.edu/cdm/compoundobject/collection/IRecorder/id/31156/rec/1

Association, Voyager Club, Fraternal Order of Police and Grace Apostolic Church." [548]

549

Captain Anthony Watkins

Born: August 5, 1916 Indianapolis, Indiana
Died: April 9, 1990 Indianapolis, Indiana [550]

---

[548] "Community Sadden by deaths of two outstanding leaders", *Indianapolis Recorder* – December 23, 1972, .1, http://indiamond6.ulib.iupui.edu/cdm/compoundobject/collection/IRecorder/id/52480/rec/1

[549] IMPD Lichtenberger History Room.
[550] "Anthony Watkins Dead at 73 'First Black Police Captain'", Birth & death dates from obituary, *Indianapolis Recorder* – April 14, 1990, .A-2, http://indiamond6.ulib.iupui.edu/cdm/compoundobject/collec:

Date Appointed: April 26, 1944
Date Retired: October 5, 1968

A graduate of Crispus Attucks H.S. Studied police administration at Indiana University and Michigan State University.[551]

1944: First assignment was foot patrol in Beat 27.

Spent 5 years in the PAL Club, directing the Lockfield PAL Club. He turned out many outstanding sports teams while there.[552] Watkins was then assigned to Juvenile Aid Division.

1953: Promoted to Sergeant. Watkins, then assigned to the Burglary and Larceny Division, was later detailed to the narcotics squad. He earned numerous awards and commendations for his work there.[553]

---

ion/IRecorder/id/83245/rec/1
[551] Ibid.
[552] "Records Support Promotions of Three Officers", *Indianapolis Recorder* – July 14, 1956, 1-2,
http://indiamond6.ulib.iupui.edu/cdm/compoundobject/collection/IRecorder/id/29075/rec/1
[553] "Anthony Watkins Dead at 73 'First Black Police Captain'", Birth & death dates from obituary, *Indianapolis Recorder* – April 14, 1990, .A-2,
http://indiamond6.ulib.iupui.edu/cdm/compoundobject/collect

<u>September 6, 1955</u>: Promoted to Detective Sergeant.[554]

<u>March 1956</u>: Assigned to newly created Narcotics Division.[555]

<u>July 12, 1956</u>: Promoted to Lieutenant, assigned to Vice Squad.

(From his 1956 promotion announcement) "A member of the force since April, 1944, Watkins directed the Lockfield PAL Club in the mid- forties, served as a detective and also in a squad car. His outstanding record includes commendations in 1949 and '52, for efficient work and thorough investigation which led to the solution of a hit and run killing and a wave of mail box thefts. He was promoted to detective sergeant Sept. 6, 1955 while a member of the narcotics bureau, rated by federal officials as one of the very top narcotics squads in the country- Watkins was cited early this year

---

ion/IRecorder/id/83245/rec/1

[554] "Records Support Promotions of Three Officers", *Indianapolis Recorder* – July 14, 1956, 1-2, http://indiamond6.ulib.iupui.edu/cdm/compoundobject/collection/IRecorder/id/29075/rec/1

[555] Jim Cummings, "New Dope Law Works Magic", *Indianapolis Recorder* - March 10, 1956, 1, http://indiamond6.ulib.iupui.edu/cdm/compoundobject/collection/IRecorder/id/28990/rec/2

by the Federal Bureau of Narcotics for his "judgment and tact" in the roundup of 20 "important" dope dealers." [556]

December 30, 1957: Promoted to Acting Captain. He was the first African-American in IPD history to hold the rank of Captain.[557]

November 1958: Promoted to Merit Captain. Again, he is the first African-American in IPD history to hold this rank, which the African-American community and the *Indianapolis Recorder* had been lobbying for since the 1920's.[558]

Captain Watkins was the founder of the "Coffee Can" fund, which was used to provide food, fuel or clothing to people in dire need.[559]

---

[556] "Records Support Promotions of Three Officers", *Indianapolis Recorder* – July 14, 1956, 1-2,
http://indiamond6.ulib.iupui.edu/cdm/compoundobject/collection/IRecorder/id/29075/rec/1

[557] "New Promotion Unprecedented in Police Dept.", *Indianapolis Recorder* – January 4, 1958, 1,
http://indiamond6.ulib.iupui.edu/cdm/compoundobject/collection/IRecorder/id/31868/rec/1

[558] "Chief of Police Recommends Officer to Board of Public Safety", *Indianapolis Recorder* – November 22, 1958, 1,
http://indiamond6.ulib.iupui.edu/cdm/compoundobject/collection/IRecorder/id/33290/rec/1

[559] "Anthony Watkins Dead at 73 'First Black Police Captain'",

Anthony Watkins earned the Robinson-Ragsdale American-Legion Post Award for cracking a gang of youths holding up cabbies at knifepoint, while he was in the Juvenile Aid Division. The promotion and career history of Anthony Watkins is detailed in *Indianapolis Recorder*, October 12, 1968. The accomplishments of Anthony Watkins at the Indianapolis Police Department cannot be exaggerated, his 1957 promotion to Captain being a historic advance for African-Americans there.

Birth & death dates from obituary, *Indianapolis Recorder* – Apri 14, 1990, .A-2, http://indiamond6.ulib.iupui.edu/cdm/compoundobject/collection/IRecorder/id/83245/rec/1

Detective Sergeant Alfred L. Finnell

Born: November 26, 1913 Indianapolis, Indiana
Died: December 2, 2005 Indianapolis, Indiana [560]
Date Appointed: April 1944

---

[560] Birth & death dates, SSDI: Issue State: Indiana; Issue Date: Before 1951.

Date Separated/Retired: June 22, 1974

Buried Crown Hill Cemetery, section 103, lot 319. [561]

<u>1951-1956:</u> Assigned to Car 27.
<u>1960</u>: Promoted to Sergeant.
<u>1969:</u> Sergeant in Investigations Division office.
<u>1971:</u> Booking Desk, Investigations Division.
October 26, 1974:
SGT. ALFRED FINNELL SR.
"An Indianapolis policeman who spent more than 30 years on the force quietly retired during the summer and is now supervisor of security at American Fletcher National Bank, Meadows Branch. Sgt. Alfred Finnell Sr., who joined the force in April, 1944, as a patrolman and retired June 22, 1974, as a detective sergeant, was a familiar face in the old Car 27 on the city's west side during his earlier years on the force. He also served a number of years under Sgt. Narvell Bennett of the vice section. Sgt. Finnell was assigned to the burglary and larceny branch at time of his retirement. He was promoted to sergeant in 1960.

---

[561] Findagrave.com

During his 30 years on the force, Sgt. Finnell and his wife. Mrs. Idovie Finnell, managed to put four children through college. They are: Alfred Finnell Jr., president of the Mapleton Fall Creek School here in Indianapolis; Mrs. Carrie Wilson, chairman of the art department at Shortridge High School; Rudolph Eric Finnell, orchestra director of Gary (Indiana) Westside High School, and Ms. Romans Finnell, who recently acquired a degree in sociology from Indiana University. Now that he is retired from the force, Sgt. Finnell hopes to get more time in on his hobbies — gardening and rabbit hunting, that is when he is not participating in church activities at Mt. Zion Baptist Church, of which he and his wife are members. He sings in the male chorus." [562]

---

[562] "Sgt. Finnell 'quietly' retires from department after 30 years", *Indianapolis Recorder* – October 26, 1974, 3, http://indiamond6.ulib.iupui.edu/cdm/compoundobject/collection/IRecorder/id/1936/rec/1

Lieutenant Thomas H. Williams

Born: About 1911 Newburgh, Indiana
Died: July 4, 1985 Indianapolis, IN.
Date Appointed: August 28, 1944
Date Separated/Retired: April 14, 1980

1949: Assigned to Car 27.
June 26, 1951: Shot in same gun battle which resulted in the death of his partner, Officer Clarence Snorden. Critically wounded, he had improved to fair condition by July 21st. He lost one eye and a partially

---

563 Chester Coates archives, IMPD Lichtenberger History Room.

severed arm. He returned to work after healing for 7 months.[564]

January 1952: Assigned to Mayor's Office as an investigator after being wounded. He served as his driver and bodyguard through 1956.

February 6, 1954: Promoted to rank of Acting Sergeant. Remains assigned to the Mayor's Office as an investigator. He had earned 6 commendations for meritorious service up to this date.

June 9, 1954: Promoted to merit Sergeant.[565] Strangely, he was demoted in 1956 from "acting" Sergeant and promoted yet again to merit sergeant in 1963. This is unusual since a "merit" rank tended to be permanent.

July 14, 1956: Demoted from Acting Sergeant to Patrolman.[566]

---

[564] "Mad Dog" Husband Kills Officer; Wounds Another", *Indianapolis Recorder* – June 30, 1951,.1, http://indiamond6.ulib.iupui.edu/cdm/compoundobject/collection/IRecorder/id/85607/rec/1

[565] "Police Sgts. Given Permanent Rank", *Indianapolis Recorder* – June 12, 1954, 1, http://indiamond6.ulib.iupui.edu/cdm/compoundobject/collection/IRecorder/id/33492/rec/1

[566] "Records Support Promotions of Three Officers", *Indianapolis Recorder* – July 14, 1956, 1, http://indiamond6.ulib.iupui.edu/cdm/compoundobject/collection/IRecorder/id/29075/rec/1

October 1963: Promoted to rank of Sergeant.[567]
1971: Held rank of Sergeant.
1971-1974: Lieutenant in the Community Affairs Office.[568]
He had been cited many times for bravery.

Patrolman William T. "Bill" Lee

---

[567] "Patrolman Thomas Williams, Sgt. David Jeter Promoted", *Indianapolis Recorder* – October 12, 1963, 2, http://indiamond6.ulib.iupui.edu/cdm/ref/collection/IRecorder/id/41889/rec/2

[568] "Public affairs office seeks closer ties between citizens and police", *Indianapolis Recorder* – January 1, 1972, 14, http://indiamond6.ulib.iupui.edu/cdm/compoundobject/collection/IRecorder/id/50479/rec/6

Born: About 1913 Jeffersonville, Indiana
Died: May 11, 1966 Indianapolis, Indiana
Date Appointed: February 25, 1945
Date Separated/Retired: May 11, 1966

Buried Crown Hill Cemetery, section 99B, lot 304.[569] Bill Lee moved to Indianapolis in 1938. He received 5 citations for meritorious service.[570] Birthplace, death date and career information comes from obituary.[571]

---

[569] Findagrave.com
[570] "Rites Set for Patrolman Bill Lee", *Indianapolis Recorder* – May 14, 1966, 1,
http://indiamond6.ulib.iupui.edu/cdm/compoundobject/collection/IRecorder/id/43913/rec/1
[571] "Rites Set for Patrolman Bill Lee", *Indianapolis Recorder* – May 14, 1966, 1,
http://indiamond6.ulib.iupui.edu/cdm/compoundobject/collection/IRecorder/id/43913/rec/1

Sergeant Thelma Marie (Johnson) Sansbury

Born: December 6, 1917 Cartersville, GA [572]
Died: February 1, 1994 Indianapolis, IN.

---

[572] Birth and death dates, SSDI: Number: 311-22-4519; Issue State: Indiana; Issue Date: Before 1951.

Date Appointed: December 16, 1947
Date Separated/Retired: May 17, 1983

Buried Crown Hill Cemetery, section 99B, lot 433. [573]
Thelma M. Johnson, daughter of Dallas and Rebecca Johnson, moved from Cartersville, in Bartow County, Georgia to Indianapolis in 1927. She graduated from Crispus Attucks H.S. in June 1937. She married Charles J. Sansbury Jr., September 17, 1938 in St. Rita's Church, Indianapolis. She then was the only African-American employee of the Indiana branch of Donna Lo Laboratories. [574]

<u>October 1968:</u> Field Investigator for Juvenile Branch. Assigned to Juvenile Branch through 1974.
<u>November 1968:</u> Became first African-American female in IPD history to be promoted to the rank of Sergeant (along with Thelma Graves).[575]

---

[573] Findagrave.com
[574] "Sansbury-Johnson Rites to Be Read Saturday, Sept. 17", *Indianapolis Recorder* – September 10, 1938, 4,
http://indiamond6.ulib.iupui.edu/cdm/compoundobject/collection/IRecorder/id/63839/rec/1
[575] *Indianapolis Recorder* – November 16, 1968, 4,
http://indiamond6.ulib.iupui.edu/cdm/compoundobject/collection/IR

Sergeant Thelma Sansbury, 1980's

Facing Page: Letter from the City of Indianapolis Director of Personnel in response to Recorder Publisher Marcus Stewart's recommendation that Thelma Sansbury be given consideration for promotion to Lieutenant, which would make her the first woman in IPD history to attain that rank.

Sergeant Thelma Sansbury & Mayor Richard Lugar – April 30, 1975

CITY OF INDIANAPOLIS

RICHARD G. LUGAR, MAYOR

ALAN R. KIMBELL, DIRECTOR
BOARD MEMBERS
GEORGE CAPOUROS
REV. WILLIAM H. HUBNUT, II, D.D.
RICHARD E. RETTERER
REUBEN L. WHITE, D.D.S.

DEPARTMENT OF PUBLIC SAFETY
ROOM 2542, CITY-COUNTY BUILDING
TELEPHONE 633-3680

November 29, 1971

Mr. Marcus Stewart
Publisher
The Indianapolis Recorder
518 Indiana Avenue
Indianapolis, Indiana

Dear Mr. Stewart:

    Mr. Bob Beckmann has informed me of your interest in a promotion for Policewoman Thelma Sansbury. Sgt. Sansbury ranks very high in the test rankings and is one of the most qualified women in the Indianapolis Police Department.

    To date, no woman has been promoted to the rank of Lieutenant. Mrs. Sansbury was promoted to Sergeant in the first year of the Lugar Administration. We are considering opening the rank of Lieutenant to women and will certainly give full consideratio to Mrs. Sansbury at that time.

Sincerely yours,

Alan R. Kimbell
Director

ARK/meg

cc: Mayor Richard G. Lugar
    L. Keith Bulen
    Mr. Robert Beckmann
    Mr. William L. Leak
    Chief Winston Churchill

---

[576] Alan R. Kimbell to Marcus Stewart, November 29, 1971. University of Indianapolis Digital Mayoral Archives. http://uindy.archivestree.com/item/recordview.php?itemid=844794&record=209177&ftype=pdf (accessed 3/29/2015). - See more

<u>1972</u>: Sergeant Thelma Sansbury tested well for the promotional examination for Lieutenant, ranking 12th. She slipped to 37th in rank in 1974 when retesting.

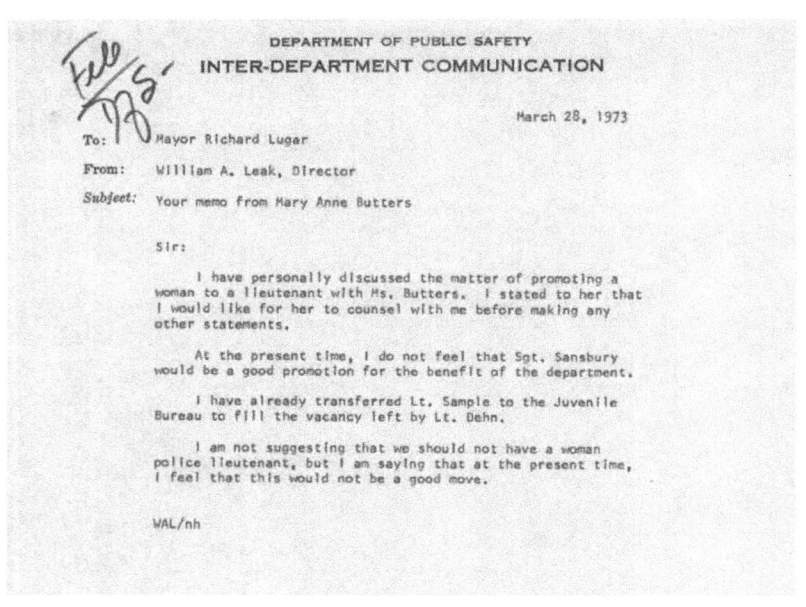

<u>March 28, 1973</u>: A letter from William A. Leak, the new Director of Personnel, which probably carried great weight with Mayor Lugar. [577]

---

at:
http://uindy.archivestree.com/item/recordview.php?itemid=844794&record=209177&ftype=pdf#sthash.yaHyc9cb.dpuf

[577] William A. Leak to Richard Lugar, March 28, 1973. University of Indianapolis Digital Mayoral Archives.

December 1974: Fran Toler, Executive Director of the Metropolitan Office for Women's Programs, wrote a memo to Mayor Lugar recommending Sergeant Thelma Sansbury for promotion to Lieutenant, citing her high test score in 1972, her college degree and that she's a "good police officer".

December 5, 1974: Mayor Richard G. Lugar interviewed Sgt. Thelma Sansbury along with two male Sergeants regarding promotion to Lieutenant. [578] Thelma Sansbury was not promoted.

April 1976: Working in the Public Affairs Office.

October 1981: Passed over for the 6th time in a bid to become the first African-American female Lieutenant on IPD.[579]

---

http://uindy.archivestree.com/item/recordview.php?itemid=73586 3&record=173951&ftype=pdf (accessed 3/29/2015). - See more at:
http://uindy.archivestree.com/item/recordview.php?itemid=73586 3&record=173951&ftype=pdf#sthash.GSIMXH7k.dpuf

[578] Schedule for Lugar, December 5, 1974. University of Indianapolis Digital Mayoral Archives.
http://uindy.archivestree.com/item/recordview.php?itemid=68327 5&record=134663&ftype=pdf (accessed 3/29/2015). - See more at:
http://uindy.archivestree.com/item/recordview.php?itemid=68327 5&record=134663&ftype=pdf#sthash.7LAfcbE0.dpuf

[579] Willie Alexander, "Time for Talk", October 3, 1981, 3, http://indiamond6.ulib.iupui.edu/cdm/compoundobject/collec

November 16, 1968:
"Sergeant" Thelma Sansbury of 3026 N. California is proud of her new rank in the Indianapolis Police Department after having earned it through her years of dedicated service with the law enforcement agency. Close friends, co-workers and admirers agreed that no one was more deserving of the step up than the charming west- side lady. She and a fellow department worker, Mrs. Thelma Graves, were the first Negro women to be promoted to the high rank.

During her 21-year association with the police force, Sgt. Sansbury has worked in many capacities. She is presently an investigator for the juvenile bureau. One of 14 women on the force, she was a patrolwoman before her promotion. Sgt. Sansbury said she has enjoyed working as a law agent especially in her current capacity. Previously, she worked in latent prints and identification. Here she would classify and read fingerprints. 'I didn't have any children and I felt I would be of service.' the friendly Sgt. Sansbury related when giving her reason for joining the department. She would advise other women to join the police department. "I think it is a promising field for Negro girls - especially those with two years of college.

'They now even have two policewomen assigned to a sector car (a car in certain districts),' Sgt. Sansbury related. In her present job, she receives complaints from civilians and requests for investigations from district cars. Oftentimes it is necessary for Sgt. Sansbury to go to homes or schools to confer with the juveniles. She gets to know some of the offenders personally through interrogation and notes that what happens to a child depends on the seriousness of the charge. She consults with the court or superior officers since a lot of children are on probation. Sgt. Sansbury averages over 40 cases a month. 'One of the most satisfying things is seeing some of the young people later on and having them show you pictures of their family. This is staying on friendly terms with them,' Sgt. Sansbury pointed out happily.

She drives an unmarked police car which varies in colors. 'I am very grateful to the mayor, chief of police, my many friends and civilians who were indirectly responsible for by obtaining this promotion,' she added. Well qualified for her promotion, Sgt. Sansbury attended police promotional schools and consistently received the highest grade for any woman except for the last time the test was given, when she ranked second. In addition, Sgt. Sansbury studied police administration courses at Indiana University. She was graduated from Crispus Attucks High School. Her working days vary with 28 days and 28 nights. Social and civic wise, Sgt. Sansbury was founder of the International Girls Aid League, a three-year-old organization which aids deserving girls through scholarships. She is a charter member of the Cameo Club and is also affiliated with the National Council of Negro Women, Holy Angels Catholic Church, and the Holy Angels Women's Club. She has also been working with Project Renewal in the area of the Broadway Christian Center. In her present job, she is the only woman in the field with a rating. Sgt. Sansbury's hubby, Charles Sansbury, is employed by the Indianapolis Board of School Commissioners." [580]

---

[580] *Indianapolis Recorder* – November 16, 1968, 4,

Official IPD retirement ceremony for Sergeant Thelma Sansbury, September 1983: Mayor William G. Hudnut & Chief Joseph G. McAtee look on.

The International Girl Aid League (IGALS) was founded by the late Thelma Sansbury in 1964, a policewoman whose objective was to give aid to young women who wanted to obtain a college education. She was executive director of this charity. This

http://indiamond6.ulib.iupui.edu/cdm/compoundobject/collection/IRecorder/id/47850/rec/4

charity was still granting sizeable scholarships the year Thelma Sansbury passed away.[581]

The members of the International Girl Aid League meet at 6075 N. Gifford Avenue in July of 1966. Sergeant Thelma Sansbury is on far left – July 1966[582]

---

[581] "Girl Aid Scholarship Dance", *Indianapolis Recorder* – October 22, 1994, B8,
http://indiamond6.ulib.iupui.edu/cdm/compoundobject/collection/IRecorder/id/75146/rec/1

[582] "The International Girl Aid League Met Recently", *Indianapolis Recorder* – July 2, 1966, 5,
http://indiamond6.ulib.iupui.edu/cdm/ref/collection/IRecorder/id/44026/rec/9

[583]

Lieutenant Chester Coates

Born: October 15, 1912 Indianapolis, IN.[584]
Died: December 8, 1982 Indianapolis, Indiana
Date Appointed: April 16, 1947
Date Separated/Retired: 1974

WWII veteran. Served in the U.S. Navy 33 months, from May 22, 1943 to November 25, 1945, with rank of Boatswain 2/c. [585]

---

[583] Chester Coates archives, IMPD Lichtenberger History Room.
[584] Birth and death dates, SSDI - Number: 303-01-0912; Issue State: Indiana; Issue Date: Before 1951.
[585] U.S., Department of Veterans Affairs BIRLS Death File, 1850-2010 [database on-line]. Provo, UT, USA: Ancestry.com

January 8, 1952: Patrolman Charles Coates appointed as Acting Detective Sergeant.

May 6, 1953: Promoted to Merit Detective Sergeant.[586]

July 31, 1954: Transferred from Detective Division to a beat on Indiana Avenue (switching with Sgt. Clarence Lewis).

July 14, 1956: Demoted from Acting Detective Sergeant to Patrolman. He remained a Detective.[587]

June 13, 1959: Chester Coates Promoted to Detective Sergeant.

Det. Chester Coates has been promoted to detective sergeant effective June 16, Chief Robert E. Reilly announced this week. A 12-year department veteran, Sgt. Coates was appointed to the force on April 16, 1947. He was commended in October of that year for the capture of William Joyner, later found to be responsible for 235 burglaries and again in 1950 for good police work and

---

Operations, Inc., 2011.

[586] "Four Police Get Permanent Rank", *Indianapolis Recorder* – May 9, 1953, 1,
http://indiamond6.ulib.iupui.edu/cdm/compoundobject/collection/IRecorder/id/31774/rec/1

[587] "Records Support Promotions of Three Officers", *Indianapolis Recorder* – July 14, 1956, 1,
http://indiamond6.ulib.iupui.edu/cdm/compoundobject/collection/IRecorder/id/29075/rec/1

devotion to duty while under fire in pursuit of a holdup man. Sgt. Coates is a Navy veteran and was recruit company commander while at Great Lakes Naval Station, 111. He lives with his wife at 1919 Miller.[588]

May 1962: Appointed to a post in the IPD Internal Security Division, first African-American to work there in the 22 years of the division's existence. [589]

May 7, 1966: Holds rank of Lieutenant.

1969: The IPD Community Relations Council was organized this year under Lt. Chester Coates. It was later renamed the Office of Public Affairs.[590]

February 23-24, 1969: Lt. Chester Coates attended a law enforcement conference to discuss the possibility of organizing a National Association of Police Community

---

[588] "Chester Coates Promoted to Detective Sgt.", *Indianapolis Recorder* – June 13, 1959, 1, http://indiamond6.ulib.iupui.edu/cdm/compoundobject/collection/IRecorder/id/36670/rec/1

[589] "Coates Named to Security Division", *Indianapolis Recorder* – May 12, 1962, 1, http://indiamond6.ulib.iupui.edu/cdm/compoundobject/collection/IRecorder/id/40526/rec/4

[590] "Public affairs office seeks closer ties between citizens and police", *Indianapolis Recorder* – January 1, 1972, 14, http://indiamond6.ulib.iupui.edu/cdm/compoundobject/collection/IRecorder/id/50479/rec/6

Relations Officers. It was held at the Gateway Hotel, St. Louis, Missouri. Lt. Coates represented IPD since he serves as the department's civil rights liaison officer.[591]
<u>1971:</u> Assigned to Car A-1 on Adam Sector.
<u>1974:</u> At his retirement, was director of IPD Community Relations section of Internal Affairs. He was one of 20 law enforcement officers selected by the FBI to write anti-riot guidelines for the federal government.

---

[591] "Lt. Coates will attend police forum", *Indianapolis Recorder* – February 1, 1969, 1,
http://indiamond6.ulib.iupui.edu/cdm/compoundobject/collection/IRecorder/id/48132/rec/1

Det. Sgt. J. Samuel "Sam" Gibbs

Born: About 1921 Tennessee[593]
Died: April 28, 1969 Indianapolis, IN.[594]
Date Appointed: April 16, 1947

---

[592] IMPD Lichtenberger History Room.
[593] Birthdate and place: 1940; Census Place: Indianapolis, Marion, Indiana; Roll: T627_1127; Page: 1A; Enumeration District: 96-193.
[594] "Rites Sat. for Sam Gibbs; veteran police officer", *Indianapolis Recorder* – May 3, 1969, 1, http://indiamond6.ulib.iupui.edu/cdm/compoundobject/collection/IRecorder/id/48369/rec/1

Date Separated: April 28, 1969 (death)

Sam came to Indianapolis around 1923 and graduated from Crispus Attucks H.S.[595]   He was a WWII veteran with the rank of Staff Sergeant.

March 1953: Promoted to Acting Detective. He was then assigned to the newly created Narcotics Squad.
Held rank of Detective Sergeant by 1957.
1961-1969: Working in Robbery.
April 28, 1969: Detective Sergeant Sam Gibbs' body was found early Tuesday morning slumped behind the steering wheel of his car, parked in the 900 block of W. 16th Street. Lieutenant Thomas Bryant had started a search for Gibbs after his wife reported he had not come home the night before.   Death was attributed to a heart attack. [596]

---

[595]   Ibid.
[596]   "Rites Sat. for Sam Gibbs; veteran police officer", *Indianapolis Recorder* – May 3, 1969, 1, http://indiamond6.ulib.iupui.edu/cdm/compoundobject/collection/IRecorder/id/48369/rec/1

Faces of IPD

Detective John Webster, Robbery, 1985. [597]

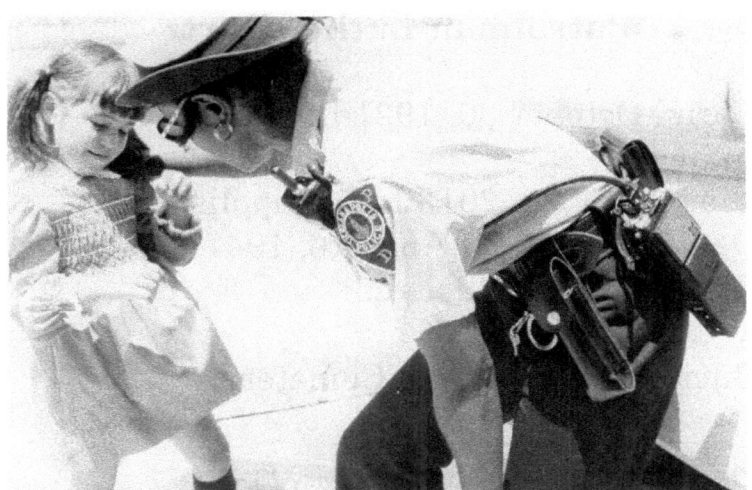

Policewoman Ella Crenshaw, 1977.

---

[597] IMPD Lichtenberger History Room.

Patrolman Luther Kurtz

Born: October 30, 1921 Indianapolis, Indiana
Died: May 22, 2013 Indianapolis, IN.[599]
Date Appointed: April 16, 1947
Date Separated/Retired:

Buried in Crown Hill Cemetery.[600]

---

[598] Crown Hill webpage, accessed May 13, 2014.
http://www.crownhill.org/obits/obituaries.php/obitID/812385/obit/Luther-Lukie-Kurtz
[599] Crown Hill webpage, accessed May 13, 2014. Birth & death dates:
http://www.crownhill.org/obits/obituaries.php/obitID/812385/obit/Luther-Lukie-Kurtz
[600] Ibid.

During WWII he was in the 3rd Army infantry and air cadet school. He served as a 1st Sergeant in Europe and won the Bronze Star.[601]

1947-1948: Assigned to Car 27.
1957-1968: Working in the Motorcycle Division.

"Luther Kurtz II was born October 30, 1921 to Luther and Mattie Kurtz, in Indianapolis, Indiana. He departed this life May 22, 2013 at the age of 91. Lukie, as everyone knew him, was a wise and funny man; he served as daddy to many. He served his country in the Army, served his community as a police officer (retired) and later went on to work and retire from the Gas Company. He was a faithful member of Pilgrim Missionary Baptist Church for over thirty years.

He was preceded in death by his parents, Luther and Mattie Kurtz, and his brother

---

[601] Opal Tandy, "New Police In Service Six Months", *Indianapolis Recorder* – October 25, 1947, 2, http://indiamond6.ulib.iupui.edu/cdm/compoundobject/collection/IRecorder/id/91109/rec/1

Homer Kurtz. He leaves to cherish his memory his one and only child, daughter Pamela J. Kurtz; four grandchildren, Rhonda (Darren) Allen, David (Jina) Helms, Rachel and Desmond Kurtz; nine great grandchildren, Chandler Jacobs, Mikala, David, Sarai, Anjayla, Anthony, Amari and Brinli Helms and Aysia Kurtz; two great great grandchildren, Mekhi Brittain and Aiden Jacobs. He also leaves behind his brothers George and William Kurtz along with his nieces, nephews, friends, and other family."[602]

---

[602] http://www.crownhill.org/obits/obituaries.php/obitID/812385/obit/Luther-Lukie-Kurtz

603

Sergeant William Fairfield Rapier

Born: November 5, 1921 Middleborough, Kentucky[604]
Died: September 9, 2002 Orange, FL.
Date Appointed: July 1, 1948
Date Retired: September 24, 1968

---

[603] A History of the Indianapolis Police Department's Black Police Officers by Captain Richard Crenshaw

[604] Birth, death data and military service dates: U.S., Department of Veterans Affairs BIRLS Death File, 1850-2010 [database on-line]. Provo, UT, USA: Ancestry.com Operations, Inc., 2011. Original data: Beneficiary Identification Records Locator Subsystem (BIRLS) Death File. Washington, D.C.: U.S. Department of Veterans Affairs.

Among the first African-American officers to patrol in Car #29, previously manned by White officers.[605] He rode a 3-wheel cycle for two years. Rapier worked with the Lockfield PAL Club 1 & ½ years.

1953: Received a citation from the Chief for his capture of a holdup man.

Officer William Rapier coaching boxing at PAL Club, 1955.

January 1958: Appointed Acting Sergeant in Juvenile.

---

[605] Opal L. Tandy, "The Avenoo", *Indianapolis Recorder* – July 16, 1949, 12,
http://indiamond6.ulib.iupui.edu/cdm/compoundobject/collection/IRecorder/id/88094/rec/1

January 11, 1958:
William F. Rapier is appointed Acting Sergeant. He remains in the Juvenile Aid Division. During the previous 10 years with IPD, he had worked with the PAL Club, as a uniformed officer and as a three wheel motorcycle officer in the Traffic Division. A graduate of Attucks H.S., 1940, Rapier was a two letter man in football. He received 8 commendations for his police work.[606]

Rapier was partners with Sgt. Clarence White while in Juvenile, see his biography for details on their major cases.

September 1972: Working as a Welfare Bureau Investigator.

World War II Career

He served in WWII for 6 years in the Navy, in the submarine service. He enlisted January 22, 1940, as a Mess Attendant 2nd Class. On November 4, 1940, he joined the crew of the U.S.S. Sacramento, a WWI

---

[606] W.F. Rapier is Upped to Acting Sgt.", *Indianapolis Recorder* – January 11, 1958, 1, http://indiamond6.ulib.iupui.edu/cdm/compoundobject/collection/IRecorder/id/31913/rec/1

gunboat. The Sacramento entered Pearl Harbor on August 15, 1941 and when the Japanese attack began on December 7, 1941, it was berthed in the Navy Yard's repair berth B-6 along with two other ships. Her battle stations were manned by 0800 hours and were firing on Japanese aircraft attacking "Battleship Row" within 2 minutes. They destroyed one enemy plane which crossed her bow and later shot down another which was attacking the U.S.S. Nevada. [607]

Rapier joined the U.S.S. Fulton, a submarine tender, May 18, 1942. He joined the crew of the submarine U.S.S. Silversides (SS-236), July 10, 1942. During his time there he participated in three war patrols. His sub sank 8 ships. On December 25, 1942 the Silversides endured a severe depth charge attack but survived. On March 8, 1943, he joined the crew of the submarine U.S.S. Tunny, (SS-282), receiving the rating of Officer's Cook 3rd Class.[608] The sub left Pearl Harbor 10 days

---

[607] Wikipedia, accessed May 13, 2014.
http://en.wikipedia.org/wiki/USS_Sacramento_(PG-19)

[608] U.S.S. Naval personnel records: Ancestry.com. U.S. World War II Navy Muster Rolls, 1938-1949 [database on-line]. Provo,

later, starting its second war patrol, which was so successful the ship received a Presidential Citation. She earned another Presidential Citation and 9 battle stars during WWII.

On February 10, 1945, Rapier joined the U.S.S. Howard W. Gilmore (AS16), a submarine tender. William Rapier made 8 war patrols on the U.S.S. Silversides and U.S.S. Tunny. Only 126 African-American stewards made more than 6 war patrols, which averaged 50 days. He mustered out October 21, 1945. [609]

UT, USA: Ancestry.com Operations Inc, 2011.
[609] Glenn A. Knoblock, Black Submariners in the U.S. Navy, 1940-1975, 389
http://books.google.com/books?id=HpDnMZVqEhIC&printsec=frontcover&dq=Glenn+A.+Knoblock,+Black+Submariners+in+the+U.S.+Navy,+1940-1975&hl=en&sa=X&ei=_s9yU8imKI2vyAS3rIDgCg&ved=0CEYQ6AEwAA#v=onepage&q=Glenn%20A.%20Knoblock%2C%20Black%20Submariners%20in%20the%20U.S.%20Navy%2C%201940-1975&f=false

Lieutenant Roger Nelson Harrison

Born: August 8, 1918 Ohio[610]
Died: November 23, 1996 Indianapolis, Indiana
Date Appointed: July 1, 1948

---

[610] Birth & death dates, SSDI: Number: 303-05-4537; Issue State: Indiana; Issue Date: Before 1951.

Date Separated/Retired: April 18, 1986

April-May 1950: Harrison was commended in April and May of 1950 for his apprehension of two holdup men and "good police work and devotion to duty while under fire in the capture of a liquor store hold-up man."[611]

1955-56: Assigned to Car 29.

July 14, 1956: Promoted to uniform Sergeant.[612]

December 9, 1961: Sgt. Roger Harrison was selected to supervise Division 5 on the Westside. This placed him in command over numerous White officers which was a first for the Indianapolis Police Department. [613]

July 15, 1967: Roger Harrison is promoted to the rank of Lieutenant. He has received

---

[611] "Records Support Promotions of Three Officers", *Indianapolis Recorder* – July 14, 1956, 1, http://indiamond6.ulib.iupui.edu/cdm/compoundobject/collection/IRecorder/id/29075/rec/1

[612] "Records Support Promotions of Three Officers", *Indianapolis Recorder* – July 14, 1956, 1, http://indiamond6.ulib.iupui.edu/cdm/compoundobject/collection/IRecorder/id/29075/rec/1

[613] "Sgt. Roger N. Harrison Named to Supervise Division 5, Westside", *Indianapolis Recorder* – December 16, 1961, 1, http://indiamond6.ulib.iupui.edu/cdm/ref/collection/IRecorder/id/39968/rec/2

5 commendations, including three for the apprehension of armed holdup men.[614]

<u>1968-1969:</u> George Sector Field Lieutenant.
<u>1971:</u> Unit C-1, Charles Sector.

On May 7, 1977, Mayor William G. Hudnut holds a press event demonstrating his new field commanders, including Captain Cephas Bandy and Lt. Roger N. Harrison to his left.

---

[614] "Promoted", *Indianapolis Recorder* – July 15, 1967, 6, http://indiamond6.ulib.iupui.edu/cdm/ref/collection/IRecorder/id/46432/rec/31

<u>1979:</u> Employed with IPD as a Lieutenant.

Roger Harrison was appointed to the rank of Assistant Deputy Chief late in his career, being one of two Black man to hold this rank in IPD history. The other was Cicero Mukes.

Deputy Chief James Vernon Dabner

Born: June 29, 1920 Indiana
Died: December 24, 1999 Indianapolis, Indiana[615]

---

[615] Birth & death dates, SSDI: Number: 317-03-6605; Issue

Date Appointed: July 1, 1948
Date Separated/Retired: 1983

1948-July 13, 1955: Assigned to Car 27.
1955-1956: Assigned as Detective in Burglary-Larceny Division.
July 6, 1957: Promoted to Detective Sergeant.
February 8, 1962: Received the Robinson-Ragsdale American Legion Post Award for solving 4 major crimes.[616]
January 4, 1967: Promoted to Lieutenant, Operations Division.
March 8, 1968: Promoted to Inspector; changed to Major, August 5, 1969. Served in Operations Division 1972-1973.
1973: Promoted to Deputy Chief.[617]

James Dabner was recognized as a very efficient officer and rose to be the highest

---

State: Indiana; Issue Date: Before 1951.

[616] "Firemen, Police Cited by Legion", *Indianapolis Recorder* – February 10, 1962, 1, http://indiamond6.ulib.iupui.edu/cdm/compoundobject/collection/IRecorder/id/40317/rec/4

[617] "Dabner to succeed Davenport in police deputy chief post", *Indianapolis Recorder* – October 27, 1973, 1, http://indiamond6.ulib.iupui.edu/cdm/compoundobject/collection/IRecorder/id/53364/rec/1

ranking African-American with IPD (1973) when he was promoted to Deputy Chief.

With Mayor William Hudnut, February 6, 1976. [618]

---

[618] IMPD Lichtenberger History Room.

Patrolman Clarence Glover Snorden

Born: November 6, 1921 Allensville, KY.
Died: June 26, 1951 Indianapolis, IN.
Date Appointed: July 1, 1948
Date Separated: June 26, 1951 (death)

Buried Crown Hill Cemetery, section 47, lot 621.

Clarence Snorden came from his native Kentucky to Indianapolis at age 3. He

---

[619] Indianapolis Metropolitan Police Department, About IMPD: In Memorium, accessed April 9, 2014, http://www.indy.gov/eGov/City/DPS/IMPD/About/Memoriam/Pages/csnorden.aspx

graduated from Attucks High School. In March of 1942 he entered the U.S. Army, serving 3 years in Italy, reaching the rank of Staff Sergeant. After being discharged in September 1945, he married Miss Harriet Roney, May 7, 1948. On July 1st of that year, he graduated from the IPD police school. On June 12, 1950, he was promoted due to meritorious service, to the permanent rank of Patrolman First Class. They had a son when he was killed. [620]

---

[620] "Mad Dog" Husband Kills Officer; Wounds Another", *Indianapolis Recorder* – June 30, 1951,.1-2, http://indiamond6.ulib.iupui.edu/cdm/compoundobject/collection/IRecorder/id/85607/rec/1

Funeral of Officer Clarence Snorden.[621]

The pallbearers were: Albert Booth (front left), Sergeant Alexander Posey (front right), Patrolmen Joseph McElroy and Chester Coates (center), Oscar Donahue (not shown) and Patrolman William Lee. Note officers saluting on left. Standing to the right are Mayor Phillip L. Bayt and Inspector J. Richard Jacob.

---

[621] IMPD Lichtenberger History Room.

Sergeant Bailey Coleman

Born: June 9, 1917 Tennessee[623]
Died: May 28, 2005 Indianapolis, Indiana
Date Appointed: November 4, 1948
Date Retired: June 24, 1981
Buried in Crown Hill Cemetery, section 100, lot 26.[624]

<u>1948:</u> Assigned to Car 27. He patrolled the streets of Indianapolis for his first nine years, before switching to motorcycles.

---

[622] A History of the Indianapolis Police Department's Black Police Officers by Captain Richard Crenshaw
[623] Birth & death dates, SSDI: Issue State: Indiana; Issue Date: Before 1951.
[624] Findagrave.com

<u>July 1, 1957</u>: Assigned to IPD Motorcycle Division.
<u>February 1968:</u> Promoted to Sergeant.
<u>June 1969-April 1976</u>: Sergeant in Burglary & Larceny.

Excerpts from a June 5, 1998 interview with Miracle Lee, *Indianapolis Recorder* intern:

"I liked the police department because it was a steady job. The only thing I had to do was keep my nose clean," said Coleman. Security was the main reason he joined the force, because Blacks couldn't get many jobs that offered what the police department offered. He explained that back then, riding the two wheeled motorcycles was a privilege because African-Americans were restricted to three wheeled cycles or just traffic duty. Riding a two wheel motorcycle allowed Bailey Coleman to do the kinds of duties that White officers were doing. He did this for seven years, then becoming a detective. He served in the detective division for 16 years. His wife, Ella C. Coleman served as a policewoman for 24 years and their son Ronald Coleman served with IPD for 22 years. [625]

June 2, 2005:
"Bailey Coleman Age 87, passed away May 28, 2005. He was a Patrol Officer for the Indianapolis Police Department. He was a member of the IPD Motorcycle Drill Team. He retired from the Indianapolis Police Department in 1981, after 33 years as Sergeant. He was a sales associate at Abernathy Realtors, and a member of the Lords and Ladies Social Club. He was married 60 years to the late Policewoman Ella C. Coleman, who passed away 55 days ago. He was a member of Mt. Paran Missionary Baptist Church for over 60 years; and the Mt. Paran Brotherhood. He is survived by two sons, Ronald Coleman (Mary) and Rev. Joel E. Coleman, Sr. (Tonya); 5 grandchildren; two great-grandchildren; and other relatives. Funeral services will be held at 12 Noon on Friday, June 3, 2005 at Mt. Paran Missionary Baptist Church, with calling from 10 a.m. until service time. Burial will be in Crown Hill Cemetery. Funeral arrangements are

---

[625] Miracle Lee, "Black officers remember integrating IPD", *Indianapolis Recorder* – June 5, 1998, 1-7, http://indiamond6.ulib.iupui.edu/cdm/compoundobject/collection/IRecorder/id/67552/rec/1

entrusted to Lavenia, Smith & Summers Home for Funerals." [626]

Lieutenant Thomas Warry Bryant Jr.

Born: July 16, 1920[627]
Died: July 7, 2004 Indianapolis, IN.
Date Appointed: February 23, 1949
Date Separated/Retired: About 1981

<u>1951-1956:</u> Assigned to Car 27.

---

[626] United States Obituary Collection, Ancestry.com, *The Indianapolis Star* – June 2, 2005
[627] Birth & death dates, Number: 718-03-3085; Issue State: Railroad Board (Issued Through); Issue Date: Before 1951.

January 1, 1959:   Promoted to Detective Sergeant.

L-R: Thomas Williams, Thomas Bryant and Chester Coates with Car 27.[628]

April 22, 1964:   Promoted to Detective Lieutenant.[629]

February 1966: Appointed head of Homicide Bureau, replacing Spurgeon Davenport.[630] He was still there in June 1969.

---

[628] Chester Coates archives – IMPD Lichtenberger History Room.
[629] "Two Negroes included among 11 new police promotions", *Indianapolis Recorder* – April 25, 1964, 1, http://indiamond6.ulib.iupui.edu/cdm/compoundobject/collection/IRecorder/id/42160/rec/1

<u>1971:</u> Serving as Lieutenant.
<u>April 1976:</u> Lieutenant in Auto Desk.

Thomas Warry Bryant, Jr. 83, passed away July 7, 2004. He was employed by the Indianapolis Police Department, where he retired as a Lieutenant after 32 years of service. He was a veteran of the United States Air Force and a member of the American Legion Tillman Harpole Post #249, and also a member of the Cosmo Knights. Services will be held on Tuesday, July 13, 2004 at 1 p.m. with calling held from 12 to 1 p.m. at Stuart Mortuary. Survivors include his brother, Brandon L. Bryant; sisters, Ramona Bryant Young and Mary Bryant Northington. Entombment in Crown Hill Cemetery Mausoleum. Final care and arrangements have been entrusted to Stuart Mortuary.[631]

---

[630] "Davenport Promoted to Captain", *Indianapolis Recorder* - February 5, 1966, 1, http://indiamond6.ulib.iupui.edu/cdm/compoundobject/collection/IRecorder/id/43671/rec/1

[631] United States Obituary Collection – Ancestry.com, from *The Indianapolis Star*.

Patrolman James Joseph McElroy

Born: March 4, 1920 New Castle, IN.
Died: June 16 1977 Indianapolis, IN.
Date Appointed: August 1, 1949
Date Resigned: June 19, 1967

<u>August 21, 1950</u>: Patrolmen Albert Booth and McElroy chased and captured two fleeing men suspected of the brutal beating and rape of a woman.
<u>October 1957</u>: Patrolled in Squad Car 27 along with Alfred Finnell.

---

[632] A History of the Indianapolis Police Department's Black Police Officers by Captain Richard Crenshaw.

Sergeant Averitte Wallace Corley

Born: October 11, 1927
Died: January 3, 2016 Indianapolis, IN.
Date Appointed: November 12, 1953
Date Retired: 1974

Averitte Corley was attending Attucks H.S. during WWII. At age 16 he dropped out and enlisted in the Army Air Corps, on March 17, 1944. When they found out how old he was, Averitte was given an Honorable Discharge.[633]

---

[633] Details of early life and college from taped interview with

In 1945, he went to the recruiting station and enlisted in the U.S. Army. However he was placed on a Navy bus. Then, a Marine Sergeant, apparently looking for Black recruits, took hold of him and the next thing he knew, he was a Marine.

Averitte Corley had become a part of a significant moment in history. Up to then, there had been no Black Marines, the USMC being the last branch of the service to integrate.

On July 1, 1945, Private Corley was at Montford Point and a Marine. Averitte was one of 20,000 African-Americans to be trained at the Montford Point facility at Camp Lejune, N.C. They were segregated from the White soldiers.

Although Mr. Corley later described the Marine training as "brutal", recruits often being kicked and slapped, he said "They tried to make us better Marines" and "We were the first blacks, and they wanted to make sure you measured up."

Purdue University – May 2, 2008 – courtesy Paula Corley.

Averitte served in the Pacific 1 year. At Saipan. His duties included guarding Japanese POWs in Saipan and guarding naval installations at Norfolk, Virginia.[634]

---

[634] Details of USMC from Indianapolis Star story October 25, 2011
https://www.newspapers.com/clip/9949992/averitte_corley_of_the_usmc_and_ipd/

Averitte Corley – USMC possibly during Korean War.

After WWII, he enlisted for 2 years, was sent to Guam and had served until August 25, 1947. After the service, he decided to go back to high school and graduate. He graduated from Jackson Central H.S.,

Arcadia, Ind. where his family had owned a farm since 1848.

He applied at Purdue University on the G.I. Bill and entered the spring Semester of 1950. He majored in Agriculture. He was short 6 hours of credits to graduate and did so in 1976 after completing some required courses. He also received a Master's Degree at Indiana University.

Averitte also was a Korean War era veteran, serving until he was discharged in April 1951.

Averitte was appointed to the Indianapolis Police Department on November 12, 1953. He spent a number of years patrolling the streets. An incident early in his career occurred on March 3, 1954. A shoplifter of a grocery at 28th and Capitol was chased by two store employees. Officer Corley joined the chase at 26th St. He continued the pursuit for four blocks until almost out of breath – then fired two warning shots into the air. The suspect surrendered in the 2400 block of Highland Avenue.[636]

---

[635] Courtesy Corley family.

During the night of November 14, 1957, Corley was parked at the corner of Capitol Avenue and 11th Street. He saw a car run the red light, strike two cars and keep going.

Corley caught up to the bogged down vehicle at Missouri Street at the Water Canal. The vehicle sped off again as Corley approached – he fired six shots, hitting the two rear tires. One of the hit and run victims then pulled his car in front of the suspect vehicle, blocking it. Officer Corley arrested the suspect on multiple charges.[637]

Averitte Corley was promoted to Sergeant by 1968.

June 1969: Sergeant in Central Records.
1969: Sergeant in Homicide.

---

[636] The Indianapolis Star – March 4, 1954, p.3
https://www.newspapers.com/clip/9958638/the_indianapolis_star/

[637] The Indianapolis Star – November 15, 1957, p.5
https://www.newspapers.com/image/105624649/?terms=%22averitte%2Bw%2Bcorley%22

Patrolman Averitte Corley[638]

---

[638] Courtesy Corley family.

Averitte Corley taking information.[639]

Congress authorized a special gold medal to be awarded to the surviving 420 "Montford Point" Marines to recognize their achievement during WWII in desegregating the United States Marine Corps. This Congressional Gold Medal, one of the nation's highest civilian honors, was awarded to 400 of them in Washington D.C., in July 2012. Averitte, who was too ill to attend the ceremony, received his from Congressman Andre Carson in Indianapolis, July 4, 2012. He then served as a grand

---

[639] Courtesy Corley family.

marshal of the Lawrence, Indiana 4th of July Parade.

Averitte Corley with his medal.

---

640 All photographs courtesy of Paula Corley.

Sergeant Richard Combs

Born: October 20, 1932 Hazard, KY.
Died: October 11, 2000 Indianapolis, IN.
Appointed: February 16, 1963
Retired: April 20, 2000

Navy veteran.
1967-74: Vice Squad member.
September 9, 1969: Promoted to Acting Sergeant, Vice Squad.

1974: Transferred to Robbery.

October 10, 1974: Worked round the clock to round up 5 gang members who raped two women & committed robberies in a 2 ½ hour spree. Commended personally by Chief Kenneth Hale.

October 23, 1987: Solved robbery case, the suspect being later charged with murdering a cabbie October 19, 1987.

1989: Richard Combs, brother Elmer and Jack Gillespie in Robbery.

Richard Combs is remembered as one of the most beloved and respected police officers in Indianapolis history. He had a saying that he frequently greeted friends with "Every day is a good day" and he lived every day to the fullest. He was known for his excellent cooking skills, particularly his chili. He was also an excellent detective.

Detective James M. Highbaugh

Born: About 1945
Died: September 8, 1982 Indianapolis, IN.
Appointed: September 12, 1966
Separated: September 12, 1979

---

641 "A History of the Indianapolis Police Department's Black Police Officers by Richard Crenshaw.iu

November 20, 1968: Named Policeman of the Month for clearing 49 cases & arresting 15 suspects.

<u>1969:</u> Patrolman, Edward-4 Sector.
<u>1971:</u> Unit F-4 on Frank Sector.
<u>January 11, 1973:</u> Investigator on Lucille Hosmer murder – thanked this day by her daughter for the quick resolution to the case.
<u>May 10, 1974:</u> Member of a 5-man unit which arrested 3 suspects involved in 30 robberies.

"He was one heck of a good officer," recalled John R. Larkins, who was Highbaugh's partner for 10 years.

Patrolman James E. Mitchell

Born: August 23, 1915
Died: April 24, 2006 Indianapolis, IN.
Date Appointed: June 4, 1943
Date Separated: January 22, 1969

He earned a degree in Real Estate from IUPUI and in 1972 joined the Jobe Realty Company.

---

[642] A History of the Indianapolis Police Department's Black Police Officers by Captain Richard Crenshaw

Patrolman Jack L. Yager

Born: March 1, 1926 Culpepper, VA.
Died: March 26, 1980 Indianapolis, IN.
Date Appointed: October 16, 1958
Date Separated/Retired: May 18, 1979

Navy veteran of WWII and Korea.
<u>May 1962:</u> Patrolmen Jack Yager and William Rowe are the first two African-American canine officers with IPD.

---

[643] A History of the Indianapolis Police Department's Black Police Officers by Captain Richard Crenshaw

<u>1969-71</u>: Patrolman, Operations Division.
<u>1971</u>: Processor, Central Records.

[644] Jack Yager & K-9 partner,
graduate from K-9 Academy May 13, 1962

---

[644] The Indianapolis Star – May 13, 1962, p.27

Officer Clara (Clay) Dodson Williams

Born: About 1931
Died: July 3, 2015 Indianapolis, IN.
Date Appointed: September 20, 1956
Date Separated/Retirement: February 8, 1978

November 29, 1966: Arrested a woman while working part-tie at L.S. Ayres, who had $102 worth of stolen goods from three stores on her.[646]

---

[645] A History of the Indianapolis Police Department's Black Police Officers by Captain Richard Crenshaw
[646] The Indianapolis Star, November 30, 1966, p.29.

<u>August 4, 1967:</u> Fired a shot at the tire of a fleeing car after a shoplifter jumped in it after ignoring her call to halt. Vehicle continued and fled.

<u>1966-1976:</u> Assigned to Burglary & Larceny Division, Center Sector, Shoplift Detail.

Clara also retired from the State of Indiana after several years of dedicated service. Clara is remembered as a beautiful lady who was partners with Officer Ella Coleman. They worked the shoplift detail at the downtown L.S. Ayres store.

647 A History of the Indianapolis Police Department's Black Police

Officer Celestine G. (Vincent) Clark

Born: October 2, 1930 Indianapolis, IN.
Died: February 28, 1997 Indianapolis, IN.
Date Appointed: April 19, 1956
Date Separated/Retired: 1981

<u>April 30, 1956:</u> Policewoman Clark spent 2 hours in an undercover capacity, catching rides with six different "bootleg" cab drivers. She caught rides at different locations in Indianapolis, then rode to 400 West Washington Street, where the Vice Squad arrested the cab driver.[648]
<u>1969-1971:</u> Assigned to Teletype. She spent many years in Teletype.
<u>1976:</u> Assigned to Background Investigations.

Celestine Geraldine (Vincent) was the granddaughter of Patrolman James S. Vincent (1879-1947) who served with the Indianapolis Police Department from 1916-1937.

Officers by Captain Richard Crenshaw
[648] The Indianapolis News, May 1, 1956, p.26

Sergeant Earl W. Martin Jr.

Born: July 10, 1927 Indianapolis, IN.
Died: February 24, 1988 Indianapolis, IN.
Date Appointed: February 1, 1958
Date Separated/Retired: July 12, 1987

1963: Detective.
September 13, 1966: Promoted to Sergeant.
1968: Assigned to Homicide-Robbery Division. He was still there in 1980.
1971: Assigned to Robbery Car 82 with Joe C. Berry.
February 23, 1972: A team of five detectives, some of whom had been working on this case for four years, arrested a man

---

[649] A History of the Indianapolis Police Department's Black Police Officers by Captain Richard Crenshaw

suspected of over 200 child molests and rapes. They were Lt. John E. Offutt, Sergeants Daniel J. Marshall, Joseph C. Berry and Earl W. Martin, along with investigator Patrolman Thomas C. Watson, all of the Homicide-Robbery Division.[650]

[651]

Patrolman Kirth Nolan Vance Sr.

Born: About 1933
Died: March 28, 2005 Indianapolis, IN.
Date Appointed: February 1, 1961
Date Separated/Retired: February 6, 1981

---

[650] The Indianapolis Star, February 24, 1972, p.64
[651] A History of the Indianapolis Police Department's Black Police Officers by Captain Richard Crenshaw

1957: PAL Club boxer.

Member of IPD Motorcycle Drill Team.

Hutton To Risk Wrestling Title Here This Week

GOLDEN GLOVES CHAMPS—Six of the Indianapolis Golden Gloves fighters who will bid for national honors at Chicago starting tomorrow night are (from left to right): Edward Byrd, Tomlinson Hall, heavyweight; Norman Johnson, St. Rita's, 147 pounds; Kirth Vance, St. Rita's, 175; Ted Simmons, Hill Community Center, 160; Mike Lewis, St. Rita's, 112; Don Chowning, Hill, 118. Vance is a replacement for Bob Johnson, Christamore, 175-pound winner here who suffered a broken right hand. Sonny Karcher, Christamore, 126-pound champ here, and Vern Lee, Christamore, were unable to be present for the picture. (Star Photo)

Kirth Vance fought in the national Golden Glove championship in Chicago, February 1958.[652]

May 14, 1962: Black police officers Joe McCoy and Kirth Vance are assigned to the Vice Squad, after being interviewed among

---

[652] The Indianapolis Star, February 23, 1958, p.22

10 Black officers, following a directive from Mayor Charles Boswell.[653]

<u>1969:</u> Patrolman, Solo cycles.

<u>1971:</u> Patrolman, Homicide.

<u>May 18, 1975</u>: Received a B.S. from IUPUI which he worked hard for.

Patrolman Johnny Clinton Nevilles

Born: January 15, 1938 Minter City, MS.
Died: April 17, 2006 Indianapolis, IN.
Date Appointed: May 16, 1962
Date Separated/Retired: February 19, 1993

<u>1969:</u> Patrolman, Central Records.

<u>1965-71:</u> PAL Club officer.

<u>1971:</u> PAL Club #8, Douglas.

---

[653] Ibid, May 14, 1962, p.21

1975: Juvenile Branch officer.
1989: Missing Persons detective.

Policewoman Ella C. (King) Coleman

Born: April 22, 1923
Died: April 3, 2005 Indianapolis, IN.[654]
Date Appointed: May 1, 1951
Date Separated/Retired: May 8, 1975

---

[654] Social Security number 310-20-8761 was issued to ELLA C COLEMAN, who was born 22 April 1923 and, Death Master File says, died 03 April 2005.

Buried Crown Hill Cemetery, section 100, lot 26. [655]

May 1, 1951: Emergency hire due to manpower shortage during Korean War. Ella Received permanent appointment on August 18, 1951.

July 13, 1953: Along with Patrolwoman Thelma Graves, was assigned to the detective division, working plainclothes detail in downtown department stores, watching for shoplifters. This was the first time a female officer had done detective work since 1921. [656]

July 4, 1955: Policewoman Ella Coleman fires two warning shots to stop a fleeing shoplifter. [657]

1955-1956: Teamed with Policewoman Thelma Graves assigned to patrol downtown stores as part of the "Center Detail", between 8:30 a.m. and 4:30 p.m.

---

[655] Findagrave.com

[656] "Two Policewomen Given Different Duties", *Indianapolis Recorder* – July 18, 1953, 1, http://indiamond6.ulib.iupui.edu/cdm/compoundobject/collection/IRecorder/id/32032/rec/1

[657] "Policewomen's Speed, Grit, Too Much For Thief", *Indianapolis Recorder* – July 9, 1955, 5, http://indiamond6.ulib.iupui.edu/cdm/compoundobject/collection/IRecorder/id/36963/rec/1

October 20, 1969: Named Policewoman of the Year at the 2nd annual Policemen's & Firemen's Awards. She was then a member of the shoplifting detail.[658] She remained on the shoplift detail through the end of her career.

She wrote a book of poetry and was a public speaker later in life. Married September 3, 1944 to IPD Officer Bailey Coleman.

Ella C. King Coleman 81, Indianapolis, died Apr. 3, 2005. Services: Noon, Apr. 9 in Mt. Paran Missionary Baptist Church, with calling there from 10 a.m. Burial: Crown Hill Cemetery. Arrangements: Lavenia, Smith and Summers Home for Funerals. [659]

---

[658] "Black police officers cited with top awards", *Indianapolis Recorder* – October 25, 1969, 1, http://indiamond6.ulib.iupui.edu/cdm/compoundobject/collection/IRecorder/id/49227/rec/62

[659] United States Obituary Collection, Ancestry.com, *The Indianapolis Star* – April 7, 2005

Officer Overa Catherine (Harris) Ward

Born: May 7, 1916 McCracken County, Kentucky [661]
Died: April 15, 2001 Indianapolis, Indiana
Date Appointed: May 1, 1951
Date Retired: May 2, 1978
June 1934: Graduated from Attucks H.S.
1948-1951: Civilian stenographer for IPD Juvenile.

---

[660] A History of the Indianapolis Police Department's Black Police Officers by Captain Richard Crenshaw.
[661] Birth & Death Dates, SSDI: Number: 315-05-5964; Issue State: Indiana; Issue Date: Before 1951.

May 1, 1951: Emergency hire due to manpower shortage during Korean War.
July 1955: Part of an undercover investigation into "bootleg" cabs.
April 16, 1956: Her son Michael Ward, age 9, was tragically struck & killed by an automobile.
October 1959: While visiting kin in Jacksonville, N.C., someone stole $20 from her at a restaurant. When she raised an issue about it, a local sheriff claimed she pulled her gun and flashed a badge. He confiscated both and mailed them back to her chief in order to humiliate her. No disciplinary action was taken against her.
1960: Identification Branch, updating civilian IPD records which hadn't been done since WWI.
February 1966: Working in Teletype Office.
June 1966: Her son Michael Ward, age 7, received severe burns after workmen ignited a fire with sparks. He survived.
October 1968: Pawn Clerk, Investigations Division.
1971: Investigations Division general office.
1974-76: Juvenile Branch.
Buried Holy Cross Cemetery, Indianapolis.

A devout Catholic, Overa Harris married June 13, 1944 to Marion F. Ward in Indianapolis.

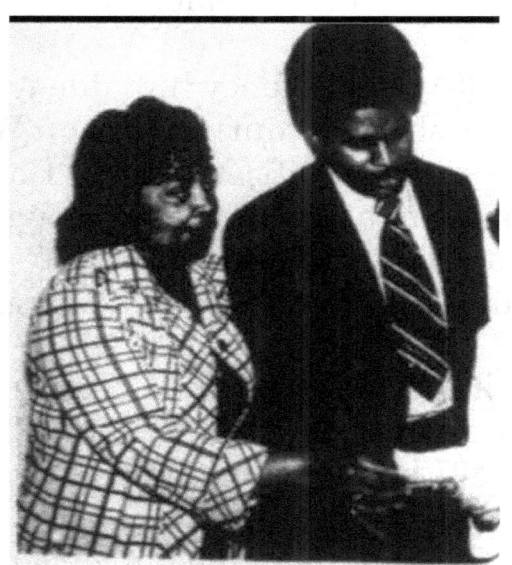

Thelma Donahue on left[662]

Policewoman
Thelma Irene (Williams) Donahue

Born: December 24, 1924 [663]

---

[662] "To Fight Crime", *Indianapolis Recorder* – August 14, 1976, 2, http://indiamond6.ulib.iupui.edu/cdm/compoundobject/collection/IRecorder/id/23788/rec/1

[663] Birth & death dates from SSDI: Number: 306-22-8289; Issue State: Indiana; Issue Date: Before 1951.

Died: December 30, 1997 Indianapolis, Indiana
Date Appointed: May 1, 1951
Date Separated/Retired: About 1960
Buried in Crown Hill Cemetery. [664]

<u>May 1, 1951:</u> Emergency hire due to manpower shortage during Korean War.
<u>January 9, 1955:</u> Officer Thelma Donahue participates in a narcotics raid along with Sergeant Thomas Williams, Albert Sheridan, William Rapier and William Rowe.[665]
<u>1956:</u> Injured while on duty. This injury kept her off duty through 1960. [666] She was the wife of Lt. Oscar Donahue.

Thelma Donahue remained involved in civic affairs after leaving IPD, chaperoning young girls on trips and being named by Mayor William G. Hudnut as Crime Watch

---

[664] Findagrave.com
[665] "State and Local Officials Drive To Hit Gamblers", *Indianapolis Recorder* – January 15, 1955, 1, http://indiamond6.ulib.iupui.edu/cdm/compoundobject/collection/IRecorder/id/34894/rec/1
[666] "Officers' Promotions Climax Behind the Scenes Struggle", *Indianapolis Recorder* – February 20, 1960, 1, http://indiamond6.ulib.iupui.edu/cdm/compoundobject/collection/IRecorder/id/38495/rec/1

Coordinator for the Butler-Tarkington neighborhood in August 1976. [667]

[668]

Officer Bessie Mae (Watkins) Matthews

Born: May 9, 1920 Hopkinsville, KY.
Died: January 14, 1998 Indianapolis, IN.[669]
Date Appointed: August 16, 1951

---

[667] "To Fight Crime", *Indianapolis Recorder* – August 14, 1976, 2,
http://indiamond6.ulib.iupui.edu/cdm/compoundobject/collection/IRecorder/id/23788/rec/1
[668] Bessie Matthews receives award at Police-Fire Awards from Joseph Shelton left, and Chief Joseph G. McAtee.
[669] Birth & Death Dates from IPD Monthly Slate.

Date Retired: June 10, 1986

Buried in Crown Hill Cemetery, section 100, lot 297. [670]

February 1966: Assigned to Teletype. Transferred out, July 1, 1970.[671]
1970-1976: Assigned to Identification & Records.

December 14, 1974:
"Officer Bessie Matthews of the Indianapolis Police Department was named last week as the first person to receive the 1974 International Police Woman of the Year Award. The award was presented Mrs. Matthews at the 21st Annual International Welcoming Dinner Saturday at Sweden House. Mrs. Matthews was cited for her work with the International Students on a person-to-person basis. She is active in other civic and community organizations and is a member of Mt. Paran Baptist Church. Assigned to the Identification and Records Branch of the department, Mrs. Matthews is also a member of the Business

---

[670] Findagrave.com
[671] Personnel records of IPD Teletype Unit, 1966-1974.

and Professional group of Mt. Paran, and The Recorder Women Sponsors." [672]

<u>1980-1986:</u> Stationed at IPD Central Desk, City-County Building.

Birth & Death dates, appointment and retirement dates from IPD Monthly Slate, 1998.

---

[672] Willa Thomas, "Mrs. Bessie Matthews, others, honored by International Students at Affair", *Indianapolis Recorder* - December 14, 1974, 4,
http://indiamond6.ulib.iupui.edu/cdm/compoundobject/collection/IRecorder/id/2073/rec/1

Patrolman Albert Alan Sheridan Jr.

Born: March 23, 1920 Indianapolis, IN.[673]
Died: November 13, 2002 Indianapolis, IN.
Date Appointed: November 12, 1953
Date Retired: September 8, 1984

Buried in Crown Hill Cemetery, plot 97, lot 1738.[674]

---

[673] Birth & death dates from SSDI: Number: 310-16-5773; Issue State: Indiana; Issue Date: Before 1951.
[674] Findagrave.com

January 1955: Conducted narcotics raids under Sgt. Thomas Williams.[675]
1955-56: Assigned to Car 29.
1958: PAL Club
1969-71: Patrolman, Operations Division.
April 1976: Assigned to Jail Division.

A 1937 graduate of Arsenal Technical H.S., Albert Sheridan Jr. started his amateur boxing career by winning the 1937 open class light heavyweight championship of Indianapolis. He repeated in 1938. He turned pro in 1940. He had numerous bouts including former heavyweight champion of the world, Ezzard Charles.

He entered the U.S. Navy in 1943 and was the service's first African-American physical instructor. After his discharge in 1945, Al Sheridan won the professional light-heavyweight championship of Indiana by defeating Tommy Charles, October 19, 1945. A big fight recalled by Al Sheridan in 1977 was against another future IPD

---

[675] "State and Local Officials Drive To Hit Gamblers", *Indianapolis Recorder* – January 15, 1955, 1, http://indiamond6.ulib.iupui.edu/cdm/compoundobject/collect ion/IRecorder/id/34894/rec/1

officer, Colion "Champ" Chaney, who he fought to a 6 round draw.[676]

[677]

Patrolman James F. "Bruiser" Gaines

Born: October 20, 1920 Indianapolis, Indiana[678]
Died: December 19, 2000 Indianapolis, Indiana[679]

---

[676] Kenny Cornell, "Al Sheridan Jr., had an outstanding boxing career", *Indianapolis Recorder* - May 21, 1977, 16, http://indiamond6.ulib.iupui.edu/cdm/compoundobject/collection/IRecorder/id/22479/rec/1
[677] IMPD Lichtenberger History Room.
[678] Birth & death dates: U.S., Department of Veterans Affairs BIRLS Death File, 1850-2010 [database on-line]. Provo, UT, USA: Ancestry.com Operations, Inc., 2011.

Date Appointed: November 12, 1953
Date Separated/Retired: February 2, 1979

Graduate of Attucks H.S. where he played on the school's football and basketball teams.[680]

Buried in Crown Hill Cemetery, section 94, lot 133.[681]

<u>1944:</u> Served in U.S. Navy, November 22, 1944 to February 21, 1946.[682]
<u>1953-1972:</u> Managed the highly successful PAL Club project, "The Dust Bowl" tournament at Lockfield Gardens, where Bruiser Gaines had lived since 1941.[683]
<u>1954-55:</u> James Gaines and partner Oscar Donahue had captured eight holdup men in 6 weeks as of November 1954[684]. They

---

[679] Findagrave.com
[680] (Ad) "Indiana Black Expo 89' & Miller Lite 14th Annual Dustbowl Tournament", *Indianapolis Recorder* – May 27, 1989, A10, http://indiamond6.ulib.iupui.edu/cdm/compoundobject/collection/IRecorder/id/84281/rec/1
[681] Findagrave.com
[682] U.S., Department of Veterans Affairs BIRLS Death File, 1850-2010 [database on-line]. Provo, UT, USA: Ancestry.com Operations, Inc., 2011.
[683] (Ad) "Indiana Black Expo 89' & Miller Lite 14th Annual Dustbowl Tournament", *Indianapolis Recorder* – May 27, 1989, A10, http://indiamond6.ulib.iupui.edu/cdm/compoundobject/collection/IRecorder/id/84281/rec/1

captured 15 holdup men in a little more than one year while assigned to Car 27.[685]

<u>1957-1958</u>: Working in PAL Club at Lockfield Gardens. He did a fine job there, then moved to PAL Club #2, at the Northwestern Community Center.

<u>April 15, 1961</u>: Patrolman James Gaines is in charge of PAL Club Number 2 at the Northwestern Community Center for past 18 months.[686]

<u>1971:</u> PAL Club #2, Watkins.

<u>May 1989</u>: Honored by Indiana Black Expo '89 & Miller Lite for his long time management of the Dust Bowl tournament.[687]

---

[684] The Saint, "The Avenoo", *Indianapolis Recorder* – November 20, 1954, 12,
http://indiamond6.ulib.iupui.edu/cdm/ref/collection/IRecorder/id/35844/rec/15

[685] "Records Support Promotions of Three Officers", *Indianapolis Recorder* – July 14, 1956, 1-2,
http://indiamond6.ulib.iupui.edu/cdm/compoundobject/collection/IRecorder/id/29075/rec/1

[686] "PAL Clubs", *Indianapolis Recorder* – April 15, 1961, 3,
http://indiamond6.ulib.iupui.edu/cdm/ref/collection/IRecorder/id/39642/rec/19

[687] (Ad) "Indiana Black Expo 89' & Miller Lite 14th Annual Dustbowl Tournament", *Indianapolis Recorder* – May 27, 1989, A10,
http://indiamond6.ulib.iupui.edu/cdm/compoundobject/collection/IRecorder/id/84281/rec/1

US Navy photo of James Gaines.

---

[688] IMPD Lichtenberger History Room.

Sergeant Colion C. "Champ" Chaney[689]

Born: November 22, 1923 Commerce, GA.
Died: March 19, 2005 Indianapolis, IN.
Date Appointed: November 16, 1951
Date Separated/Retired: 1990

---

[689]

Colion "CHAMP" Chaney Tribute Page - Facebook

Source for birth and death dates, obituary. Buried Crown Hill Cemetery.[690]

<u>December 1953:</u> Newly appointed director of the Douglass-Hill PAL Club, teaching boxing.

<u>1955-1956</u>: Director of the Tomlinson Hall PAL Club #10.

<u>1971:</u> PAL Club #11, St. Rita.

<u>1982</u>: ERB Officer of the Year.

Promoted to Sergeant.

Former heavyweight champion of Indiana (1948).

Champ Chaney and some of his trainees, 1955

---

[690] http://www.memorialobituaries.com/memorials/memorials_print.cgi?memid=150167 Accessed June 3, 2014.

COLION CHANEY
"The Commerce Comet"

[691]

Boxing Career of Colion Chaney [692]

Colion Chaney's first professional fight was against Al Sheridan. This was a hard fought battle which lasted 10 rounds and ended in a bloody draw. Sheridan would later join the Indianapolis Police Department.

"That first fight was one I'll never forget," Chaney related. "I was only 23 years old then." He began gaining notice in the

---

[691] Ron Woods, "The Commerce Comet' Recalls His Narrow Miss at Joe Louis", *Indianapolis Recorder* – July 13, 1963, 11, http://indiamond6.ulib.iupui.edu/cdm/compoundobject/collection/IRecorder/id/41505/rec/1

[692] Ibid

boxing world in 1947. Although he was nicknamed "Champ" in the boxing world, he preferred the "Commerce Comet", the name of his birthplace in Georgia.

Chaney then signed to fight Lee Omo at the Outdoor State Arena, Milwaukee.

Chaney defeated Mose Brown of Pittsburg, ranked No. 2 in the light heavyweight division, followed by Clayton World, ranked No. 5 in the heavyweight division. As related in his interview with Ron Woods in 1963:

"I immediately went into training because they told me I would have to fight Jack Buddy Walker, the No. 5 ranked heavyweight. At that time (1948) Jersey Joe Walker was the No. 1 challenger to Louis' crown. Eventually, I fought Walker and knocked him out in two rounds at the Philadelphia Arena.

The year was still 1948; the place, Indianapolis, Indiana. Chaney was to fight Sid Peak, a bruising heavyweight, for the vacant Indiana heavyweight title. Peak, incidentally, was also the No. 3 ranking heavyweight contender. Peak simply was incapable of stopping the onslaught of Chaney's hard jabbing and lost a unanimous decision. Now Chaney not only was recognized as the Indiana champion, but also gained the No. 3 ranking to Joe Louis' crown."

Chaney's next bout was with Willie Barrow. Continuing with Ron Wood's article about Chaney: "In the eighth round of that fight Barrow hit Chaney with a stiff right that "almost unjointed my jaw." But Chaney came back in the ninth, ducked a left jab, threw a right cross of his own, and threw another right on the chin, buckling Barrow's knees. A left to the liver, and a right cross to the chin, dropped Barrow to the canvas. Chaney floored Barrow four more times in the ninth before he KO'd him. "My fight with Barrow was the hardest one of my career," Chaney related. "He was probably the hardest puncher in boxing." Unfortunately, however, for Colion Chaney, Willie Barrow was as close as he was to get to Joe Louis.

"I gained recognition for a shot at Louis' title alright," recalled Chaney. "But the most discouraging thing happened—Joe Louis retired, leaving the title vacant." This meant the process of elimination. Unfortunately, it also meant the end of the road for the Commerce Comet . . . for Chaney was nosed out of contention by the more popular Ezzard Charles, who signed to fight Jersey Joe Walcott for Louis' vacant throne. Chaney revealed that after the first Walcott-Charles bout—which Ezzard won for the title—the two fighters fought three more times breaking even. By the end of their last fight the aging Chaney had dropped almost into oblivion. For the record: Colion Chaney had 119 bouts. He won 99, lost 18, had two draws, and scored 40 knockouts.

"Maybe I didn't get a shot at the title," Chaney was saying. "But I know I've had my share of thrills and excitement."

On November 16, 1951, he joined the Indianapolis Police Department and was immediately assigned to the PAL Club (Hill Community Center), where he helped organize boxing and a variety of recreational activities. A great lover of children this kindly, giant of a man is devoutly concerned over the influences organized boxing today has on the younger generation.

"I feel a youngster should know how to defend himself, but by all means he must be properly trained. The fight game today is doing more to tear down a boy's character than it is to build it up. Boxing has become a business. And the fight managers are using these kids as adding machines." [693] Colion Chaney trained many champion boxers in his time with the PAL Club, but none is more famous than Marvin Johnson, three time Light Heavyweight champion of the World. Chaney spent his entire career with the PAL Club.

---

[693] Ron Woods, "The Commerce Comet' Recalls His Narrow Miss at Joe Louis", *Indianapolis Recorder* – July 13, 1963, 11, http://indiamond6.ulib.iupui.edu/cdm/compoundobject/collection/IRecorder/id/41505/rec/1

Sergeant Colion Chaney of IPD.[694]

---

[694] IMPD Lichtenberger History Room.

Lieutenant David Square Jeter Sr.

Born: January 17, 1918
Died: April 11, 1990 Springfield, Fairfax Co., VA.[695]
Date Appointed: September 16, 1952
Date Separated/Retired: January 3, 1985

Buried in Crown Hill Cemetery, section 225, lot 159B.[696]

<u>1955-1956:</u> Teamed with Alfred Finnell in Car 27.
<u>February 1960:</u> Promoted to Sergeant.[697]

---

[695] Birth & death dates from SSDI: Number: 310-03-7416; Issue State: Indiana; Issue Date: Before 1951.
[696] Findagrave.com

October 1961: Cited for apprehending three men wanted for a series of robberies.[698]

February 1963: Commended by Chief of Police Robert Reilly for "quick thinking and immediate pursuit of two hold-up suspects.[699]

March 1963: Commended by Chief of Police Robert Reilly for "alertness and strict adherence to duty" in the apprehension of a suspect in the hold-up of a Wake-Up Oil Station.[700]

March 1963: David S. Jeter was named to head one of IPD's all vehicle Vice Units, a city wide assignment. This was said to be a first for an African-American to head a Vice Unit.

October 1963: Promoted to Lieutenant.[701]

1971: Lieutenant, Unit G-1 on George Sector.

Lt. Jeter spent his last years with IPD in charge of the Property Room.

---

[697] "Patrolman Thomas Williams, Sgt. David Jeter Promoted", *Indianapolis Recorder* – October 12, 1963, 2, http://indiamond6.ulib.iupui.edu/cdm/ref/collection/IRecorde-/id/41889/rec/2

[698] Ibid.
[699] Ibid.
[700] Ibid.
[701] Ibid.

Officer Emelie Estherjane (Chowning) Weathers-Kerr

Born: May 2, 1922 Indianapolis, IN.
Died: October 17, 2004 Indianapolis, IN.[703]
Date Appointed: March 22, 1954
Date Separated/Retired: December 31, 1957

In 1936, the Crispus Attucks H.S. yearbook described student Emelie Estherjane Chowning as a participant in several school plays, whose ambition was to become a

---

[702] A History of the Indianapolis Police Department's Black Police Officers by Captain Richard Crenshaw
[703] Birth & death dates, SSDI: Number: 303-20-9890; Issue State: Indiana; Issue Date: Before 1951.

lawyer.[704] She later spelled her name as Emily. She graduated in January 1940, receiving a special award in English.[705]

September 1940: Enrolled in Indiana University.[706]
November 19, 1941: Participated as a model in a fashion show put on by the Alpha Chapter of Sigma Gamma Rho Sorority. [707]

Married 1942 to Edward E. Weathers. Two children, Patricia Elizabethgene and Edward Eugene.[708] Remarried to Kelly Kerr.

---

[704] http://indiamond6.ulib.iupui.edu/cdm/compoundobject/collection/CAttucks/id/1328/rec/7
Accessed June 3, 2014.
[705] "Largest Class of Graduates at Attucks", *Indianapolis Recorder* – May 20, 1939, 2,
http://indiamond6.ulib.iupui.edu/cdm/ref/collection/IRecorder/id/72036/rec/2
[706] "Annual Fall Exodus to School Has Started for Young People, *Indianapolis Recorder* – September 21, 1940, 4,
http://indiamond6.ulib.iupui.edu/cdm/compoundobject/collection/IRecorder/id/89104/rec/1
[707] *Indianapolis Recorder* – November 15, 1941, 5,
http://indiamond6.ulib.iupui.edu/cdm/ref/collection/IRecorder/id/93225/rec/9
[708] http://www.crownhill.org/obits/obituaries.php/obitID/776914/obit/Edward-Weathers

July 2, 1955: Patrolwoman Emily C. Weathers assists in a raid conducted by the IPD Narcotics Detail.[709]

August 2, 1955: Officer Emily Weathers assisted the IPD Narcotics Detail in another drug raid, this one capturing a woman described as Indianapolis "biggest dope dealer".[710]

February 4, 1956: On Saturday night on this date, Officer Emily C. Weathers, 32 and Officer Barbara Sneed, 25 were transporting two children to the guardian's home. The vehicle skidded on an icy spot on E. Washington Street at N. Emerson Avenue. It crashed into a utility pole. Officer Weathers was knocked unconscious and received chest injuries. Four days later she was in serious condition in General Hospital. Officer Sneed received slight head and chest injuries, a deep cut

---

[709] "Barber, 2 Men Nabbed in 2 Dope Raids", *Indianapolis Recorder* – July 9, 1955, 1-2,
http://indiamond6.ulib.iupui.edu/cdm/compoundobject/collection/IRecorder/id/36963/rec/1

[710] "Woman 'Biggest Dope Dealer'", *Indianapolis Recorder* – August 6, 1955, 8,
http://indiamond6.ulib.iupui.edu/cdm/compoundobject/collection/IRecorder/id/35081/rec/1

under her chin, and lacerations on the knees. The children were not hurt.

Officer Weathers was injured several months previously in an accident while she and a partner were chasing a bootleg cab. She was not driving at that time.[711] Emily Weathers appears to have left the force after this car accident. She remained very involved in club and social activities through the 1960s. Her husband Edward was an executive at Eli Lilly & Co.

Emily Weathers-Kerr Age 82, Indianapolis passed Oct 17, 2004. She was a retired Police Officer with the Indianapolis Police Department and a member of Nu Corinthian Missionary Baptist Church. Emily is survived by her husband Kelly; children Edward E. Weathers (Cecelia), Patricia E. Weathers-Brownlee; four grandchildren and two great grandchildren. Services: Friday Oct 22, 2004 at 1:00 p.m. in the Peace Chapel of Crown Hill Cemetery,

---

[711] "2 Policewomen Hurt In Crash", *Indianapolis Recorder* - February 11, 1956, 3,
http://indiamond6.ulib.iupui.edu/cdm/compoundobject/collection/IRecorder/id/28922/rec/1

with calling from 11:30 a.m. Arrangements: Crown Hill Funeral Home.[712]

Policewoman Sarah Lee Jones

Born: About 1928 Hopkinsville, KY.
Died: July 27, 1986 Decatur, IL. [713]
Date Appointed: March 22, 1954
Date Retired: September 7, 1985

---

[712] http://www.memorialobituaries.com/memorials/obits_display.cgi?action=obit&memid=136318&clientid=crown

[713] Birth & death dates, SSDI: Number: 303-20-9890; Issue State: Indiana; Issue Date: Before 1951.

May 7, 1954: Sarah Lee Jones graduated from the Madam Walker College of Beauty Culture.

July 9, 1955: During a crackdown on illegal taxi cab drivers, Policewoman Sarah Lee Jones was forced to draw her weapon on Roy Woods, 26. She got into his car at 23rd and Martindale, directing him to the 2500 block of Guilford Avenue, where Officer Chisley was waiting. As the cabbie pulled up on Guilford Avenue, he recognized Chisley and sped off with Jones in the car. He tried to push Officer Sarah Lee Jones out of the car and she pulled her gun. Woods skidded to a stop and got out and ran, later giving himself up.

For many years, Sarah Jones was solely in charge of the IPD Missing Persons Branch.

1969 to 1976: Assigned to Juvenile Branch.

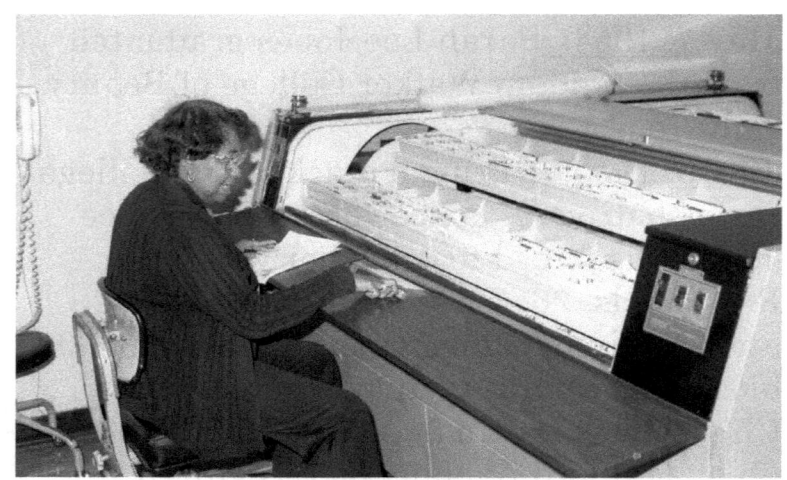

Officer Sarah Jones, working in Identification, 1980's.[714]

Sarah L. Jones is buried in Crown Hill Cemetery. She was a longtime church organist her in Indianapolis, where she lived 53 years and in Decatur, Illinois, where she moved after retiring.

---

[714] IMPD Lichtenberger History Room.

Detective Sergeant Albert S. Taylor

Born: July 5, 1926
Died: June 2, 2010 Indianapolis, Indiana[716]
Date Appointed: September 16, 1952
Date Retired: February 18, 1975

Buried Crown Hill Cemetery.
February 1954: Partner of Officer Arthur E. Carter in Car 29.[717]

---

[715] Photograph courtesy of Anna Green Hamblen.
[716] Birth & death dates from SSDI: Issue State: Indiana; Issue Date: Before 1951.
[717] Jim Cummings, "Cop Dismissed", *Indianapolis Recorder* – March 6, 1954, 7,
http://indiamond6.ulib.iupui.edu/cdm/ref/collection/IRecorder/id/34528/rec/31

February 1961: Working as a Robbery detective.[718]

October 1963: Promoted to Sergeant.[719]

June 5, 1968: Detective Sergeants William Kaiser and Albert Taylor make an arrest to solve the murder of Ulysses Randall, 46, a week earlier. [720] Detective Sergeant Taylor was assigned to the IPD Homicide Division through 1973.

---

[718] *Indianapolis Recorder* – February 4, 1961, 1, http://indiamond6.ulib.iupui.edu/cdm/ref/collection/IRecorder/id/39430/rec/36

[719] "George P. Stewart II, "As We See It", *Indianapolis Recorder* – October 12, 1963, 9, http://indiamond6.ulib.iupui.edu/cdm/ref/collection/IRecorder/id/41889/rec/41

[720] "Arrest ends manhunt in bizarre case", *Indianapolis Recorder* – June 8, 1968, 1, http://indiamond6.ulib.iupui.edu/cdm/ref/collection/IRecorder/id/45492/rec/43

Patrolman Phillip Connaly Parker

Born: August 6, 1928 Indianapolis, IN.
Died: February 2, 1994 Indianapolis, IN.
Date Appointed: January 5, 1953
Date Retired: January 31, 1974

U.S.M.C. veteran in Korean War.

December 1955: Walking District Day Shift, North.
August 12, 1958: At 3 a.m., Officers John Bailey and Phillip Parker were ordered to check the Cotton Club on Indiana Avenue when a man there reported he was robbed while sleeping. While taking the report in

the back of the club, Lt. Forrest Euliss of the Vice Squad asked them, "Didn't you see these people dancing in here?"

Both officers said they were busy taking the report and didn't see the couple dancing, who were interracial. Lt. Euliss arrested the couple for obscene conduct. IPD suspended the two officers August 13th for neglect of duty.[721] Both men were given 60-day suspensions in September.

<u>May 13, 1962:</u> Along with Jack Yager, became the first Black officers to graduate from the IPD K-9 Academy.[722]

<u>1968-1988:</u> Employed by U.S. Postal Service.

<u>1969-71:</u> Patrolman, street patrol.

---

[721] The Indianapolis Recorder, August 16, 1958, p.1
[722] The Indianapolis Recorder, May 19, 1962, p.1

Officer Barbara (Taliaferro) Sneed Chism

Born: December 9, 1930 District of Columbia
Died: February 28, 2003 Indianapolis, Indiana[724]
Date Appointed: June 20, 1955
Date Retired: August 17, 1979

<u>1940:</u> Barbara, age 9, living with parents Wendell & Helen Taliaferro, living in Prince George's County, Maryland. [725] Her

---

[723] A History of the Indianapolis Police Department's Black Police Officers by Captain Richard Crenshaw
[724] Birth/Death dates from IPD Monthly Slate.
[725] Year: 1940; Census Place: , Prince George's, Maryland; Roll: T627_1557; Page: 15A; Enumeration District: 17-36.

father, who went to college, worked for the U.S. Department of Interior and her mother was a teacher.

A very active member of Gamma Phi Delta Sorority.

<u>1952:</u> Resided Washington, D.C.
<u>February 4, 1956:</u> Slightly injured in an on-duty car accident. [726]
<u>October 1968-June 1970:</u>   Serving in Juvenile Aid Division.[727]

---

[726] "2 Policewomen Hurt In Crash", *Indianapolis Recorder* - February 11, 1956, 3, http://indiamond6.ulib.iupui.edu/cdm/compoundobject/collection/IRecorder/id/28922/rec/1

[727] October 1968 IPD Monthly Slate.

Teletype in early 1970's [728]
L-R: Policewomen Barbara Sneed and Diane Pemberton.

June 19, 1970: Assigned to Teletype, transcribing police reports. She was still there in 1975, just before all policewomen were replaced in "Teletype" by civilian employees. She was described by her former supervisor, Lieutenant Chalmer Byrne as a "good worker, very efficient and a nice person to work with."[729]
April 19, 1976: Assigned to Special Services.

---

[728] IMPD Lichtenberger History Room.
[729] Interview with Chalmer Byrne, March 29, 2003

Barbara was married first to Jacque Sneed, son of legendary Lieutenant George Sneed. [730]

Barbara E. Taliaferro Chism, 72, Indianapolis, died Fri., Feb. 28, 2003. After 24 years of service, she retired from the Indianapolis Police Department in 1979. Mrs. Chism was a member of St. Rita Catholic Church, the Fraternal Order of Police, Gamma Phi Delta Sorority and the Ladies Auxiliary of St. Peter Claver #97. Services: Noon, Sat., March 8 at St. Rita Catholic with calling there from 10 a.m. until service. Burial: Crown Hill Cemetery. She was preceded in death by husband, James Chism. Survivors: daughter, Helen R. Smith; grandson Michael D. Hart; granddaughter Mignon R. Holder; great-grandchildren Kelan Holder, Kameron Hart, Ko'Keyto Holder, Guan Maxie and Lamont Maxie. Arrangements handled by Williams and Bluitt Funeral Home.[731]

---

[730] "Four Appointed to Police Department", *Indianapolis Recorder* – June 11, 1955, 7, http://indiamond6.ulib.iupui.edu/cdm/compoundobject/collection/IRecorder/id/36895/rec/1

[731] Findagrave.com, *The Indianapolis Star*, March 5, 2003

Officer Barbara Sneed, 1974, with Lt. Chalmer Byrne in the Reporting Center, also known as "Teletype."

Policewoman Maria (Legg) McElroy

Born: June 7, 1929 Indianapolis, IN.[732]
Died: June 17, 1989 Indianapolis, IN. [733]
Date Appointed: September 18, 1956
Date Separated: January 31, 1969

Daughter of Sidney and Marguerite (Baker) Davis.

<u>July 1953</u>: Miss Maria Legg, daughter of Mrs. Sidney Davis of Indianapolis, is the

---

[732] "Birthdays", *Indianapolis Recorder* – June 5, 1943, 5, http://indiamond6.ulib.iupui.edu/cdm/compoundobject/collection/IRecorder/id/95842/rec/1

[733] St. Luke Necrology, accessed April 12, 2014, https://mpcms.blob.core.windows.net/c2d03185-4103-4d8a-908a-104f4f87bdc4/docs/5c6db8cb-2dc6-4bc9-936e-20e0d7034b7b/st.-luke-necrology.pdf

first "colored" student to be received into the Order of the School Sisters of Notre Dame, Milwaukee, Wisconsin. She received the habit and white veil of a novice nun this month. She is a member of St. Rita Catholic Church, Indianapolis. [734]

September 25, 1954: TAKES VEIL: MILWAUKEE, Wis. — "With her parents and friends present for the ceremony, Miss MARIE LEGG of Indianapolis recently became the first Negro to join the School Sisters of Notre Dame, a very large teaching community in this city. Known in religion as Sister MARY MARTYN, she attended Attucks High School in Indianapolis and is a convert of that city's St. Rita's Catholic Church. Her mother, Mrs. SIDNEY DAVIS, lives at 814 E. 17th street, Indianapolis. Sister Mary Martyn who did her practice teaching at St. Benedict the Moor School in Detroit, at present is continuing college work at St. Mary's, Elm Grove, Wis." [735]

---

[734] "Catholic Girl Receives White Habit of Novice", The Baltimore Afro-American, July 21, 1953, 7, accessed June 4, 2014, http://news.google.com/newspapers?nid=2205&dat=19530721&id=q_glAAAAIBAJ&sjid=bfUFAAAAIBAJ&pg=6458,7757505

[735] "Takes Veil", *Indianapolis Recorder* – September 25, 1954, 2,

June 3, 1956: Graduated from Marian College, Indianapolis, Indiana, B.A. [736] She was then writing a book on sociology.

A poem by Maria Legg while in Marian College:

In black nakedness She stood, Bare arms uplifted,
Begging Spring to come and clothe Her bareness With an emerald robe.

- Maria Legg[737]

October 19, 1956: "Maria Legg, a policewoman here in the city, hopes soon to go into the Juvenile Aid Division. Next year she will begin graduate work in social studies." [738]

---

http://indiamond6.ulib.iupui.edu/cdm/compoundobject/collection/IRecorder/id/33747/rec/1
[736] 1956-06-01 The Phoenix, Vol. XIX, No. 7 (June 1, 1956), accessed June 4, 2014,
http://replica.palni.edu/cdm/ref/collection/MCNewspaper/id/218
[737] The Fioretti, Vol. 13, 1955-1956, 32, accessed June 4, 2014, http://palni.contentdm.oclc.org/cdm/ref/collection/p15705coll7/id/899
[738] '56 Grads Report Progress in Careers, Study, Homemaking", 1956-10-19 The Phoenix, Vol. XX, No. 1 (October 19, 1956), 3, accessed June 4, 2014,

July 1957: Employed as a policewoman with the Indianapolis Police Department.[739]

July 12, 1958: She made an off-duty arrest of a man who was causing a disturbance and assaulted her.[740]

October 25, 1958: Maria Legg married Aloysius A. McElroy (1921-2006) in Indianapolis, Indiana.

1959-1969: Officer Maria McElroy assigned to Teletype Office of IPD, typing police reports. [741]

1969: Begins a new career teaching developmentally disabled grade school children.

1985: President of St. Peter Claver Catholic Charities, Indianapolis, Indiana.

1989: Member of St. Luke Catholic Church at death.

---

http://replica.palni.edu/cdm/compoundobject/collection/MCNewspaper/id/268

[739] "The Avenoo", *Indianapolis Recorder* – July 20, 1957, 12, http://indiamond6.ulib.iupui.edu/cdm/compoundobject/collection/IRecorder/id/31373/rec/1

[740] "Three-Block Chase Ends With Youth's Capture", *Indianapolis Recorder* – July 12, 1958, 1, http://indiamond6.ulib.iupui.edu/cdm/compoundobject/collection/IRecorder/id/32810/rec/28

[741] Personnel records of IPD Teletype Unit, 1966-1974.

February 2015: Marianna Fall and her son Khadim came from Cincinnati, Ohio to view the IMPD Black History exhibit. Marianna's mother was former IPD Officer Maria McElroy.

742

Patrolman Warren Edward Greene

Born: January 24, 1922 New Rochelle, New York[743]
Died: December 20, 1975 Indianapolis, Indiana
Date Appointed: September 20, 1956

---

[742] IMPD Indianapolis Metropolitan Police Department – About IMPD: In Memorium, accessed May 13, 2014.
http://www.indy.gov/eGov/City/DPS/IMPD/About/Memoriam/Pages/wgreene.aspx

[743] Birth and death dates: Indianapolis Metropolitan Police Department – About IMPD: In Memorium, accessed May 13, 2014.
http://www.indy.gov/eGov/City/DPS/IMPD/About/Memoriam/Pages/wgreene.aspx

Date Separated: December 20, 1975 (his death)

1955: Arrived in Indianapolis. He had served 10 years with the New York Police Department.[744]

April 6, 1957: After a series of robberies and beatings, three suspects were spotted by officers in the 500 block of North Alabama Street. One of the suspects was apprehended by Patrolmen Alfred Finnell & Warren Green on Illinois Street. [745]

Officer Warren E. Greene was dispatched December 20, 1975 to a disturbance call at 324 W. 26th Street at 4:12 p.m. With him was Officer Ronald McClain, a rookie. Clifford Howard was shot by his Uncle John G. Howard with a .38 revolver. When the officers arrived, they found Clifford Howard lying in a pool of blood. Directing Officer McClain to return to the squad car and call for an ambulance, Officer Greene started to administer first aid.

---

[744] Indianapolis Metropolitan Police Department – About IMPD: In Memorium, accessed May 13, 2014.
http://www.indy.gov/eGov/City/DPS/IMPD/About/Memoriam/Pages/wgreene.aspx

[745] The Indianapolis Star – April 7, 1957, p.12.

Warren Greene checked for a pulse as John G. Howard came out of a hiding place. Officer Charles Kaiser arrived on the scene and heard Officer Greene telling John G. Howard to put the gun down. Kaiser heard shots and saw Officer Greene fall before he could assist him.

Officer Kaiser fired his revolver 6 times, knocking Howard down. As he reloaded, Officer Ernest Todd arrived on the scene. While covered by Officer Todd, Officer Kaiser started to administer first aid to Officer Greene. Officer Todd went to John Howard who although down, was still holding his weapon. Howard pointed it at Todd, who fired one shot, striking Howard in the head, killing him. Officer Greene was transported to Wishard Memorial hospital, where he died of two gunshot wounds to the chest. Clifford Howard also died. During his funeral services, IPD Sergeant Jacqueline Winters sang two heartfelt solos. Officer Warren Greene was buried in Washington Park North Cemetery.

His trainee, Ronald McClain remembered his last moments with Warren Greene: "You know, the last thing Greene was doing before he was killed was showing concern over the wounded man and trying to talk Howard into putting his gun down. He was that kind of police officer." [746]

Warren Greene loved working the streets. "The street people were his people", a fellow officer said. He was described as a "cop's cop" by Deputy Chief of Operations David H. Elmore. [747]

---

[746] The Indianapolis Star – December 24, 1975, p.3.
[747] The Indianapolis Star – December 22, 1975, p.33.

Warren Greene doing preventative maintenance on his take home vehicle, 1970. [748]

---

[748] A History of the Indianapolis Police Department – 2000.

Patrolman John M. Morris

Born: About 1931 Chicago, Illinois
Died: July 28, 1967 Indianapolis, IN.
Date Appointed: January 28, 1958
Date Separated: July 28, 1967 (his death)

Buried Crown Hill Cemetery, section 99, lot 82.[749]

<u>1958:</u> Moved to Indianapolis.
<u>1958:</u> Earned the Robinson-Ragsdale Award.
<u>July 9, 1958:</u> While on a run to investigate a report of rowdy drunks, Officer John Morris was shot and wounded by Charles Hall. He was slightly wounded by a

---

[749] Findagrave.com

shotgun blast, on his hand and chest. Hall was sentenced to 1-10 years in January 1959.[750]

November 1965: Injured slightly in car accident.

July 28, 1967: Fatally injured in a car accident. Morris, who was off duty, was driving a panel truck north on Orchard Boulevard. He was struck by a car going west on 34th Street. Following this accident, Morris' truck crashed into a parked truck. Morris was thrown from his truck and suffered internal injuries and died as a result. The car that initially crashed into Morris' truck was arrested for driving under the influence of alcohol. Morris was an ordained minister of the Westside Baptist Church. [751]

Earned two commendations.

---

[750] George P. Stewart II, "Rookie Policeman Barely Escapes Death", *Indianapolis Recorder*, July 12, 1958, 1, http://indiamond6.ulib.iupui.edu/cdm/compoundobject/collection/IRecorder/id/32810/rec/1

[751] "Policeman in 3-car crash dies of injuries", *Indianapolis Recorder* – August 5, 1967, 1, http://indiamond6.ulib.iupui.edu/cdm/compoundobject/collection/IRecorder/id/46483/rec/3

Policewoman Joan M. Rayford

Born: November 7, 1931 Indianapolis, IN.
Died: April 19, 1995 Indianapolis, IN.
Appointed: February 16, 1960
Retired: March 31, 1986

<u>1959:</u> Graduate of Butler University.
<u>1960-68:</u> Assigned to "Teletype", Vice and Narcotics branches.
<u>1968-1976:</u> Juvenile Aid Division.
<u>1971:</u> Assigned to Car 121, Intake & Child Abuse.
<u>1982:</u> Part of a four-person detective unit searching for missing persons, a rarity in police agencies at that time.
Officer Joan M. Rayford spent most of her career in the Juvenile Branch.

MARCH 11, 1972

Policewoman Joan Rayford's day may begin as early as 6 a.m. in the juvenile branch of the Indianapolis Police Department. She plans to see the cherry blossoms in Washington, D.C. during her April vacation. — The NEWS Photo, Bob Doeppers.

L-R: Chief of Police Joseph McAtee, Joan Rayford & Mayor William H. Hudnut. This is her retirement ceremony.

Buried in Crown Hill Cemetery.

---

[752] IMPD Lichtenberger History Room.

Sergeant Harry C. Dunn

Born: February 7, 1929 Nashville, TN.
Died: August 17, 1998 Indianapolis, IN.[753]
Date Appointed: January 31, 1961
Date Retired: April 16, 1993

Buried Crown Hill Cemetery, section 97, lot 465. [754]

Harry Dunn graduated from Pearl High School, Nashville, Tennessee.[755]

---

[753] Birth & death dates, SSDI: Number: 410-30-6482; Issue State: Tennessee; Issue Date: Before 1951.
[754] Findagrave.com
[755] Annette L. Morris, "IPD Officer is truly 'an officer and a gentleman'", *Indianapolis Recorder* – December 5, 1987, 1B, http://indiamond6.ulib.iupui.edu/cdm/compoundobject/collection/IRecorder/id/61547/rec/1

Harry "Dynamite" Dunn boxed pro from 1949-1950, with an 11-3 record. He held the Indianapolis Golden Gloves Championship from 1947-1953.[756] He won the Amateur Athletic Association (AAA) Championship in Boston, Massachusetts.[757]

<u>1965:</u> Assigned to Homicide & Robbery Division. He was partners with Sergeant Clarence White through 1966.
<u>October 1968:</u> Working as a full-time detective in the Homicide Division.

---

[756] Annette L. Morris, "IPD Officer is truly 'an officer and a gentleman'", *Indianapolis Recorder* – December 5, 1987, 1B, http://indiamond6.ulib.iupui.edu/cdm/compoundobject/collection/IRecorder/id/61547/rec/1
[757] BoxRec, accessed May 11, 2014. http://boxrec.com/list_bouts.php?human_id=162252&cat=boxer

Faces of IPD

Homicide Detectives Alonzo Watford (left) and Robert C. Green receive awards from Mayor William H. Hudnut.

PAL Club event, Officer Marilyn Gurnell on drums.[758]

---

[758] IMPD Lichtenberger History Room.

Homicide Detectives, early 1970's. Sitting at desk, on left: Robert C. Green, James O. Wyatt. Sitting at desk, on right: Howard Kramer, Harry C. Dunn. Standing: Robert Terminstein, John Offutt, James Strode. [759]

June 1970: Honored jointly with Detective Sergeant John Offutt as "Officer of the Month" for their role in arresting 6 suspects in the brutal rape and assault of a north side couple.[760]

---

[759] 2000 IPD History Book.
[760] "Sgts. Offutt and Dunn named 'Officer of Month' by Mayor", *Indianapolis Recorder* – June 6, 1970, 1, http://indiamond6.ulib.iupui.edu/cdm/compoundobject/collect

December 1970: Transferred from Homicide & Robbery to Burglary & Larceny.

1971: Partnered with Sgt. Alonzo Watford in Robbery.

January 19, 1973: Commended for being part of the Homicide Unit which solved 100% of murder cases in 1972.

March 8, 1974: Investigations Officer of the Year at Policemans and Firemans Awards.

May 10, 1974: Member of a 5 man unit which arrested 3 suspects involved in 30 robberies.

March-August 1975: Held rank of Acting Lieutenant, head of the Homicide Branch.

January 10, 1976: Passed over as head of the Homicide & Robbery Branch. "Dunn is the best damn homicide and robbery investigator in the whole department and there are no two ways about it." "Over the past 5 years, Dunn has been credited with solving more homicides and robberies than any other member of the division." [761]

---

ion/IRecorder/id/49942/rec/1

[761] "Black Cops 'Hoppin' Mad' at lack of appointments", *Indianapolis Recorder* – January 10, 1976, 1,
http://indiamond6.ulib.iupui.edu/cdm/compoundobject/collection/IRecorder/id/6806/rec/1

July 1987, L-R: John Offutt, unidentified, Harry Dunn.[762]

<u>1986</u>: Assigned to Community Relations.[763] Quote: ""I am always fair because my first sworn oath is to help, assist and as a last resort, to arrest," exclaimed Dunn. "I live by this. Spurgeon Davenport trained me a long time ago to practice that everyone is innocent until proven guilty and I still practice that philosophy today." [764]

---

[762] IMPD Lichtenberger History Room.
[763] Annette L. Morris, "IPD Officer is truly 'an officer and a gentleman'", *Indianapolis Recorder* – December 5, 1987, 1B, http://indiamond6.ulib.iupui.edu/cdm/compoundobject/collection/IRecorder/id/61547/rec/1
[764] Ibid.

Police recruiting at Christ Church Cathedral, April 25, 1987. L-R: Mayor William Hudnut, Sgt. Matthew Steward & Sgt. Harry C. Dunn. [765]

---

[765] IMPD Lichtenberger History Room.

Faces of IPD

Det. R.C. Green receiving Officer of the Month Award for February 1977 from Mayor William G. Hudnut. [766]

Officer Horace Johnson

---

[766] Mayor Hudnut Archives.

Detective Willie Norman Larkins

Born: July 13, 1938 Indianapolis, IN.
Died: June 25, 1997 Indianapolis, IN.
Date Appointed: September 20, 1965
Date Retired: March 31, 1995

<u>1969</u>: Patrolman, Edward-4 Sector.
<u>1969:</u> Along with other IPD officers, was one of the founders of "The Guardians", an organization of African-American officers in Indianapolis who created recreation and camping opportunities for local youth. It was a local affiliate of a national organization.[767]

<u>1971:</u> Unit E-11, Edward Sector.

<u>December 7, 1971:</u> Detective R.C. Green received a tip regarding 4 suspects involved in the robbery-murder of a tavern owner Lloyd Shackelford. He passed this onto Det. Willie Larkins and Sgt. Alonzo Watford. They along with the IPD Task Force, conducted simultaneous early morning raids on three residences where 3 suspects were found.[768]

<u>February 1972:</u> Assigned as detective in IPD Homicide.[769]

<u>January 6, 1973:</u> The "crack brother-team" of John and Willie Larkins, assigned to the Homicide Division, along with Lt. John E. Offutt, work the murder case of James A. Anderson, 61, found shot inside his service

---

[767] Donald Carpenter, "Are Certain Crime Patterns by Design?", *Indianapolis Recorder*, October 9, 1982, 17, http://indiamond6.ulib.iupui.edu/cdm/ref/collection/IRecorder/id/28415/rec/5

[768] "Youth 16, Two Others, Held in Tavern Murder", *Indianapolis Recorder* – December 11, 1971, 1, http://indiamond6.ulib.iupui.edu/cdm/ref/collection/IRecorder/id/51471/rec/55

[769] *Indianapolis Recorder* – February 12, 1972, 1, http://indiamond6.ulib.iupui.edu/cdm/ref/collection/IRecorder/id/50583/rec/53

station on December 31, 1972. He later died in the hospital after giving a death bed description of the suspect. The Larkins brothers concentrated on this case for 24 hours a day until they uncovered the suspect, who they believed was now on the run.[770]

September 1, 1973: Off Duty Detective Willie Larkins, assigned to the burglary division, received information from an informant that led him to apprehend Willie Jones, wanted for the February 22, 1969 murder of Claude Johnson at the Tally Ho Tavern (100 feet away from where Detective Larkins found him.[771]

December 1975: 37 members of a panel submitted the names of Deputy Chief James V. Dabner, Lt. John Offutt and Detective Willie Larkins to the City as candidates to be interviewed for the vacant Chief of Police position. Larkins was not interviewed

---

[770] "Dope addict hunted in station murder", *Indianapolis Recorder*, January 6, 1973, 1, http://indiamond6.ulib.iupui.edu/cdm/ref/collection/IRecorder/id/51774/rec/56

[771] "Police Nab Suspect in 1969 Murder", *Indianapolis Recorder*, 1, http://indiamond6.ulib.iupui.edu/cdm/ref/collection/IRecorder/id/53214/rec/11

because IPD required a rank of Lieutenant or above of candidates.[772]

February 1, 1977: Rated as one of the best detectives with IPD, Willie Larkins is chosen to participate in the House Select Committee investigating the assassinations of Robert F. Kennedy and Dr. Martin Luther King Jr. At this time he was described as being the highest decorated officer in IPD history, with 50 commendations and as well as one from the F.B.I. [773]

September 1977: Willie Larkins files suit against IPD in federal court over discriminatory hiring and promotion practices. The NAACP joined this suit on September 14th.[774]

---

[772] "37 member panel aiding in selection", *Indianapolis Recorder*, December 13, 1975, 1,
http://indiamond6.ulib.iupui.edu/cdm/ref/collection/IRecorder/id/5659/rec/16

[773] "Larkins 'Surprised' about murder probe appointment", *Indianapolis Recorder* – February 5, 1977, 2,
http://indiamond6.ulib.iupui.edu/cdm/compoundobject/collection/IRecorder/id/21015/rec/18

[774] Marcus Mims, "Local NAACP takes over Black Policeman Suit", *Indianapolis Recorder*, 1,
http://indiamond6.ulib.iupui.edu/cdm/ref/collection/IRecorder/id/22814/rec/24

<u>1978:</u> Willie Larkins and other IPD African-American officers filed suit against the City of Indianapolis charging discrimination in their hiring practices. In 1978 a Consent Decree was signed between the parties, a successful outcome for the officers.[775] In October of 1983, 71 African-American officers reactivated the group "The Guardians", in order to charge the city and IPD with failing to live up to the decree. Willie Larkins was spokesman for the group, who charged there were the same number of African-American officers in 1983 as when the decree was signed. The city and IPD disputed this. [776]

<u>December 1981:</u> "During the past year, the racial situation on the Indianapolis Department has deteriorated to the point where now, blatant racism exists within the department, and the community, with no

---

[775] http://www.nytimes.com/1985/05/05/weekinreview/indianapolis-defends-its-hiring-plan.html Retrieved May 11, 2014

[776] Lamont Curry, "Guardians, Police Dept., headed for another racial suit?", *Indianapolis Recorder*, 1, http://indiamond6.ulib.iupui.edu/cdm/ref/collection/IRecorder/id/2210/rec/14

respect to the rights of the blacks on the Indianapolis Police department." –
March 16, 1986: Received a Certificate of Appreciation on Black Law Enforcement Recognition Day.

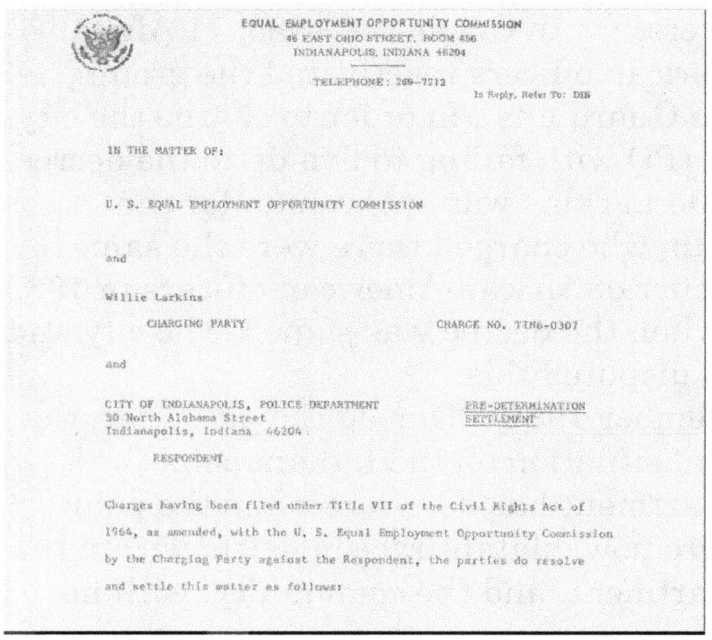

Cover page of original settlement between Willie Larkins and the City of Indianapolis. [777]

---

[777] Hudnut Collection. University of Indianapolis Digital Mayoral Archives. http://uindy.historyit.com/item/?itemid=660203 (accessed 4/5/2017). - See more at: http://uindy.historyit.com/item/?itemid=660203#sthash.6tzBlHtW.dpuf

Willie Larkins, IPD officer and candidate for Marion County Sheriff.[778]
1989: Quad III operations officer.
November 1996: Elected to Washington Township Board, serving as Constable.[779]

July 5, 1997: "Larkins was a true hero" "The Black Police Association acknowledges the passing of a true local hero in the fight for fairness in law enforcement in Indianapolis. The late retired officer Willie Larkins was a pioneer in the struggle for equal opportunity in law enforcement and equal treatment under the law by our criminal justice system. Mr. Larkins was the main reason for the Indianapolis police and fire departments having an increase in minority hiring from 1979-1993, due to his filing a law suit on behalf of these departments which eventually led to a federal consent decree.

---

[778] "Officer Says IPD Has Two Sets of Standards", *Indianapolis Recorder*, December 5, 1981, 17, http://indiamond6.ulib.iupui.edu/cdm/ref/collection/IRecorder/id/27732/rec/4

[779] Amos Brown, "Wrap-up of the 1996 Campaign", *Indianapolis Recorder* – November 16, 1996, A7, http://indiamond6.ulib.iupui.edu/cdm/ref/collection/IRecorder/id/68295/rec/3

He fought for the rights of officers and citizens to be treated fairly by our public safety institution and even sacrificed his own career to do so after his retirement. He was saddened by the fact that many Blacks who benefited from his many years of work never publicly or privately thanked him. Mr. Larkins made it possible for the Indianapolis community to have a chief Toler and chief Allen.

His many contributions were never acknowledged. Mr. Larkins was a mentor, friend, and father figure to many Black and white officers. While other high ranking Black and white officers avoided dealing with issues of racism and discrimination, officer Larkins dealt with the issues head on and pushed for positive change in the areas of hiring, promotion, community relations and public policy. It's too bad he was never given credit for the pioneer that he was. He once said "The agent of change gets nothing, while others reap the benefits of change." [780]

---

[780] "Larkins was a true hero", Indianapolis Recorder – July 5, 1997, A3,
http://indiamond6.ulib.iupui.edu/cdm/ref/collection/IRecorder/id/68618/rec/70

Faces of IPD

Patrolman Robert B. Turner receives the Officer of the Month award from Mayor Richard G. Lugar.[781]

---

[781] The Digital Mayoral Archives Collections. University of Indianapolis Digital Mayoral Archives. http://uindy.archivestree.com/collections/ (accessed 4/11/2014).

Sergeant Paul Hooks explains to rookie Patrolwoman Ruth Corbitt how to fill out an accident report. Jim Burres photograph for *Indianapolis Recorder*, November 30, 1968.

Newly promoted Sgt. Charlotte Frazier & Deputy Chief Robert Turner.

Major Cicero Claude Mukes [782]

Born: November 11, 1930
Died: October 9, 2002 Indianapolis, Indiana[783]
Date Appointed: May 16, 1962
Date Separated/Retired: 1995

Buried Crown Hill Cemetery, section 28, lot 255. [784]

---

[782] Photograph courtesy of Societe de Police
[783] Birth & death dates from SSDI: Number: 315-22-1481; Issue State: Indiana; Issue Date: Before 1951.

[784] Findagrave.com

Served in U.S.A.F. December 15, 1949 to December 14, 1953. [785]
Korean War USAF veteran.

1964: Cited for bravery after struggling with a theft suspect over a gun and capturing him.
1969-71: Serving as Narcotics Sergeant.
June 1974: Working in the Community Relations Bureau.[786]
April 1976: Sergeant in the Background Investigations unit.
November 17, 1978: Promoted to Lieutenant, David Sector.[787]
1978: The City of Indianapolis signs a consent decree in response to a discrimination suit filed by 7 IPD African-American officers, including Cicero Mukes.

---

[785] U.S., Department of Veterans Affairs BIRLS Death File, 1850-2010 [database on-line]. Provo, UT, USA: Ancestry.com Operations, Inc., 2011.

[786] "IPD bureau works to prevent crime and improve community relations", *Indianapolis Recorder* – June 22, 1974, 17,
http://indiamond6.ulib.iupui.edu/cdm/compoundobject/collection/IRecorder/id/4035/rec/17

[787] "Blacks receive IPD promotions", *Indianapolis Recorder* – November 25, 1978, 18,
http://indiamond6.ulib.iupui.edu/cdm/compoundobject/collection/IRecorder/id/25370/rec/1

Mukes was quoted as saying in a 1985 interview about the decree: ""There's no way in the world I would even have made captain if it hadn't been for that consent decree," said Major Mukes last week. "If they took it away, by attrition alone we'd have a 95 percent white Anglo-Saxon Protestant police department going into lower-income neighborhoods. And that would be chaotic." [788]

<u>November 6, 1979:</u> Shot in the face, seriously wounded in same incident which killed Officer Jerry Griffin.[789]

<u>December 1980:</u> Held appointed rank of Assistant Deputy Chief.

<u>October 1981:</u> Promoted to Captain.[790]

<u>August 1986:</u> Held rank of Major.

---

[788] http://www.nytimes.com/1985/05/05/weekinreview/indianapolis-defends-its-hiring-plan.html Retrieved May 11, 2014.

[789] "Black police lieut. among 4 wounded", *Indianapolis Recorder* – November 10, 1979, 1, http://indiamond6.ulib.iupui.edu/cdm/compoundobject/collection/IRecorder/id/21938/rec/1

[790] Willie Alexander, "Time for Talk", October 3, 1981, 3, http://indiamond6.ulib.iupui.edu/cdm/compoundobject/collection/IRecorder/id/27544/rec/24

1989-1990: Captain, commander of Internal Affairs.
1992: Field Captain on West District.

Instrumental in instituting the Field Training Officer program for the Indianapolis Police Department.

Cicero Mukes.[791]

---

[791] IMPD Lichtenberger History Room.

Major Cicero Mukes [792]

---

[792] IMPD Lichtenberger History Room.

Faces of IPD

Patrolman Samuel Drake – 1969 [793]

---

[793] Photograph courtesy of Samuel I. Drake.

Detective William E. Durham

Born: August 25, 1936 Campbellsburg, KY.
Died: November 24, 1996 Indianapolis, IN.
Appointed: May 16, 1962
Retired: 1995
Nickname: Beechie.
1959-1961: U.S. Army.
1969-1971: Patrolman in Juvenile Aid Division.
June 11, 1976: Det. Sgt. Alonzo Watford & Det. Durham charged a 14-year old with rape & robbery.
November 4, 1979: Chosen as part of a 3-man detail to investigate gang activity on the near-Northside & near Northeastside. Father of IMPD Officer Melony D. Moore.

Detective Joe Cephas Berry

Born: June 16, 1931 Caskey, KY.
Died: July 1, 1988 Indianapolis, IN.
Date Appointed: September 18, 1956
Date Retired: April 24, 1977

1967: Held rank of Sergeant.

Joe Berry was a long time Homicide and Robbery investigator and was rated highly for his detective skills.

Sergeant Joe W. McCoy

Born: August 27, 1935 Pulaski, TN.
Died: September 4, 2016 Indianapolis, IN.
Appointed: February 1, 1961
Retired: 1991

Served in USMC 1955-1959.

<u>1964:</u> Assigned to Robbery-Homicide.
April 5, 1968: Promoted to Sergeant, Homicide.
October 10, 1974: Worked round the clock to round up 5 gang members who raped two

women & committed robberies in a 2 ½ hour spree. Commended personally by Chief Kenneth Hale.

May 18, 1975: Received a B.S. from IUPUI which he worked hard for.
Teamed with Det. R.C. Green in Homicide for 20 years, one of the best in IPD history.

From Joe W. McCoy's obituary:

"Joe was raised by his beloved step-father, Robert Smith and his favorite uncle Elease Campbell both of Indianapolis.

Joe attended elementary school in Pulaski and later moved to Indianapolis enrolling in Crispus Attucks High School, graduating in 1955. He enlisted in the Marine Corp, was an MP and was honorably discharged in 1959. While stationed at Camp Lejeune in North Carolina, he married his high school sweetheart, Eleanor Lanier McCoy. Joe and Eleanor were married in the Catholic Church where he was confirmed in faith by Father Munshower, attending Saint Thomas Aquinas Church. Eleanor and Joe, remained married for 30 years and had one Daughter Monica McCoy -DeLaPaz.

Joe, honorably served on active duty in the United States Marine Corp for (4) years and was a Military Police officer. After his discharge he joined the Indianapolis Police Department (IPD) in 1961, and enjoyed an illustrious career. Joe worked in narcotics and robbery and was later promoted to Detective Sergeant of Homicide and was appointed Special Deputy as Marion County Coroner, for the State of Indiana. During these years he continued his education, graduating from Indiana University with a Bachelor of Science Degree in Criminal Justice. Joe was part of the security detail that protected the Reverend Dr. Martin Luther King and Presidential Hopeful Robert F. Kennedy…. In. After retiring from (IPD) in 1991, Joe worked for Indianapolis Power & Light Security, his second retirement was in 2004.

Joe, enjoyed restoring antiques cars, especially 1934 Fords. He also purchased and traded many antique, new and used cars, in which his daughter Monica was a grateful recipient of! Joe loved all of his family, served his community….. He loved jazz, Nat king Cole and "Don't Stop the

Music" by Yarbrough and Peoples. He liked watching westerns, but his all-time favorite was "Shane." He made his police buddies laugh when they were dealing with difficult situations on the job"

Detective Sergeant Clarence R. Grant

Born: December 27, 1931 Savannah, GA.
Died: February 11, 2005 Indianapolis, IN.
Appointed: May 16, 1962
Retired: 1990

June 23, 1963: Rookie Patrolman Richard Jeter and two other police officers, Clarence

Grant and Donald Floyd, were sent to the 600 block of Blake Street, on a report of a man with a gun. The man's wife met them at the door and directed them to the back yard, where her husband was sitting in a chair with an automatic pistol in his hand.

As they approached, the man rose and fired three shots at them, then ran into an alley. Patrolman Grant warned the others, "Wait, let's see if he's in here", referring to a pick-up truck that they saw the suspect climb into.

Approaching the truck, the suspect again fired several more shots. The police officers returned a volley of bullets, puncturing the truck and hitting the suspect twice in the left side and once in the left shoulder.

The suspect was apprehended after running from the scene and survived.[794]
1966: Detective in Vice Branch.
1968-71: Sergeant in Vice Branch.
1971: Promoted to Lieutenant, Vice Branch.

---

[794] The Indianapolis News, June 24, 1963, p.20
https://www.newspapers.com/image/105143546/?terms=%22richard%2Bjeter%22

July-Aug. 1972: Acting Vice Squad Captain.

1974: Reduced to Sergeant, transferred to Robbery, working there until 1981.

October 10, 1974: Worked round the clock to round up 5 gang members who raped two women & committed robberies in a 2 ½ hour spree.

September 19, 1978: Two men were arrested for the murder of a liquor store owner killed during an attempt robbery earlier in the week. Sgt. Grant & Det. James Parnell were assigned to the case and filed warrants on September 18th for their arrests.

1984-1989: Quad II district detective.

Policewoman Rosemary Anthony Simpson

Born: July 10, 1929 Indianapolis, IN.
Died: December 29, 2014 Indianapolis, IN.
Appointed: February 16, 1963
Retired: July 11, 1984
Badge No. 310
Rosemary was popular as well as a child prodigy finishing her high-school education with honors at 16 years of age and completed her ROTC.

In the fall of 1946, Rosemary applied and was accepted to Indiana University.

In Rosemary's sophomore year, she met and wedded Mr. George McErvin Simpson, a WWII veteran in the U.S. Navy.
Rosemary Simpson was an early detective in the Juvenile Aid Division. She was a founding member of the IPD Child Abuse Unit.

<u>1971:</u> Juvenile Branch, assigned to Car 121, Intake & Child Abuse.
<u>June 24, 1971</u>: One of two policewomen detailed to provide security at the Hilton Hotel for the visit of President Richard Nixon to Indianapolis.
<u>1976:</u> Along with Officer Norma Bacon, the only African-American female in the Homicide & Robbery Unit.

Buried in Crown Hill Cemetery.

Detective Sergeant
Richard Cartwright Jeter

Born: September 12, 1938 Indianapolis, IN.
Died: October 22, 1994 Indianapolis, IN.
Date Appointed: February 16, 1963
Date Retired: August 9, 1985
U.S. Navy veteran.
Graduate of Indiana University.

1971: Detective A-112 on A Sector.
November 17, 1978: Promoted to Sergeant.
February 1983: Juvenile Sergeant.

Son of Lt. David S. Jeter of IPD.
Richard was a member of the Allen Chapel AME Church, where he was trustee emeritus and superintendent of its adult Sunday School.

Patrolman Lyman T. Battle

Born: March 21, 1935 Cincinnati, Ohio
Died: November 11, 2007 Indianapolis, IN.
Appointed: September 20, 1965
Retired:
<u>1963:</u> Employed as medical technician.
<u>1968:</u> Walked a beat downtown, night shift.
<u>October 26, 1969:</u> Performed incredible lifesaving feats at the scene of a 4-car accident where 9 were killed. First Black officer to receive the Valor award.
<u>March 23, 1970:</u> Honored by Red Cross.
<u>September 22, 1971:</u> Applied external massage to a 5-year old girl whose heart stopped after being struck by a car.
1971: Unit E-5 on Edward Sector.

March 23, 1972: Nominated for the Red Cross Hall of Fame.
1983: Community Service Award, Police-Fire Awards.
1984: Vice-president of the Police Athletic League.

Lyman Battle at a 1980 PAL softball game.[795]

1989: Member of the IPD Warrant Unit.
January 29, 1994: One of six recipients of the 3rd annual Living Legends in Black awards, for making a difference in their community.

---

[795] IMPD Lichtenberger History Room.

Detective Ned H. Wyatt

Born: December 16, 1935 Newburn, TN.
Died: June 23, 2001 Indianapolis, IN.
Date Appointed: September 5 1967
Date Retired: July 21, 1988
1971: Detective, Sector B.

After retiring from IPD, Ned Wyatt worked as a security guard for Indianapolis Power & Light Co. for 10 years, retiring in 1988.

Patrolman Ronald R. Coleman

Born: About 1944
Died: August 3, 2012 Indianapolis, IN.
Date Appointed: September 5, 1967
Date Retired: July 1, 1989

<u>1974:</u> Assigned to Solo motorcycles.

Son of Sergeant Bailey Coleman of IPD.

Patrolman William Luther Armor

Born: December 21, 1946 Anniston, AL.
Died: December 1, 1997 Indianapolis, IN.
Date Appointed: October 21, 1968
Date Retired: May 20, 1994
Air Force veteran of the Vietnam War.
<u>February 10, 1978:</u> Using information obtained by Detectives Clarence Grant and William Armor, Patrolman R.D. Davidson arrested a suspect in the February 4th beating and robbery of the owner of a cleaners at 1602 N. Alabama Street. [796]
<u>1986</u>: ERB Operations Officer of the Year.

---

[796] The Indianapolis Star – February 12, 1978, p.48, https://www.newspapers.com/image/105931721/?terms=%22william%2Barmor%22

After retiring as a sworn officer, William served as a civilian wagon officer for IPD.
1989: Quad II operations officer.
Brother of IPD Officer Fred Armor.

Detective Ernest Lee Miller

Born: About 1948
Died: September 17, 2014 Indianapolis, IN.
Date Appointed: September 22, 1969
Date Retired: December 1, 1997

1971: Unit E-9, Edward Sector.
March 5, 1979: Receives a Valor Award at the American Legion's Spartan Awards dinner. He received this for his actions in December 1978. He had arrived at a restaurant to see an employee being held at gunpoint by two armed men. The men

ignored his orders and one of them fired at Patrolman Miller. Miller then wounded the shooter and arrested both men.[797]

April 19, 1979: Above, Patrolman Ernest L. Miller received a commendation for valor. He earned it for a confrontation he had with an armed robber.[798] Patrolman Charles Shue awaits his valor award.

---

[797] The Indianapolis Star, March 6, 1979, p.11.
https://www.newspapers.com/image/106981038/?terms=%22ernest%2Bmiller%22

[798] The Indianapolis Star, April 20, 1979, p.10.
https://www.newspapers.com/image/107188510/?terms=%22ernest%2Bl%2Bmiller%22

1983-1997: Detective in Robbery.

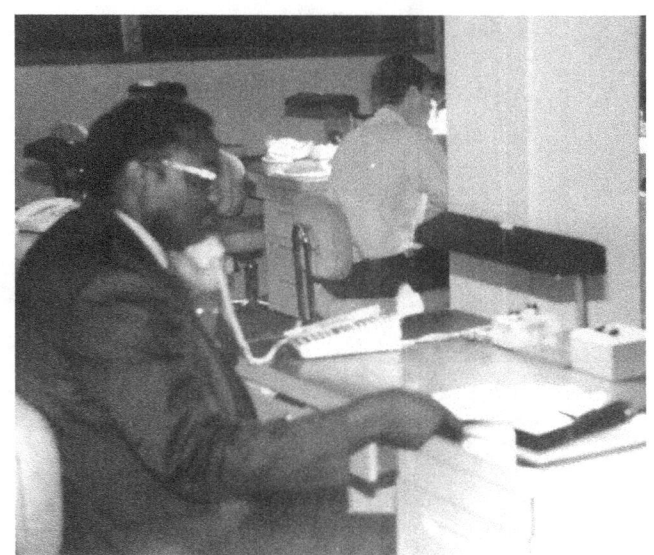

Ernie Miller 1987 Pan Am Games Task Force and at work, below. [799]

---

[799] IMPD Lichtenberger History Room.

Lieutenant Vernon D. Pullings

Born: May 11, 1936 Dayton, OH.
Died: September 17, 2000 Indianapolis, IN.
Date Appointed: September 12, 1966
Retired:

<u>1969</u>: Promoted to Detective Sergeant in Robbery.

December 9, 1966: Received the Mental Attitude award for his Recruit Class.

<u>March 9, 1970:</u> Sergeants Joe McCoy and Vernon Pullings arrest two suspects, who admitted pulling six holdups.[800]

<u>April 27, 1970:</u> McCoy and Pullings arrest two suspects in a Village Pantry robbery.

---

[800] Indianapolis Star, March 10, 1970, p.10, https://www.newspapers.com/image/106842372/?terms=%22vernor%2Bd%2Bpullings%22

One of the suspects admitted to committing 17 holdups to support a drug habit.[801]

August 21, 1980: Promoted to Lieutenant. An Edward Sector Sergeant, he remained in Operations.

Vern Pullings spent the remainder of his career as a shift Lieutenant in the IPD Communications Branch. Vern has been described as being a great guy and very "old school."
Father of IPD Officer Jerry Pullings.

---

[801] Indianapolis Star, April 28, 1970, p.19, https://www.newspapers.com/image/106861932/?terms=%22vernon%2Bd%2Bpullings%22

Sergeant Willie J. Jackson

Born: December 17, 1943 Baird, MS.
Died: March 15, 2008 Indianapolis, IN.
Date Appointed: July 7, 1975
Date Retired: December 21, 2007

USAF veteran.
1989: Quad IV Sergeant.
2002: Traffic Supervisor.
Willie played pool and bowled.
Willie was a member of the IPD musical group, "Shades of Blue."

Mayor William H. Hudnut & IPD Drill Team member Willie J. Jackson, Phoenix

Willie singing at a New Years event.

Asst Chief Robert G. "Bobby" Allen

Date appointed to IPD: September 1, 1961
Date Separated/Retired: October 20, 2006

<u>April 1976:</u> Sergeant in Special Investigations.
<u>November 17, 1978</u>: Promoted to Traffic Sector Lieutenant.
April 16, 1986: Promoted to Captain, assigned to Traffic Division, the first African-American to hold that rank in that division.
<u>March 1988:</u> Major Robert G. Allen appointed Commander of the Traffic

Branch, replacing retiring Major Robert Robinson.

At work, April 3, 1990 during President George H.W. Bush visit.[802]

<u>October 1995:</u> Serving as Assistant Chief of Police. "I also want white people to know that each person will be treated fair and equitable, regardless of race, color and creed. I am very sincere about the things that need to be done in the community. And, when I say community, I mean the entire community."- Robert G. Allen.

<u>1996:</u> Appointed Acting Chief of Police after resignation of Chief of Police. Held this

---

[802] IMPD Lichtenberger History Room.

position until Michael Zunk was appointed Chief of Police in January 1997.
<u>February 1997:</u> Appointed Assistant Chief of Police.

Bobby Allen is fondly remembered as a good man and leader. He was known for managing traffic for major events downtown in a skilled way for many years.

Sergeant Jacqueline Jean Winters

Date appointed to IPD: February 16, 1960
Date Separated/Retired: 1980

1953 Graduate of Attucks High School.

January 9, 1955: Jacqueline Winters is vocalist for the Duke Hampton Band as they played at the Walker Casino.

March 8, 1959: Model at a fashion show, "Preludes to Fashion of '59". [803]

Jackie Winters was brought up in a household which encouraged the children to achieve, such as her brother Ronald, who became a noted minister and was an assistant to Senator Vance Hartke, or her brother David, who served as an Indianapolis Firefighter.

Jackie first began singing when she was 4 years old. She has sung all types of music, from opera to country and western. Jackie, who had just turned 17 and her sister Ruth, performed in a chorus line for "A Night on the Riviera", performed for 300 young people at the Senate Avenue Y.M.C.A., December 22, 1951. She also modeled in a fashion show that evening.

She was a good student, making the Honor Roll her senior year at Attucks H.S.

---

[803] "Elaborate Props to Be Background For 'Preludes to Fashion' Review", *Indianapolis Recorder* – February 21, 1959, 4, http://indiamond6.ulib.iupui.edu/cdm/ref/collection/IRecorder/id/37067/rec/5

> JACQUELINE WINTERS, up and coming young vocalist will soon make a name in the local musical world. I understand talent scouts from a nationally known recording company are very much interested in her singing career. Miss Winters appeared at the recent Recorder Xmas Benefit Show. Much luck! ... Ruby Taylor, 88'er and thrush, i-

The Indianapolis Recorder – January 8, 1955

She sang at the Walker Casino, January 9, 1955, performing "Let me Go" and many other songs. At this time, she was attracting the attention of a national recording company. [804]

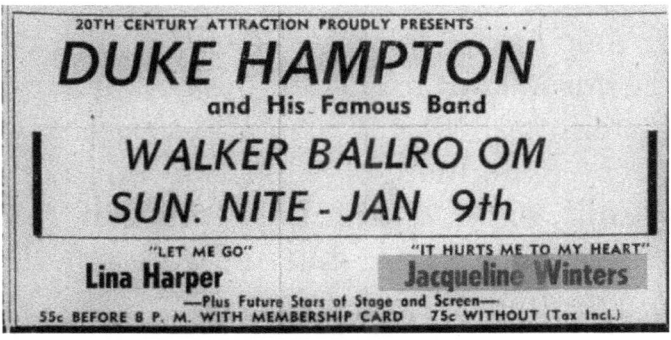

The next record of her performing is at the High Toppers club for its "Teenage Rhythm and Blues Show" in August of 1955. Miss

---

[804] "Duke Hampton's Band at Walker Casino – With Lina Harper, Jacqualine Winters, Popular Vocalists", *Indianapolis Recorder* – January 8, 1955, 12, http://indiamond6.ulib.iupui.edu/cdm/compoundobject/collection/IRecorder/id/34877/rec/1

Winters performed at the Frontiers Artists and Models Ball and Revue, at the Indiana Roof, September 8-9, 1958. She played the "Orbit Girl", described as "exciting and spectacular." She modeled at various venues, after graduating from the Loretta Young Way Modeling school, from 1959-1963.

Jackie became an Indianapolis Meter Maid in January 1958 with a goal of becoming a member of the Indianapolis Police Department. The salary was $3,430. She described one of the pitfalls of the job was being cussed out and even pushed around. "One fellow shook my arm and swore at me," she explained, because the red flag only said "expired" and not "violation." The maids received their share of wolf whistles from passing cars as well.

Miss Jacqueline Winters has found a clear case of overtime parking and writes out a ticket. She hopes to become a regular policewoman later.

Photos from an Indianapolis Star Magazine article on Meter Maids – August 9, 1959.

When Jackie was about 13, she first met Sergeant William Rapier, an African-American IPD officer who came to her home on a run. She asked him how she could become a police officer and he advised her to "Treat your parents right, have a good character, act right at school and help other people. The main thing is to mind your parents, stay in the church and don't have a criminal record."

So, in 1960, when she was appointed to the police department, then Sergeant Rapier saw Jackie and said, "I know you." She replied, "Yes, I was the girl you talked to when you came to our house." Rapier said, "You made it."

Recruits Jacqueline Winters & Joan Rayford, 1960.[805]

In August of 1961, Jackie flew to Washington D.C. to visit her brother, the Reverend Ronald Winters who pastored there. She also took in the usual sights but made a point of going to the Women's Bureau of the Washington Metropolitan Police Department.

---

[805] Authors collection.

"CHARMING Miss Jacqueline Winters, daughter of Mrs. Leontine Winters, boards a TWA Airline plane for New York City— the first destination of her two-week vacation. The well-known policewoman plans to visit friends and the famous opera star, Leesa Foster Esposito, while in New York City. She will extend her Eastern journey by departing for Washington, D.C, to visit her brother, Rev. Ronald Winters. The pretty Miss Winters was very stylish en-route in a red mohair suit created by "Rocile" of this city and a red velvet hat by Michael Torre. *Indianapolis Recorder* – October 19, 1963" [806]

---

[806] *Indianapolis Recorder* – October 19, 1963, 5, http://indiamond6.ulib.iupui.edu/cdm/compoundobject/collection/IRecorder/id/41712/rec/17

Friendship with Leesa Foster Esposito

An interesting episode in the life of Jacqueline Winters began when she attended a local church recital of Elizabeth "Leesa" Foster Esposito, who came in from New York. Leesa was a Black opera and nightclub singer, born in Alabama and she was married to an Italian man. After bearing two sons in Denmark, she moved to NYC in 1963.

Jackie met Leesa at the church and they exchanged numbers. She encouraged Jackie to come to NYC and meet Dorothy Dandridge. In 1953, Leesa had played "Ruby" in "Porgy and Bess" and was understudy to the actress playing Bess. She tested for the lead role in the 1959 movie version but lost out to Dandridge. She stayed with Leesa in Yonkers, N.Y. and occasionally babysat for her two sons, Giancarlo "John Carlos" and Vincent Esposito, who Jackie describes as "beautiful boys," when Leesa went to Paris, France. This was in 1963.

The women stayed in touch and about 1970, Leesa called Jackie and said, "I want you to come to New York City." By now the Espositos had moved there because Leesa's son John Carlos had been doing Broadway plays, showing a lot of talent. After the 1965 death of Dorothy Dandridge. Leesa tried to get a part meant for Dandridge but her complexion wasn't light enough. The producers wanted someone who looked like Dandridge. "Jackie, you've got it all. You've got the complexion they want. You've got the voice. You just need to know some technical things. Pack your bags and come out, I'm going to make you a movie star", she said.

Jackie says today, "I wouldn't leave the department. I had 10 years on. "She got mad at me," Jackie recalls. Today, America knows the boy that Jackie babysat as the memorable bad guy "Gus Fring" on *"Breaking Bad"*, as played by Giocarlo Esposito.

Patrolman Jackie Winters typing a police report in the Teletype Office, March 1965.[807]

---

[807] IPD Historical Photograph Archives.

Police Career

October 1968: Patrolwoman working in Juvenile Aid Division.[808]

1969: Promoted to Sergeant.

1974: Working in Personnel Office.

1976: Assigned to Public Affairs Office.

April 5, 1977: Sergeant Jacqueline Winters of the IPD Public Affairs Division gave a speech at a dinner meeting of En Ami Chapter of the American Women's Association. The topic of her presentation was "Protection of Businesswomen". In addition, she sang two songs.[809]

---

[808] October 1968 IPD Monthly Slate.
[809] "Women's Assn to hear policewoman", *Indianapolis Recorder* – April 2, 1977, 6,
http://indiamond6.ulib.iupui.edu/cdm/ref/collection/IRecorder/id/24698/rec/3

Jacqueline "Jackie" Winters, still strong of mind and body, 67 years after being appointed to the Indianapolis Police Department, recalled her days as a one of the early policewomen, while at an F.O.P. Retired Officers meeting. She is a 50-year member of the F.O.P. She said that being a policewoman as "a dream" of hers as youth. While wanting to do police work on the streets however, she, like all Indianapolis policewomen in those years, was assigned to a desk job, "Teletype", typing police reports.

She happened to be in a downtown department store one day when she heard and saw the evidence of a major theft going on. She made the arrest and this got her transferred out of Teletype after 8 months.

During her years in the Juvenile Branch, she helped break up gangs, investigated cross burnings and neighborhood disputes. In 1968, newly elected Mayor Richard Lugar talked to her because he wanted to break the color line – no African-American policewomen had yet been promoted to Sergeant. He told her to pass the promotional exam and he would promote her. She did and she was promoted, breaking the color line along with Thelma Sansbury and Thelma Graves. For a number of years, Jackie worked hard in the early days of neighborhood crime prevention while the head of the Crime Watch Task Force for Edward Sector Team Policing.

She was asked to sing the national Anthem at Bush Stadium (for the 3rd time), July 12, 1974 and at the National NAACP Convention in Indianapolis, July 5, 1973. Jackie continued to perform, being a trained operatic singer and being a deeply spiritual person, has done many performances in a church setting.

In the IPD Crime Prevention Office.

Singing in church.

[810] Photos courtesy of Jacqueline Winters. Interview with Miss Winters conducted May 11, 2017.

Captain Clarence A. White [811]

When Clarence A. White got out of the service, he was looking for a job.[812] There wasn't that many jobs "that Black men could take pride in." He tested twice for the Fire Department but failed the test. After briefly working for the City Sanitation

---

[811] Courtesy Clarence White Jr.
[812] This chapter is drawn from an interview conducted with Clarence A. White Sr., April 17, 2017.

Department, his wife came to Clarence and said, "Uncle Spurgeon wants to talk to you." Spurgeon Davenport was a Sergeant in the IPD Homicide Division and had served with distinction since 1937. Over coffee, the men talked about opportunities on the police department and Clarence White said, "I don't want to work for the police department", detailing some recent scandals about drunkards and gambling.

Spurgeon Davenport said, "Any place you go to work you're going to find people that shouldn't be in those positions and that's the same thing with the police department. You've got good guys and bad guys. If you stop and think, how many you know that you know now, have they ever been wrote up or having problems?" White said no. "It's the bad ones you hear about", said Davenport. Clarence White told him that he'd think about it.

After about a year, Spurgeon Davenport called for another meeting. After a long talk, White said he'd take the test. He passed with a score of 98 – the same questions were on this test as on the two IFD tests he had failed. He was appointed to the police department on January 5, 1953.

Rookie Officer Clarence White - 1953[813]

After being appointed to the Indianapolis Police Department, Clarence White undertook the six-week training course. After four weeks, he was pulled to work with two Vice Squads. He eventually was put on a beat, sometimes walking, sometimes riding in a squad car. "When I

---

[813] IMPD Lichtenberger History Room.

went on in 1953, there were only two squad cars. There was one detective car, for burglaries and things that they used to go and talk to their people (Black detectives).

Cars 27 and 29

"Car 27's district ran from Michigan Street, north, daytime to 22nd Street and Senate Avenue, over to Fall Creek, make the curve and come back. Car 29 ran from 22nd, north to 34th Street, from Illinois to West Street, up to the cemetery (Crown Hill). At night, when people got off from work, Car 29 was cut down from there, we ran from 16th Street to 22nd Street. The White car that came in was Car 34. They ran from Fall Creek, up to the White area. Car 29 wasn't allowed to run in the White area at night time because the White men were back", said Clarence White in an interview conducted with the author on April 17, 2017. Clarence White rode in Car 27 with Patrolman Alfred Finnell for a period of time.

When I came on, there was a 'gentleman's agreement'. Blacks weren't supposed to arrest whites. I DID. My first night, working the beat, I was with an officer whose dead now – Bill Bragg. This gentleman, tie, drunk as he could be, we was walking the beat, working 11 to 7. This guy stumbled up to me by the Walker Theater and said, 'Officer, I want you to go over with me to that cab company.' It was called United, a Black cab company, the largest Black cab company in the city at that time." The man told Officer White, "I went over there to get a cab. They've got 10 or 15 cabs over there and they refused to put me in one of their cabs. I want you to go over there and make them take me home.' I said, 'I can't do that. I can't make…where'd you come from? "

The man came on a Red Cab and had run up a large bill and they'd put him out in the middle of the triple intersection of Indiana Avenue, West Street and North Streets. He was standing in the middle of the street at 12 o'clock midnight. He turned to Officer

White on the corner and yelled, "I know why you won't lock me up. I'm drunk. I'm WHITE and you're not allowed to lock up a White man. I'm drunk and in the middle of the street. I'm going to get hit-" White said, "Uh, uh, don't do that." "Oh yes I am." The drunken man countered.

Clarence White said he was frustrated. He learned later this man who was telling him what he couldn't do was the Vice President of Eli Lilly & Co. He brought him to the corner and pulled out a pad of arrest slips. "I pulled it out and started writing. My partner said, 'White, what are you doing?' "I'm going to send him to jail." White said. "Don't do that", said Officer Bragg, continuing, "You know you've got to call the Lieutenant." "I'm NOT CALLING the Lieutenant!" said Clarence White. "I'm not calling anybody. Here's a man standing in the middle of the street. What if he got hit by a car? It'd been on us" replied the rookie and he sent him to jail.

As Clarence White recalls now, "For three months, the Black officers wouldn't have anything to do with me." Two days later, a White Sergeant named Sanders, in charge of a Squad found him on the beat and told him the Judge wanted Officer White to call him. Officer Bragg said, Sh- , its hit the fan now. Don't you mention my name, don't you say nothin' that I was involved in that arrest."

Sgt. Sanders also questioned Officer White about why he didn't call him before arresting the man. When White replied he didn't have time, the Sergeant said, "YOU had time to call me." White asked, "What was I supposed to do, leave him out in the middle of the street and call you to tell you I'm locking up this man and while I'm on the phone he gets hit by a car?" Sgt. Sanders said angrily, "Don't you sass me. Don't say another word."

When he met the judge, he found out the arrested man couldn't find his car and wanted to know where it was. After reminding the judge that he had testified about the man arriving in a Red Cab, the judge apologized for taking him off his beat.

However, before White left, the judge asked him. "Have you had any problems with the higher echelons in the police department about that arrest?" "I lied", recalled Mr. White. He told the judge, "Uhhh, no, I haven't (debating about mentioning Sgt. Sanders)" He didn't want to cause turmoil within the department and didn't say anything more.

When the author asked Mr. White "When did this gentleman's agreement end, roughly?" He answered, "It ended when I made the arrest." My arrest was made, that ended that period. We never had any more say-sos about the arrests. But I caught the dickens for making that arrest."

He eventually found himself riding in Car 27 with a veteran officer. On the night of December 4, 1953, an incident occurred which for the first time; Clarence White reveals the full details of for this history. They were patrolling that night along Northwestern Avenue (now known as Dr. Martin Luther King Jr. Street) and had passed by Freije's Grocery, at 1625

Northwestern. The store was lit up like someone was working, with fully stocked shelves.

They passed by a fourth time at 3 a.m. and Officer White noticed something strange. "Look at that store", he said. The shelves were completely empty. His partner pulled the squad car around to 17th Street and parked. "White, I'm going to check the back end.

"I got out of the car, watching the store to see if anybody runs while he's in the back", Mr. White recalled. From behind him, White heard his partner say, "White, take this guy and put him in the back seat."

"All I did was I turn and said, 'Get in.' My partner turned and said, I'm going to go and see if there's anybody else and went back. I turned around and he says 'M.F., if you turn around I'm going to blow your brains out.' I looked and there's a gun pointed at me. I said, I don't have my gun this evening. You know, I was in a rush, I'm a rookie, I enjoy coming to work and I forgot my gun. He said, 'You lyin S.O.B. You cross-draw.' He took his gun and hit me on the head, then said, 'Pull your coat back.'"

This revealed Officer White's revolver on his hip. The suspect said "I want that gun" and White complied, as the suspect stepped out of the squad car, saying, "Now run." White didn't want to run because he felt he would be shot as he did. Standing by the car door, White dove over the hood of the car, injuring his shoulder. By the time he got up and grabbed his shotgun, the suspect had fled. White got on the radio and hit for headquarters, which brought squad cars from all points of town. Mr. White says now, "I don't know where my partner is and to this day I think my partner set me up so that guy could get away.[814]

While all the available IPD vehicles were screaming to the area, one car that pulled up was that of the number one number's runner in Indianapolis, "Slim" Williams. A

---

[814] His partner was implicated in a 1955 jewel theft when he and another IPD officer let the suspect go but took the jewels from him. He was arrested, suspended and indicted for this incident.

man that many police respected for his cordial manner, Williams asked White how he was and then offered him a .32 revolver he had with him. White declined and Williams said, "Take it, you're gonna need it."

The suspect was later identified as Venyua A. Lawrence, 27. He boldly returned to the scene and stood amongst the onlookers. He asked one of them if he'd take him to 25th Street, which the man agreed to do. He car jacked him and left him tied to a tree north of Lebanon, Indiana. Lawrence was apprehended by the State Police near Lafayette, Indiana.

The story that hasn't been told is what Clarence White endured during the ensuing investigation. White was called at home and told to come down to headquarters and identify a suspect. There he met two detectives, one of whom was "nasty", named Carmichael. He said to White, "We don't see any marks on your head so are you lying?" White replied, "Somebody *hit* me and I'm not changing." Carmichael said,

"There's no laceration." "I don't care what it was, he hit me, he took the gun and slapped me across the head because I wouldn't give him my gun." The suspect was sitting in the room during the long session of White being accused of lying, which went on for hours.

On the trip to headquarters prior to this grilling, the patrolman driving White said to him, "White, on the way down I'm going to give you some advice. They're going to put you in an interrogation room with a two-way glass in it. They're going to put this guy in that room. They're going to talk to the two of you, both of them, for a few minutes and then they're going to leave and you'll hear the door lock. Now, after they walk away they're going to walk around and they're going to watch you. Walk over; don't say one word to that guy. Double your fist and knock the hell out of him. Knock him out of that chair. He's not going to fight you." Remembering this conversation in 2017, Mr. White says, that now that he was alone in the interrogation room with the suspect, "I thought about that and I looked over at this guy for thirty minutes. Am I going to do what this patrolman says? No, I'm not going to do it. "

After 30 minutes, the two detectives came back in and one of them said, "Well, we want you to say he didn't hit you. "He hit me." "You're lying," the detective replied. About 5 a.m., the detective said, "I'm going to send you home. You come back tonight and when you do you better tell me he didn't hit you. I'm going to request they suspend you for 30 days for lying.

When he was getting ready to go to work he got a phone call from his wife's Uncle Spurgeon Davenport. According to Mr. White, his wife's father and Uncle Spurgeon were powerful people in the Republican Party. "Clarency, I got word that this Carmichael is going to have you suspended. The chief's going to suspend you. Don't say one word. He's going to call you back in. When you get there, sit down. Don't say one word, don't even look at him. When he tells you he's filed papers and is going to suspend you, you get up and you walk out of that interrogation room. If he tells you to stop, you say 'Don't put your hands on me.' The head of the Republican Party, who is the most powerful figure in the city of Indianapolis, will take care of you. Don't worry. Don't argue with him."

In the interrogation room, Patrolman White was sitting there, waiting for Detective Carmichael to tell him this and was waiting to get up and walk out. However, nothing was said. "He got the word", Mr. White says. The word came from the Chief of Police and the Mayor, "Don't you put your hands on White." After White was promoted to Captain, Carmichael, then retired, came down to police headquarters and told him, "White, I know you don't like me. But I've got some words I'd like to give you. I admire you. You didn't waver; you didn't act like you were afraid of me."

White responded, "What would I be afraid of you for? I was telling the truth. But I felt like *punching you right dead in your mouth*." Carmichael laughed at that and said, "Well, you could have. Tell you what; I'm the sheriff over in the next county. I need some help. Why don't you come over and work part time?" "*I wouldn't work for you*", Mr. White said, laughing as he recounted this story.

Clarence White recalls that the White officer who suggested to him in the squad car ride that he slug the suspect who stole his gun, his face is fixed in his memory for another reason. "He raped two Black women, *prominent* women. The husbands were prominent. The women were stopped because they came out of a place at 25th and Northwestern at 3:30 in the morning. One of them looked like she was White. 'What you doin' here?'"

The women said they were down there to see somebody. They told the woman with a darker complexion, "You got her down here because you're showing her the ropes?" Mr. White continued, "They took them over to Northwestern Park and raped *both of them*. The woman was a prominent school teacher. I went to school with her. I still foam at the mouth that nothing was done. Ten years ago, that man killed himself." The case was covered up according to Mr. White after some political payoffs were made.

The Way IPD Worked in the 1950's

"Davenport was the main cog of Black officers. Claude White was a detective and he used to call me 'nephew'. He'd take me to the side and take me someplace where they sold coffee. He'd talk to me and go over different things within the police department. I liked him. Claude White, Plez Jones, (Preston) Heater, George Sneed. Sneed took me under his wing. He used to call me all the time. I was kind of proud of Sneed. They trampled on him. They gave him a car. He had a chauffeur that drove. He'd pull that car up to Senate and Indiana Avenues and park in front of Doyle's Restaurant.

"When I first came on I made a count of the number of Black officers. There was 28 or 29. The detectives back then were hard-nosed. If you saw them on the street you couldn't tell them from a thug."

Doyle's, where Black officers converged to turn in their daily reports to Sneed.[815]

Then all the walking beat officers and all the squad cars – there was only two squad cars, 27 and 29, would pull up.

Twenty-seven would pull up and park and give what they'd done to him and we who were walking would give what we'd done to him. Then he said 'I've got to leave this corner for about an hour. I've got to go up north and meet Car 29'. When he got finished with Car 29 he'd come back and park. He didn't patrol, nothing."

[815] https://jazzindianaavenue.files.wordpress.com/2010/04/georges-bar.jpg

Then he had a walking district called District 34, which I walked for two months. It was a punishment district. It ran from 16th Street north to 34th. It ran from College Avenue east, over to Martindale. That was a punishment district. I walked day time and middle shift. When I got ready to go to Late Shift, they pulled me and put me on District 32, over off the Canal and 16th Street. Those were the walking punishment beats for Blacks. If you done something wrong or something they didn't like, they'd put you in those different districts.

"The Avenue"

"Friday and Saturday, the Avenue (Indiana Avenue) was packed. You couldn't walk down the Avenue. White people, Black people. Then this Sergeant Sanders, said, 'White, come here. Move those people along.'" White replied, "For what? Where do I move them?" They're not moving fast enough" said the Sergeant. Patrolman White asked him one day, "I've been on Washington Street, from Meridian, east, it's packed. I don't see no squad cars down there making them people keep walking." The Sergeant replied, "I done told you about being a smart aleck with me." Every weekend, the Avenue was packed.

In late 1955, PAL Club Sergeant Schmidt came to him and said, "White, your background fits you in the PAL Club. We'll, we figure you do. Clarence White didn't want to be in the PAL Club (Police Athletic League). This officer had an authoritative manner which was insulting. White spent a year in the PAL Club, from 1956-1957, spending time at the Hill Center. [816]

Officer White was then moved downtown to Tomlinson Hall in 1958. He hated that assignment but carried his duties out. One night when he got home from work, his wife said, "You're building is on TV." It was on fire. [817] "Did you set it on fire because you were trying to get out", she asked. Clarence said no. It was determined the

---

[816] White was in PAL Club, March 1956-August 1957.
[817] Tomlinson Hall burned the night of January 30, 1958.

fire was started by a pigeon taking a lit cigarette to feather her nest in one of the building's eves.

Clarence White remembers: "Well, I had no place to go. They didn't want to mix me with the other plethora of officers. They wouldn't put a black with a white back then. So they put me in Juvenile. I became a Juvenile Investigator.[818] I was partnered with Officer by the name of Rapier (William Rapier) and we worked several cases."

One of the cases he handled involved a White teen from Shortridge High School. He had reported being kidnapped and taken to the 6000 block of Pennsylvania Street and being beaten, then ejected from the car. Detective White and his partner immediately noticed that the boy's arms didn't look like they were slashed with a razor blade, as he had claimed. They talked to his physician who said it looked like his arm had been scratched with a safety pin. They talked to the boy several times and

---

[818] Rapier & White in Juvenile, April 1959.

told him they were going to charge him with filing a false crime report.

The boy's father was a prominent attorney. He wanted White and Rapier fired. "I am an upstanding law abiding citizen and a white man and this officer is accusing my son, who is very well thought of at Shortridge High School."

The Chief of Police called in the detectives, who explained that it was obvious the cuts were not deep and were self-inflicted. The father went to the Mayor and asked the two detectives be terminated for accusing their son of lying. Within a week, the son went to his father and told him he was lying. "Those officers are telling you the truth. These are not razor cuts", he said. He had some friends drive him to the 6000 block of Pennsylvania, let him out and then had a person in the area call the sheriff. It developed that the boy was gay and had been caught in a compromising situation in a school bathroom. Three boys blackmailed him for two months and he stole change from his father to pay the blackmailers.

The father called another meeting with the Mayor and the Chief of Police. He wanted the detectives at the meeting. He apologized to the two officers. After the hour-long meeting, he called Detective White over and said, "Listen, I am so sorry to cause you this much headache. Can I do anything for you?" Since he had put Clarence White through a fair amount of grief, he said, "Yes, they're going to transfer me to PAL and I want to stay in Juvenile as an investigator. He said, "You got it."

A major case Detectives White and Rapier worked was the brutal beating and rape of a young woman in a park at Delaware and Vermont. This was April 30, 1959. The beating was so severe her eye had to be placed back in the socket surgically. They got a call to an apartment on Capitol Avenue. The caller was a grandmother whose grandson lived with her. She said something was wrong because his jeans and shirt were bloody when he came home but he had no marks on him. The tub was full of bloody water after he threw them in it.

White and Rapier interviewed the juvenile with his grandmother's permission and he admitted beating the young woman. This led Inspector Noel Jones to call the detectives in. He said, "You two guys are working better than the Homicide and Robbery details. I'm going to pull you out of Juvenile and put you on the street, working 11 p.m. to 7 a.m. on homicide and robbery cases. They did that for a year, making some good drug arrests.

Then Inspector Jones came to White and said, "We'll put you in Homicide and promote you to Sergeant." White resisted this promotion. He was told to take the promotion test, scored a 45 and failed, not wanting the promotion. Jones called White in, told him he had set the class up for him and ordered him to retake it or take a 30-day suspension. This time White scored a 98 which infuriated the Inspector, due to the obvious ruse on the original test. Jones said "I should suspend you for 90-days but I picked you for Homicide. You'll be the youngest man in Homicide."

White and Detective Sergeant James V. Dabner got a case involving prostitution in 1961. The suspects were five men, all of whom lived in Ohio – Columbus, Dayton, Akron and Cleveland. After obtaining warrants from the prosecutor, they went to Columbus first. They first went to the police department and spoke to the Vice Squad.

With seven Columbus detectives, they were taken to the African-American section of town. They were directed to the local streetwalkers, who they were told, would give you the guys you want if you talk to them. Columbus police called in four girls who met the detectives at a bar. The Columbus detectives told the girls what the Indianapolis detectives wanted and ordered them to give them the information they needed. If they didn't, they would shut down every street corner they worked on.

Dabner and White got a name, arrested him and brought him back to Indianapolis. Obtaining the name of the next man from the head of the IPD detective division, they went to Cleveland to find him. Coming through Columbus, they found the first man was now out of jail and back in Columbus. They proceeded to Cleveland. Sgt. Dabner told the owner of a hotel there that "We're coming back, we want a room."

About 4 p.m. they were having dinner when a clerk came in paging Clarence White. Puzzled, since nobody knew he was there, he went to the front office of the hotel. The caller told him "Don't come back to Columbus with that prisoner." "Why?" he replied. "The F.B.I. just came in here and locked up everybody that you all interviewed before you left. They closed the hotel down. They closed the two bars that we hung out in."

White said to himself, "What's going on?" The detectives brought their man back to Indianapolis, bypassing Columbus. They now had two more cities to go, Akron and Dayton. Jim Dabner wanted to go back through Columbus. "Why do you want to do that?" asked White. "I want to talk to the lady and find out why they closed her down" he replied. They went to Akron this time and there, White got another call at the hotel. "Don't bring your prisoner back through Columbus. Everybody came in a second time and locked up every Tom, Dick and Harry, including the boy that owned the hotel. This happened three times as they picked up four prisoners in Ohio.

Clarence White started thinking, "Was the F.B.I. following us?" Although he F.B.I. was known to just pull information from you but not tell you what they were working on, Sgt. White went to two agents he knew. He asked them, "I know I haven't done anything. Why are they following me and my partner every time we go to Ohio?" The agent replied, "White, I can trust you. Those guys you locked up in Indianapolis and eventually, you'd have wound up making trips to Los Angeles, California. There's a group called 'The Magnificent Seven.' Everybody you were locking up was a part of that Magnificent Seven'."

The gang was running what is now called a human trafficking operation using prostitutes. That's how they made their money. The truth was that the F.B.I. was using Sergeants Dabner and White to get their suspects for them. The agent revealed that they eventually broke that ring, with their help, but they didn't know it. The F.B.I. announced this case being broken on August 12, 1961. The news was carried in *JET Magazine*, August 31, 1961:

> **FBI Cracks White Slave Ring In Los Angeles**
> An alleged white slave ring, headed by a Negro group known as "The Magnificent Seven," was cracked by the FBI in Los Angeles. Its members, whom FBI agents said "talked big, sported fancy clothes and drove big cars," were listed as Glenn D. Smith, Jerry Mosley, William J. King, Willie C. White, Kenneth Jones, Richard Strickland and Melvin M. Brown. They were charged with having transported women from Cleveland for purposes of prostitution. One of the men, King, identified himself as a minister's son and said he formerly sang with The Spaniards. [819]

The city of Indianapolis was shocked by the brutal murder of shoe cobbler Joseph H. Hammer, age 67, on August 7, 1962. He had been robbed during the crime. On August 8th, Sgt. Clarence White questioned tavern patrons and got the nickname of a customer in the bar that had a blood stained man with him. Late that afternoon, White

---

[819] Jet Magazine – August 31, 1961.

found the customer and later, the suspect, William C. Edmonds. [820]

The crime was solved due to a vital clue of a billfold found in a West 21st Street tavern by Sgt. Alfred Finnell and the work of Detective Sergeants James W. Rogers, Howard D. Kramer, Clarence White and James Mullen. Chief Robert Reilly commended the officers for a job well done, as did the Indianapolis Recorder newspaper.[821]

Control of the City

"When I went on the force, the Irish controlled the city administration. They controlled the city. Then along came the Italian immigrants who moved into the northern part of Virginia Avenue. They forced the Irish further south." Eventually the Italians took control of the south side and they controlled the city of Indianapolis. They called themselves the little Italian mafia in that area.

---

[820] The Indianapolis Star – August 9, 1962.
[821] The Indianapolis Recorder – August 18, 1962.

I was working in Homicide, one of the cases I had was a robbery on Virginia Avenue. I went down to Little Italy to talk to the guy. I walked in and found all these important men with high collars and ties, playing poker. One of them, who had a cigar the size of a rope, said "What do you got?" White replied, "There was a robbery here." "There's no robbery here. Stop the investigation. That's my son, he's lying. There was no robbery here." White said, "But I've got to talk to him." The man said, "You don't talk to him. Leave the premises NOW. Don't come back." White said to himself, "Who's going to tell me 'don't come back.'" Two days later he went back. The same scene played out. Clarence White explained in 2017, "What he was trying to do was to protect the illegal gambling that was going on there.

"I got a call from the Chief of Police Robert Reilly. They spoke in Reilly's office and the Chief said "Sgt. White, you have a legitimate case. You were told not to come back. Why did you come back?" He replied,

"That's my case. I didn't finish the investigation." The Chief said, "Well, that man owns several blocks in that area. You've got to honor that. I know it's wrong but you've got to honor it. White "backed off" the case.

After Clarence White retired, he was working security at Merchant's Bank. While eating lunch one day, a little man came up and looked long at him. He said, "White, you in Homicide?" "Yeah". "Were you a sergeant?" he asked. "Yes", White replied. "Did you ever, go to 'such and such' and were told to leave?" "Yes." The man said, "Do you know who that was?" "No." Saying the man's name, he replied, "He controlled 'Little Italy' down here. He was the main one. You came back the second time, right?" White replied, "Yeah." The man said, "If you had come back a third time they would have found your body in White River or somewhere. He reported you." White said, "Yes he did."

He worked several murder cases while in Homicide. One of them involved a woman of foreign birth, who was waiting to catch a bus at 34th and College. A man abducted her, raped and murdered her. He then dumped her body under the bedroom window of a female employee of the IPD Identification Branch, who heard nothing.

Sgt. White arrested a man later, for breaking into cars. While searching his nearby apartment, White found a collection of buttons from a woman's coat. The murder victim's coat was missing its buttons. The man apparently collected "trophies" from his victims. White matched the buttons with the victim's coat. Sgt. White determined that the suspect was working as a dishwasher at a nightclub on College Avenue. He theorized that after closing up the nightclub, he got on a bus and found the victim as she was getting on the bus.

The prosecutor said, 'Nobody saw him there. You can't pinpoint him getting off the bus grabbing the woman.' So he would not give him an affidavit for prosecution. Prior to the trial, Sgt. White talked to the judge of his trial for breaking into cars. He told him the evidence he had linking him to the recent murder. The judge said,' tell you what I'll do. I'll give him a sentence of 10-25 years', which he did. That was not the norm for breaking and entering a car.

Howard Smiley Murder Case

One murder case assigned to Sergeants James V. Dabner and Clarence White was that of Howard Smiley. He was found crawling in his driveway at 2:15 a.m., October 30, 1962 by his wife in the 400 block of West Hampton Drive. He had been shot four times. Dabner and White worked around the clock on this case. [822] Detectives got a break when they traced an old .22 rifle found at the murder scene and traced it to an Army Surplus store. The identified a "strong suspect" who was shot and wounded slightly on October 31st, while struggling with an IPD officer investigating a burglary. Dabner and White identified the suspect.

---

[822] The Indianapolis Recorder – November 7, 1964 p.1

Claypool Hotel Robbery

On the morning of November 25, 1964, two men walked into the auditor's office at the Claypool Hotel, armed with .45 automatics. They ordered three employees to lie down on the floor. A forth employee who walked in while the robbery was in progress, was also ordered to the floor. They rifled the hotel safe and made their getaway with $5,000, without being noticed. Lt. Spurgeon Davenport, in charge of Homicide and Robbery, suspected they were from out of town due to the fact they didn't show their faces and the large caliber weapons they carried, not the norm for Indianapolis criminals.

Investigating this case were Detective Sergeants James Rogers, Clarence White and James Dabner. They quickly found that one of the probable suspects checked into the Claypool early the morning of the robbery, accompanied by a woman. Tracing the suspect's movements, back in time, they learned he, another man and the woman checked into the Plaza Hotel on Indiana

Avenue the day before the robbery. One of the men and the woman then checked into the Claypool at 1:45 a.m. the day of the robbery.

The suspect came back after the robbery and checked out of the hotel. Sgt. White figured this for an inside job. They sent warrants to the Columbus Ohio, Police Department requesting the arrest of the two men. On December 3, 1964, Sergeants Dabner and White left for Columbus to pick up their prisoner. They brought back John W. Smith, 27 the next night. Lt. Davenport credited the three detectives with "excellent detective work" for the swift identification of the holdup suspects. [823]

While in Homicide, he was partnered with Detective Harry C. Dunn. In 1965 they were investigating a series of robberies in the vicinity of the former Indianapolis Hebrew Congregation at 10th and Delaware. White saw a man there who "looked like he

---

[823] The Indianapolis Recorder – December 5, 1964, p.1
http://indiamond6.ulib.iupui.edu/cdm/ref/collection/IRecorder/id/42696/rec/29

stepped out of Vogue, the way he was dressed. Shoes shined, tinted sunglasses, shirt and a tie." They saw him at the synagogue all the time. White told Dunn, "Something's going on there."

He said in 2017, "We had a report of food being delivered and the guy was robbed. So we're going in that church." The detectives were surprised when they opened the door to see there was no floor. They almost fell headlong into the subbasement.

Dunn and White went to the prosecutor with what they had a series of robberies that seemed to be coming from this church. They couldn't get a warrant for the "minister" of the church. Turned out he was a respected citizen who worked for the city as Director of the Human Rights Commission.

Undeterred, the two detectives went back to the 10th and Delaware church several times. They figured out that the scheme that was going on was to order food to be delivered there, whereupon the delivery men would be robbed.

The members of the church had ripped up the first floor and the pews and burned them in a bonfire for heat on the dirt floor. They had talked to two ladies on Puryear Street about the case and one of them called them in to complain about them messing with the reverend. They told her of their plans to lock him up along with the date.

They had been told by Prosecutor Noble Pearcy "Don't you lock that man up." Dunn and White decided to go over his head. The day of the arrest was to be on a Holiday. They decided to go in early. When they got there, the basement was empty. The fires were smothered. During the night, the reverend had brought in 15 buses on Alabama Street and Puryear.

The entire congregation of 145 people they were told went to California. "We tried our best to get warrants filed on him for habitual criminal", Clarence White says. The 145 people had signed over all their property and social security checks to the reverend it was revealed later. The Reverend Jim Jones established his People's Temple in Ukiah, California in July 1965. The ladies on Puryear Street died in Guyana, November 18, 1978 along with 907 other members of the People's Temple.

The Forrest Arthur Murder Case

On November 2, 1967, Forrest Arthur, 49, owner of a north side hardware store, was shot three times during a robbery of his store. He identified one man of the three who robbed him as the trigger man before

---

[824] Wikipedia.

dying 10 days later. The case was assigned to Harry Dunn and Clarence White.

They credited Detective John Offutt, who wasn't assigned to the case, for supplying the name of an important eye witness to the crime. They had already received the names of three suspects from an informant, but he had not witnessed the crime, so they had to wait. The witness provided by John Offutt corroborated the same three suspect names. The first suspect was arrested November 24, 1967. The 2nd turned himself in. The 3rd was arrested as he stepped off a Greyhound bus from Tennessee, where he had gone after the shooting. [825]

Homicide Investigation Techniques

African-American detectives had the inside track on their White counterparts when it came to informants and Mr. White remembers them pairing Black detectives with White detectives so they could learn

---

[825] The Indianapolis Recorder – December 2, 1967

some of their techniques. On one occasion however, the administration didn't seem to understand.

He recalls when Inspector Noel Jones came to him and said "White, you guys are cleaning up cases like mad here. But there's one thing I don't like you guys doing and I'm going to put a stop to it. Stop going in those taverns."

I said, *"But that's where we get our information from."* Jones said, "You go into taverns?" Sgt. White said, *"I don't drink.* I don't see what the others are doing. I get me a glass of Pepsi or Coke; fill it up about half way like I've got a drink. I walk around; sit at the table and talk." Jones replied, "I don't like that." White countered, "That's how we get our information."

Mr. White recalled that "Davenport was good at that. I had informants that I could go to if something happened. Within 10 or 15 minutes, I had the case solved. That's how we worked. But Noel Jones tried to put a stop to it. Somebody went to the Mayor and complained and Jones backed off of how the Black detectives were doing their work."

In 1968, there was a shortage of Black officers in the uniform division. While in court, waiting to testify to a grand jury, he was told by Deputy Chief Raymond Strattan, 'Sergeant White, we're going to promote you to Lieutenant. He responded by saying he didn't want it. "Well, think about it," Strattan responded and left. Minutes later, the door opened and Strattan said, 'You're promoted to Lieutenant, report tomorrow in uniform.' This was April 5, 1968, the day after Dr. Martin Luther King Jr. was assassinated.

After being laid up for a year due to severe injuries suffered in a three car accident while on duty,[826] he came back and was assigned to Juvenile as a shift Lieutenant. He loved this assignment.

---

[826] September 12, 1968: Received head & hip injuries in an accident at 20th and Park.

On September 9, 1969, the day that an Allegheny Airlines jet collided with a student pilot and crashed near Shelbyville, Indiana, Deputy Chief Spurgeon Davenport called Lt. White at work and asked him if his uniform was "straight" because he was going to be promoted to Captain and back in uniform. "I don't want it, he responded. Davenport said, 'I can't help it. The Chief appointed you and you're going in uniform.'

Lieutenant White was promoted to Acting Captain. The department made him a Merit Captain on November 25, 1969. When interviewed for this book, Mr. White said that full integration of the Indianapolis Police Department occurred in 1969. This is when Black and White officers worked together regardless of assignment. There were still some areas where Black officers weren't assigned to however. Mr. White was detailed for a year of college education in Michigan, preparing for his duties as a Captain.

As one of two Black men on the Indianapolis Police Department with the rank of

Captain, now that Anthony Watkins had retired (the other was Spurgeon Davenport, Deputy Chief was his appointed rank), the department brought Clarence White into the presence of five men who were or became President of the United States. He shook the hands of Dwight D. Eisenhower, Lyndon B. Johnson, Richard M. Nixon, Ronald Reagan and Nancy Reagan and George H.W. Bush. While White considers this as a rewarding experience, as time went on, he came to find it unpleasant as he realized why he was being pulled from all the manpower of IPD to meet these dignitaries, to show IPD was integrated.

Prostitution

When Clarence White was still in Homicide just before he made Captain, he got a run to a nice house at 22nd and Park. A man said he was robbed. He went to the house and a beautiful African-American woman dressed like a maid with a mini-skirt answered the door.

After explaining that he was checking a case of a robbery there, another woman dressed in a see through negligee came to the door and asked "What is it you want at this door? You shouldn't be here." White replied, "Checking a case lady." The woman answered angrily, "Ain't nobody been robbed here." White realized this must be a "whore house" and closed the case because the victim wouldn't talk to him.

Shortly afterward Clarence White was promoted to Captain. There were two Captains, one over the south side, one over the North side of Indianapolis, which is what he was assigned as. This included Washington Street north to the city limits and to the city limits on the east and west sides of town. To this day he doesn't know why he did it, but on a Sunday morning Captain White went to Roslyn Donuts and got a half dozen, some coffee and a paper. He then parked in front of the house at 22nd and Park to eat them.

After fifteen minutes, the district Sergeant pulled up. Knocking on the window of White's car, he said, "Hey Cap, how are you?" After telling him congratulations on being promoted to Captain, the Sergeant said, "Sorry, I got some bad news. Headquarters just called and told me to tell you to move out from in front of that house there." Surprised, White responded, "They told you to tell me to move out from in front of this house." White said "Uh, huh" and explained he had a run there several months prior. The Sergeant explained that this was a whore house and the lady who owned it called to complain. He also explained about the high level cliental which patronized it, including city officials.

Captain White told the Sergeant, "I'm not moving from this location. You call headquarters and if they tell you to tell me again to move, that I'm going to call him at headquarters and tell him to send three Sergeants in the surrounding districts and I want every car in the Edward Section in front of this place, PDQ.

Monday morning, when he went to work, he was told immediately, "Captain White, you're now the South District Captain. After two months on the south side, he was again placed on the north side. He went back to that house and dared them to call headquarters on him.

Captain Clarence White spent the last year of his career as were other Captains, being assigned to housing projects, not a rewarding duty. On October 14, 1974, he retired. During his career he had received three departmental commendations and earned the American Legion's Robinson-Ragsdale award in 1962. This was the highest award an IPD officer could receive at that time.

Today, Clarence White remembers what he told his wife about police work when she said "You never talk about your work." "What's to talk about? When I go to work, I step into the gutter. I work in the gutter for 10 or 12 hours. When I get ready to leave, I dust myself and step back on the curb. Streetwalkers, the rapes, the homicides.

We're involved in all of that. I loved it and when they moved me into uniform, it was like taking candy from me." Mr. White says "My 22 years on the police department was very rewarding." At age 90, he lives completely independently and has a crisp memory for details.

Captain Clarence White and his sons Clarence "Lonnie" White Jr. & Rodney White

Detective James Melvin Compton

Born: May 29, 1946 Indiana
Died: March 16, 1976 Indianapolis, IN.
Appointed to IPD: February 1, 1971
Date of Separatation: March 16, 1976 (His death).

Answering complaints from administrators of Crispus Attucks High School about a man named Del Anthony Boatright selling marijuana to students, a team of IPD Narcotics detectives went to his house at 2145 Gent Avenue on March 16, 1976 to serve a warrant. He was thought to be there with two other men. Detective James M. Compton Jr., aged 29, had been assigned to the Narcotics Division for 6 weeks.

At 10 p.m. Detective Compton knocked on the door of the Gent Street address and announced that he was a police officer and had a warrant. A shotgun was fired through the screen door. Compton was struck in the head and chest. Falling to the ground he crawled to the middle of the front yard. He was administered first aid by another officer while the other two detectives of the team returned fire, striking Boatright.

Both Detective Compton and Del Boatright were sent to Wishard Hospital, where the suspect died at 11 p.m. James Compton died about an hour later. Compton was a Vietnam veteran who was wounded in action, 1967. He had been appointed to the Indianapolis Police Department on February 1, 1976, after serving as a police officer for two years in the state of Kansas. He was buried in New Crown Cemetery.[827]

---

[827] Indianapolis Metropolitan Police Department Webpage, which used source of Source: *The Indianapolis Star*, March 17, 18, 20, 1976; Indianapolis News, March 19, 1976, photo of officer, accessed April 9, 2014,
http://www.indy.gov/eGov/City/DPS/IMPD/About/Memoriam/

Detective Otha Stanley "Stan" Anderson

Born: July 24, 1944
Died: June 18, 2009 Indianapolis, IN.
Date appointed to IPD: January 21, 1977
Retired: March 31, 2008

Stan served in the U.S. Army.
Officer Anderson was patrolling when he received a run of two men holding up a 7/11 Supermarket with a shotgun. He arrived in time to observe the suspects jump into their vehicle. Officer Anderson pursued them at

Pages/jcompton.aspx

high speed, one of the men firing repeatedly at him, missing. The suspects ran into a stop sign. One fled, but Officer Anderson apprehended the other man.[828]

<u>August 27, 1981:</u> Received a Certificate of Commendation from IPD.

February 1, 1986: Honored with Certificate of Appreciation from Veterans of Foreign Wars.

<u>March 16, 1986:</u> Received a Certificate of Appreciation.

March 1, 1990: Upon investigating a house where poltergeist activity was occurring, he was quoted as saying "A vase flew across the room and two objects flew right by my head."

<u>May 26, 1995:</u> [829], Patrolman Anderson happened to be watching a Value City store monitor while off duty. He observed a man shoplifting. Outside the store, the man tried to steal a car and threatened "Stan" Anderson with a knife. Anderson shot and wounded the suspect in the elbow and leg.

---

[828] Justia US Law, http://law.justia.com/cases/indiana/supreme-court/1987/49s00-8607-cr-00690-2.html, retrieved August 20, 2014.

[829] The Kokomo Tribune, May 26, 1995.

1990-2001: Stan was working as a Detective with the East District.
He was married to Cheryl L. Anderson, an officer with the Indianapolis Police Department.

Patrolman Otha "Stan" Anderson, 1985, Below, receiving VFW award, 1986. [830]

---

[830] IMPD Lichtenberger History Room.

Sergeant James Lewis Johnson

Born: September 20, 1945 Indianapolis, IN.
Died: July 14, 2012 Indianapolis, IN.
Appointed to IPD: January 29, 1968
Retired: 2005

<u>1969:</u> Edward Sector
<u>1969-72:</u> Vice Squad.
<u>1973:</u> Robbery-Homicide.
<u>1986:</u> Narcotics.

From top left: James L. Johnson, Robert Patterson, Deborah Saunders & Frank Jameson.

From his obituary:
"He graduated from Arsenal Technical High School in 1963 and from IUPUI in 1976. He married his caring and loving wife, Carol, in Las Vegas on Valentine's Day in 1996. Indianapolis was his home for his entire 66 years of life. It is here that he chose to use his key traits: stubbornness, hard work, and compassion to serve and protect both his family and his community.

JJ proudly served 37 years on the Indianapolis Police Department and earned his Sergeant's badge in 1983. James

Johnson profoundly believed that there were ALWAYS two sides to every story. As a police officer, his incredible ability to listen, acknowledge, and mediate both sides earned him the nickname "the silver tongue."

James also pursued his interest in real estate, working as a realtor at Walt Howard Realty. He purchased his first property at the age of 18 and worked hard managing and rehabbing his numerous rental properties. Sports were a major source of enjoyment for James. He coached youth basketball and baseball, his favorite moments being coaching his 2 sons through their championship games to several titles over the years.

James loved his family, cherished his friends and respected his fellow man. James is preceded in death by his sister, Berkley Johnson Banks; and brother, Virgil Tucker. James is survived by wife, Carol Ann Johnson; stepmother, Ethel Johnson; sons, James L. Johnson III (Stephanie) and Mark A. Johnson; daughters, Nicole Rowe (Vequin) and Tracie Ford (Sherrell); sisters, Helen Cornelius, Sharron Davis (Tyree),

Estralita Ward, Charlene Puckett, Connie Pettis (Chester), and Leona Drake; brothers, Orvil Tucker, Norvil Tucker, Ronnie Tucker (Linda), Thomas Tucker (Mary), Kevin Tucker, and Aaron Tucker. James is also survived by 16 grandchildren and a host of nieces and nephews.

On July 14, 2012, James as always, saw two sides. And with the same love, care, and dignity he showed in life, he, again, acknowledged both sides… this time he chose heaven. We will all forever cherish the values, the strength, and the dignity that James Johnson showed us throughout his life and now as he rests in peace.

Faces of IPD

Clockwise from left: Joseph Shelton, Major Richard Benton, Captain James "Sonny" Wyatt.

Assistant Chief John Offutt [831]

Lieutenant William Bryant. [832]

---

[831] IMPD Lichtenberger History Room.
[832] IMPD Lichtenberger History Room.

L-R: Chief Paul Annee, Officers James Traut & Deborah Hogue, Mayor William H. Hudnut. The officers earned medals for taking a man out of a burning building on July 4, 1988.[833]

---

[833] Quarterly Awards, December 15, 1988.

L-R: James Toler, Richard Crenshaw. Richard Crenshaw helped found "The Guardians" and earned the IPD Medal of Honor. He reached the rank of Major.[834]

---

[834] Ibid.

L-R: Harry Gurnell, Deborah Saunders. [835]

L-R: Detective Wallace Shobe, Michael Darst. [836]

---

[835] IMPD Lichtenberger History Room.

Patrolman Colonel Barton. [837]

---

[836] IMPD Lichtenberger History Room.
[837] Ibid.

Two pioneers at IPD – Lt. Patricia Holman and Chief James Toler upon her promotion to Deputy Chief – a first for a Black woman here. [838]

Vice Officers – L-R: Gwen Black, Ron Harrod and Charles Coldman.[839]

---

[838] IMPD Lichtenberger History Room.
[839] Ibid.

Top: Officer Charles Martin standing, Jesse Beavers in car.
Bottom: Sergeant Leetta (Davenport) White. Both photos taken about 1985.[840]

---

[840] IMPD Lichtenberger History Room.

Top: L-R: Robert Patterson & Frank Jameson.
Bottom: L-R: Rickie Clark and William Benjamin with citizen.[841]

---

[841] IMPD LIchenberger History Room.

Mayor William Hudnut & Officer Felix Howard of the Drill Team, 1976. [842]

---

[842] "Mayor Hudnut and Indianapolis Police Motorcycle Drill Team, Circa 1976, Img. 17." Indianapolis Police Motorcycle Drill Team, 1976, Box 017, Hudnut Collection. University of Indianapolis Digital Mayoral Archives. http://uindy.historyit.com/item/?itemid=660203 (accessed 4/5/2017). - See more at: http://uindy.historyit.com/item/?itemid=660203#sthash.6tzBlHtW.dpuf

Officer Cynthia White – 1980's [843]

Officer James Harris

---

[843] IMPD Lichtenberger History Room.

Officer Alfred Watson

Officer Jerome Moore

Officer George Grant

L-R: Officers Curtis Hanks, Michael Adkins and Anna Bies at IPD sponsored Auto Show.

Lt. Paul Harden

Sgt. James A. Smith

Sgt. Alonzo Watford

Lt. Steve Odle   Capt. Cephas Bandy

L-R: Donald Floyd, Richard C. Jeter and Clarence Grant.

FACED GUNMAN: Patrolmen Donald Floyd, Richard C. Jeter and Clarence Grant are pictured following a gun duel with a 33-year-old Eastside man on this city's Westside shortly after noon Sunday. The policemen said that they had gone to 657 Blake on a report of a man threatening his wife with a gun. When they arrived the man, identified as William King, 1522 E. 18th, opened fire on them. After a brief chase and more gunfire, King was apprehended after being shot three times, but not seriously. He was arrested on three charges. (Recorder photo by Houston Dickie)

L-R; Officers John Chandler and Thomas C. Watson, September 30, 1967. The two officers were one of many integrated teams assigned to high crime areas. Watson was then a rookie.

African-American members of the recruit class appointed February 16, 1963.

Bailey Coleman, Audry Jacobs and Bill Cobb, July 25, 1967. At the time, it was thought these were the first African-American officers assigned to the motorcycle division - Guy Luster being long forgotten by now.

February 11 1961 - Indianapolis Recorder
"Veterans Fete Rookies"
"Six of seven new additions to the Indianapolis Police Department were welcomed to the force in grand style recently when a high ranking veteran officer hosted a dinner in their honor. The veteran is Captain Anthony Watkins, the first and only Black police captain on the force.
"Other veteran officers were also invited to the dinner. The new officers were sworn in January 31, 1961. Shown in the photo left to right are:
Sgt David Jeter, veteran, Sgt. James Dabner, veteran, Joe McCoy, rookie, Captain Watkins
Cephus Bandy, rookie, Paul Hooks, rookie
Keith Vance, rookie, Edward Lipscomb, rookie
Paul Dean, rookie, Lt. Oscar Donahue, rookie.
Joseph Shelton, a rookie, was not present when the photo was taken on February 6th.

IPD Officer William Rowe with Chief Robert Reilly. May 19, 1962 Indianapolis Recorder article below: "NEGRO COPS IN CANINE CORPS: Police Chief Robert E. Reilly awards diplomas to the first two Negro police officers initiated into the 14 man-dog teams of the Police Department's canine corps. It marked the ending of a rigid training program for the officers and dogs which began early this year at Ft. Benjamin Harrison. The officers are William Rowe (pictured) and Jack Yager. Inspector Daniel T. Veza, an early supporter of the mondog teams, said there are plenty of volunteers for the next training school expected to be started this year.

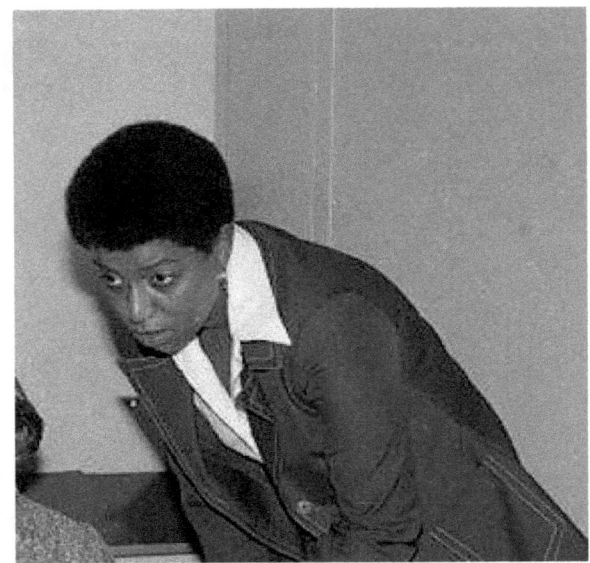
Detective Norma Bacon, Sex Crimes.

Curtis Hanks and Karen Arnett at Heather Hills School event.

Lt. Clarence White of Downtown Bicycle Patrol, 1995. Bottom, John Patterson of Mounted Patrol.

Sergeant Kirby Crawley

Sergeant Rhonda Reynolds, 1985.

Officer Kimberly Hale appointed to IPD.

Florence (Hobbs) Lackey.

Lt. Dianna Ferguson-Mosley

Assistant Chief Deborah Saunders

These policewomen appointed during World War II were the first African-American women to join IPD since 1922. This photograph was taken in September 1944. L-R: Beatrice Warfield, Georgia Rogers, Sarah Mize, Thelma Graves, Ora Phillips. Officer Jacques Durham standing behind them, taught them marksmanship.

Black History Month Dedication, February 6, 2017.
L-R:
Chief of Police Bryan Roach
Deputy Mayor David Hampton
Chaplain Pat Holman
Retired Detective John Larkins
IMPD Detective Cheryl L. Anderson
Retired Detective Robert C. Green
Retired Major Richard Crenshaw
Retired Sergeant Jacqueline Winters
Mayor Joe Hogsett
Retired Officer Larry Hoskins
IMPD Lieutenant Brownie Coleman
IMPD Captain John Walton

www.ingramcontent.com/pod-product-compliance
Lightning Source LLC
Chambersburg PA
CBHW060102170426
43198CB00010B/732